Pleasant Bay

STORIES FROM
A CAPE COD PLACE

Jimmy McClennen, watching his Bay, 1922.

Pleasant Bay

STORIES FROM
A CAPE COD PLACE

BY
MARCIA J. MONBLEAU

Acknowledgements

This book is written for and published by Friends of Pleasant Bay.
My sincere thanks to the Directors for allowing me this chance
to become better-acquainted with the place they hold dear.

I am especially grateful to:
Jay Harrington and Skip Norgeot, for rides on the Bay;
The historical societies of Chatham, Harwich and Orleans;
Robert Hardy, for his kindness in sharing photo negatives;
Pam Eaton, for her generosity in making prints of the above;
All those who loaned pictures, including Barbara Melcher and Erica Parra;
Merv Hammatt, for his drawings of Bay boats;
Lucretia Romey, artist and friend, for her illustrations;
Kevin Wright and Maureen Goodwin, talented friends, then and still;
Carla Scopeletis, who actually enjoys proofreading;
Pat Carroll, for listening and reading and for being here;
Families of those who have 'crossed the bar," for allowing us to reprint some words about the Bay,
All the folks who talked with me along the way,
And to my parents, the Reverend Charles H. and Lola G. Monbleau, who I hope would have liked this.

M.J.M.
Bog House
Harwich Port
October, 1999

Front Cover –"Eugene's Dory," *by Philip Nickerson, courtesy of the artist's wife, Joyce.*
Back Cover – *Gordon Baker, with Carrie, Howard and Anne Van Vleck, racing on Pleasant Bay.*

First Edition

ISBN 0-9676220-0-X

Contents

To Begin With...

If you'd like to learn everything there is to know about the geology of Pleasant Bay, about its remarkable Indian history, rich biological diversity or maritime heritage, there are books that will take you on thorough and scholarly tours of those subjects.

This is not one of them.

But in these pages, it is hoped, may be found a sense of the Bay, an emotion having to do with it, a look at where it came from and where it wanders. Above all, this is about people who love the place, who were born to it or discovered it for themselves-- people who have sailed, fished, worked Pleasant Bay or simply found contentment in being close enough to look at it day after day.

This book is about community and family, about growing up, passing along and passing on. For many, the Bay has been the center of childhood, the core of memory, the place they come back to.

These are a few of the many things I didn't know awhile ago, things I learned along the way.

It was with some concern that I sat down to write about Pleasant Bay, because this was unfamiliar territory. I grew up nearly ten miles away, after all, and that was a far piece. The last one off the Harwich school bus was Sally Dybing; in winter, she didn't get home to Wequassett Inn until after dark. Places we couldn't reach by foot or bike were places we rarely saw.

And although childhood was filled with love and giggles, warmth and good adventures, although I spent summers up to my widow's peak in Nantucket Sound, with water in my ears and seaweed in my bathing suit, the only boat I ever owned was in the bathtub. That fact alone would have kept the wonders of Pleasant Bay well beyond my reach.

How, then, to write a book about a foreign place?

It seemed clear. You don't have to know everything. Just find the people who do. Ask them. Listen carefully. And let them tell it their way.

On May 2nd of this year, I took the first step--three of them, in fact--down a short ladder at the end of Portanimicut Road and into Jay Harrington's fishing boat.

From that day to this, it's been a pleasant ride.

Mare's tail clouds streaked the sky that Sunday in May when I met the Bay. Things flew overhead, swam or crawled below and stared at us from the banks as we meandered. Places I'd seen from land were all around and at every turn: Arey's, Paw Wah and Lonnie's ponds. Sampson's and Hog islands, The River. Pochet. Big and Little Sipson's. The Narrows. Jay maneuvered his boat with ease and consideration, so my head wouldn't fly off in the cold east wind. And I looked--and listened.

Conversation, education and much pointing filled the afternoon. We leaned over the side to see Moon Jellyfish, Horseshoe Crabs and eelgrass. We looked up to watch Ospreys watching us, and over to where Egrets seemed to be tiptoeing through marsh grass. To the east, beach shacks were dots against the horizon.

I began--just began--to get the picture, and on the way home the car felt dark and close and airless.

As it happened, I didn't "sit down" to write about the Bay, but got up, headed off and looked for it. I went down dirt roads that twisted through the woods, got lost a time or three, tracked handmade name signs and, more often than not, emerged on the edge of one water place or another, all this in search of folks who would tell their stories.

The payoff was enviable. I sat on a fine old summer porch at Minister's Point, under the trees at the edge of Meeting House Pond, low near glassy water just south of Bassing Harbor and high on a bluff at The Narrows. I stared out a window overlooking the Head of the Bay, wore a mosquito net hat to walk on Pochet Island, saw the ghost of a World War I air base and could almost hear the high laughter of sailing campers as they shot across the finish line seventy years ago.

Slowly, patterns appeared, and with them continuity. Generations, like the tide, flowed in and out. The community of Pleasant Bay became evident. None of that should be pointed out on this page. It's a matter of discovery along the way, as it was for me.

Those in the know have their own opinions of where Pleasant Bay begins and ends. For the purposes of this book, it starts at Meeting House Pond in Orleans and ends at Chatham Light.

Some years ago, Alan McClennen wrote up a short history of the Bay. I have borrowed from that, freely and without shame, believing, absolutely, that Mr. McClennen knows whereof he speaks.

It's a well-known fact on Cape Cod that you never should make nasty comments about the plumber to the librarian, because they're probably cousins. That theory of relativity holds true here, as well. Don't assume that different last names mean different families. Scratch around Barley Neck and Pochet, and you're apt to turn up Paysons, even if their names now are Barrington, Parker and Thomsen. Wade through Pleasant Bay camping history, and a Hammatt or Melcher may bob to the surface in more than one place.

By the same token, one Nickerson and another Nickerson are not necessarily from the same Nickersons, at least not in the past hundred years or so.

The idea is to not get a muscle cramp trying to figure it all out.

Just float along.

Some folks represented here have long since departed these shores. To leave them out of a book about Pleasant Bay would be both a shame and a mistake, so included are good words from Sears Nickerson, Lawrence Brooks, Eleanor Gilbert Parker, Geneva Eldredge, Ernie Kendrick, Gilbert Payson, Emma Augusta Rogers and Josh Nickerson.

In two cases, we have borrowed from published material. Our thanks to Jean (Nickerson) Primavera for permission to include excerpts from the work of her father, Warren Sears Nickerson. Similarly, we are grateful to Judge Brooks' grandson and editor, Lawrence A. Carter, for welcoming us to the pages of the judge's memoirs.

Joe Nickerson and his grandfather Rufus are part of this book, so it seemed only fitting that another discovery along the way was the artistry of brother and grandson Philip Nickerson, whose painting of Eugene Eldredge's dory graces the cover.

The careful reader may well pounce on errors that are entirely the fault of the writer. But some things that might look wrong--spelling, style, word use--have been left as put down in the first place. Emma 'Gustie Rogers wrote years ago about "water melon," "base ball," the "school house" and someone cutting grass with a "sythe," which, it could be argued, makes a lot more sense than "scythe." Sears Nickerson used the old spelling of "Nawset" now and again, as was his right as historian. I have not altered, tidied up or presumed to correct anyone, nor did I want a book riddled with one stuffy "[sic]" after another.

One more decision regarding style may offend experts. It's never been made clear to me why the full names of some animals and birds are not capitalized. Anyone who's ever seen a Great Blue Heron cannot possibly think of it as a lower-case creature. The same goes for Snowy Egret and Diamondback Terrapin. So wherever it's been my right to do so, their names have been capitalized.

While it may not be this writer's business to sound a warning note, perhaps someone ought to. Sadly, it may already be too late. We're losing our history, because we're not paying attention.

Before the advent of a thousand things that plug in but drop dead when the power fails, the kitchen table was the home entertainment center. Or the porch. Maybe the couch by the fireplace. Folks talked. They told stories and did so with an accent and manner peculiar to the place. They dispensed village and family lore, over and over, and with the repeating came the remembering, and the memory was made solid and sure.

Today, the younger the person you talk with, the less you'll learn about the past. Somebody still may be telling stories.

But is anyone listening?

In mid-September, I went down that Town Landing ladder and into Jay's boat again. This time, we headed to Sipson's Island, walked to a sitting spot at the high place and looked off at the sweep of the Bay. This time, two things were different. The wind whipped warmer than it had in May. And I was just a little smarter about the view.

I still don't have a boat.

But I know now where I'd go if I did.

M.J.M.

The Bay

Pleasant Bay is a large estuarine embayment at the elbow of Cape Cod. The name means different things to different people. Some think of it as the cow-head shaped body of water west of Nickerson's Neck in Chatham and the islands: Strong, Sipson's and Little Sipson's. Others think of it as the whole area from the inlet at Chatham to Meetinghouse Pond in Orleans.

A Passing Glance

From available writings, the first use of the name is not known, but it appears on the map of Eastham and Orleans dated May 22, 1795.

The Bay—along with its tributary watersheds—lies in Chatham, Harwich, Brewster and Orleans. The estuary is about ten miles long and four miles wide, and at high tide has 7,285 acres. There are 56 miles of shoreline.

Those are the basics. The particulars are vast, complex and alive with all that nature creates, for this remarkable place—small as some would measure it—is a world of barrier and coastal beaches, freshwater streams and springs, coastal dunes, salt marsh, salt ponds, fish-spawning and nursery areas, shellfish beds and home for rare, threatened or endangered species. Deer, foxes, rabbits, raccoons, skunks, woodchucks and coyotes live on the Bay's uplands and islands, along with more than 200 species of birds that have been observed, more or less annually, around the area.

We are the most recent—and most threatening—newcomers to this world. Artifacts unearthed around the Bay prove that others were here first, perhaps as long ago as 6000-8000 B.C.

Geologists are used to thinking about the entire history of an area, including deeply-buried rocks which date back hundreds of millions of years below Cape Cod. But because these rocks aren't exposed on the Cape, they are left undescribed, lying below several hundred feet of Pleistocene glacial and coastal deposits.

The last continental glacier to spread over the entire New England area is known as the Late Wisconsin advance. This ice sheet, flowing south to southeasterly in direction, scraped, scoured and delivered to Cape Cod the sand, gravel boulders and clay that make up the entire area. The melting of this one-to two-mile thick ice sheet provided abundant water for reworking the glacial till deposits. At the same time, it caused the sea level to rise many fathoms. This helps explain the many kettle holes, ponds, outwash plains and channels.

As the ice retreated from the Bay area, beginning perhaps 16,000 years ago, the exposed, thawed but unvegetated land was reworked by prevailing winds. Over the next 10,000 to 12,000 years, the continental glaciers melted off North America, so sea levels rose. Extensive marine flooding of the coastal lands turned established woodlands into salt ponds and islands and eroded sanded flats and shoals. It may have been only a few thousand years ago that the Bay was changed from a series of fresh-water kettle ponds and hills into a growing saltwater embayment with ever-diminishing islands but growing salt marshes.

The earliest human habitation of land around the Bay is not carved in stone, but arrowheads and archaeological treasures found in shell middens indicate that Native Americans hunted game in the vegetation that followed glacial retreat. Early Irish North Atlantic fishing crews may have had contact with Indians prior to the Viking explorers who built North American settlements around 1000 A.D. The first European visits were recorded in the 17th century. Captain Thomas Dermer entered the Bay in 1619 and called it "Monomock." William Bradford came to "Manamoyick Bay" on a corn-buying voyage in 1622.

At that time, there probably was an entrance to the Bay southeast of Hog Island in Orleans, for there—on the outside of Nauset Beach—were found the keel and lower ribs of the *Sparrowhawk*, the ketch that went aground inside the harbor in December of 1626. The ship was repaired with supplies brought from Plymouth by Governor Bradford, but a following gale did so much damage that the *Sparrowhawk* was abandoned inside the inlet. Her bones were exhumed this century—on the Atlantic side of the beach—by storm wave action and now are exhibited at Pilgrim Hall in Plymouth.

When Champlain stopped by Nauset Inlet and "Port Fortune" (Chatham) in 1606, he made drawings of fairly sizeable Indian settlements there. But he or other Europeans must have left something behind, because those villages no longer existed by the time the Pilgrims arrived. The Indian population had been decimated by some foreign disease to which they had no immunity.

Indians here fished, hunted and raised corn. The land was wooded and kept that way, although undergrowth was burned regularly to make hunting easier. Tribes were headed by sachems who apparently had the right to sell land to white men.

Colonists from Plymouth began to settle in Nauset in 1644. In 1647, a Joseph Rogers came to Pochet, which may make him the earliest white settler in the Pleasant Bay area. William Nickerson built his house at the head of Ryder's Cove in 1664, and industry arrived a year later when a man named Baker built a tar kiln on the north side of what now is Tar Kiln River.

It took the new settlers just one century to alter completely what had been left the same by Indians for thousands of years. The virgin forest was turned into houses, barns, boats, saltworks, windmills and firewood. More land was cleared for farming, the forest topsoil depleted and the area's ecology remodeled entirely and permanently.

By the middle of the 19th century there began a new invasion. Railroad tracks were laid, and on them traveled vacationers, some of whom would become summer residents (not to be confused with tourists). Increasing numbers of affluent people escaped the city heat and came to row, sail and swim the waters of Pleasant Bay. New boarding houses flung open their doors. On Nickerson's Neck, the Hotel Chatham went up with a flourish in 1890 and closed almost before the paint dried.

As summer "cottages" blossomed around the Bay, pleasure-boat sailers became racers. In 1902, Pleasant Bay Yacht Club opened on a bluff north of Wequassett House. It would close in a few years but be replaced by Chatham Yacht Club on the Eastward Ho! shore.

The "Bell Boys" arrived at Little Pleasant Bay in 1900. Portanimicut's campers wore white middies, long sailor trousers and white caps. The first Cape Cod camp was open for only a dozen years, but it led the way. Thousands of children from around the world would come to five sailing camps on the Bay over the next 80 years.

Long before campers, racing sailors and holiday swimmers, the Bay was home base for fishing boats of all styles and sizes. In small cat and sloop-rigged sailboats, men set out, navigated over the treacherous Bar and—equipped only with experience, intuition and perhaps a compass—sailed east, probably drifted in the fog, fished all day and then, with unerring skill, maneuvered back over the shoals to safe harbor.

These were the near-shore fishermen. There were those, too, who sailed in larger sloops, yawls and schooners to work on the Grand Banks. And before the Cape Cod Canal opened in 1914, before the railroad came and a passable road system was built, traders moved goods by boat. Coastal shipping was vital to commerce in the 18th and 19th centuries.

The Bay area was home to not only fishermen and traders, but to lifesaving crews and Coast Guard men who were there because the open Atlantic off Orleans and Chatham was one awful place to be in the wrong sort of weather. Lifesaving stations dotted the shoreline, and men patrolled the Outer Beach in blizzard and nor'easter. Surfboats, breeches buoys and extraordinary courage were the tools of their trade.

Early in this century, the gas engine began popping up—and frequently pooping out—on the Bay. Power boat racing was tried in the late '20s, much to the annoyance of sailboat-owners who began to get that run-down feeling. But engines soon were being installed in both old catboats and new hulls designed for motoring.

The fishing fleet evolved with other technical advancements, but radios and radar still haven't made fishing a hazard-free business. The shoals continue to migrate, and storms are as powerful as they were a hundred years ago when lifesavers shot breeches buoys into the night. For anyone on a boat, the sea remains both the best of partners and the worst of enemies.

As late as 1944, there were fewer than 150 shore-front houses on the Bay, from Morris Island in Chatham to Meetinghouse Pond in Orleans. Post-war development began to fill in the landscape. The closing of the camps and development of their acreage brought another dramatic change.

Some areas, now protected, are not likely to change much. Nauset Beach is owned by Chatham and Orleans and is within the Cape Cod National Seashore. Pochet, Hog and Sampson's islands have been privately owned by the Pochet Island Trust since 1885 and have a permanent conservation restriction with the Department of the Interior. Little Pochet Island was given to the Town of Orleans by the trust in 1961, for conservation and recreation purposes. Strong Island was purchased by the Chatham Conservation Foundation in the early 1970s, and Little Sipson's Island was bought by the Orleans Conservation Trust in 1991.

The view of Pleasant Bay from the shore hasn't changed much over time. The view of the shore from the Bay is a different story.

The Indians wouldn't know the place.

You can divide geology into two chapters anywhere on Cape Cod. The first one is Glaciation.

The glacier got here about 21,000 years ago. By 18,000 years ago, it had retreated away from the Cape and into the Gulf of Maine. There was a tremendous amount of glacier melt-water around and a great deal of sediment coming out from under the glacier. The initial Bay or lowland was the result of a large ice mass sitting there. When that ice melted, the outwash surface collapsed down.

The Big Melt

In the Gulf of Maine, we've had a rising sea level for the past 18,000 years. Early sea-level rise was very rapid and gradually slowed through time. Recent sea-level rise was very slow, although records show a more rapid rise over the past 100 years. We don't have a perfect date as to when Pleasant Bay was submerged, but a good guess would be 6,000 years ago. That's chapter two—marine submergence of the glacial Cape.

Pleasant Bay is surrounded by outwash that was deposited by meltwater draining from the Cape Cod Bay glacier lobe. Once the ice front backed away from the Cape, all glacial deposition ceased.

The Cape is composed, in a very general way, of loose sand grains that have no resistance to wave attack. Waves began to erode glacial deposits and redeposited them to form the barrier spits and barrier beaches.

When you start to have wave erosion of a glacial landscape, the headlands erode. The Pleasant Bay barrier island, formed with a proper lagoon behind it, is composed of beach deposits, dune deposits and marsh deposits.

Pleasant Bay is there because the ice kept glacial sediment from being deposited. There is less sediment in the Bay than in the uplands around it.

We don't have watersheds on the Cape; we have water table. If we do get a stream, it's either tidal or a valley that reaches the water table. You can't have surface water on the Cape, because that water drains through that loose sand to the water table. In order to have a pond, you have to reach the water table.

Kettle holes are sites of buried ice blocks. Kettle ponds on the Cape are windows to the water table.

Pleasant Bay might have been described as a large kettle hole at one time. But we don't know where the seaward edge of that kettle hole was. Or, it might just have been open to the south channel.

If Indians were here, say, 9,000 years ago, they didn't have far to go to get to the sea because of the Gulf of Maine. There were embayments separated by headlands. From Eastham northward, those headlands have been eroded, so you have a smooth cliffed coastline.

On the assumption that sea level will continue to rise, the Cape will continue to wear away. However, we're due for another ice age. If that happens, sea level will drop and the Cape will get larger.

If sea level continues to rise, the people who really need to worry are those who live on the rockbound coast of New England because that area can't adjust to increased levels.

But sea level cannot continue to rise much. There is a finite amount of water on earth, and we're close to maximum sea level.

The Cape is going to wear away—no question. Beneath are loose sand grains, and loose sand has no strength. But that's an advantage, too, because the shoreline can adjust. All the erosion is a process of adjusting to sea level change.

Robert N. Oldale
(geologist, now retired from the United States Department of the Interior)

Photo by Richard C. Hiscock.

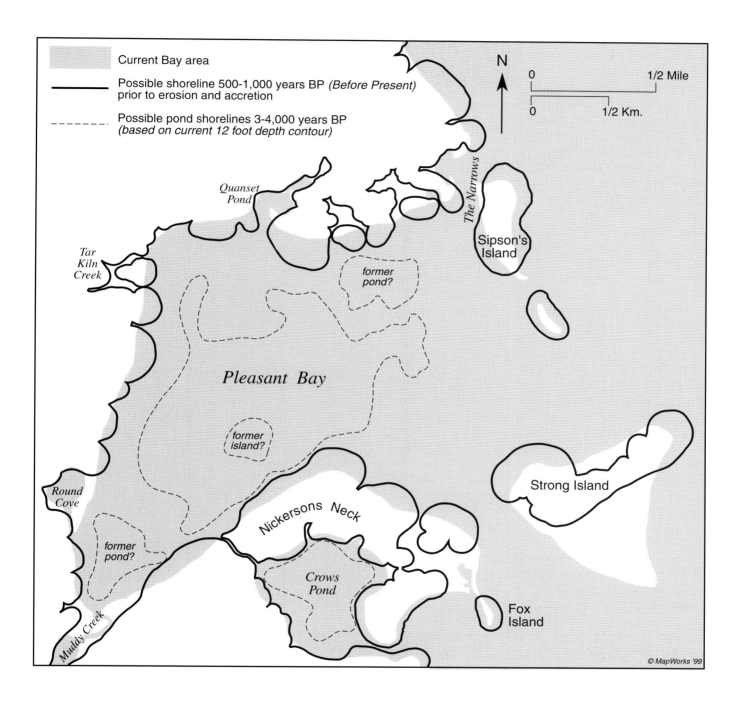

Current Bay area

Possible shoreline 500-1,000 years BP *(Before Present)* prior to erosion and accretion

Possible pond shorelines 3-4,000 years BP *(based on current 12 foot depth contour)*

N

| 0 | 1/2 Mile |
| 0 | 1/2 Km. |

Quanset Pond

Tar Kiln Creek

The Narrows

Sipson's Island

former pond?

Pleasant Bay

former island?

Strong Island

Round Cove

former pond?

Nickersons Neck

Crows Pond

Muddy Creek

Fox Island

© MapWorks '99

The Bay itself lies like a great blue patch on the ragged elbow of Cape Cod. Of all the bays, coves, creeks and salt-water ponds which fray the weather-beaten shoreline of the Cape, the waters of Pleasant Bay and those of Nawset Harbor are the only ones emptying directly into the Atlantic. Around and outside of it all simmers the lace-like tracery of the breakers on the Back Side forever and ever weaving new patterns of white.

The amateur boatman is hard put to find a rock or shoal on which to wreck his craft. Except for a few scattered boulders close in on the West and Orleans Shores and the sandy shoal of the Middleground off the elbow of the Clam Point, the whole Bay west of a line from Great Point to Big Sipson's is free from hazards.

I suppose the basin of The Bay is a product of the last ice age, when Cape Cod was part of the terminal moraine of the great glacier. When the edge of the ice cap retreated northward under pressure of warmer skies, it probably left a huge chunk of ice wedged in behind the old clay beds which geologists claim were here before the last ice period. When this huge cake finally melted, it left the kettle hole which holds The Bay. Every pebble and rock on its shores and every handful of sand from its banks tells the story of the long glacial trail which ended here.

I believe The Bay must look today much as it did thousands of years ago to the first roving red Indian who scouted ahead of his migratory tribe and peered out from behind some early savin bush or clump of beachplum bushes on its virgin waters. It undoubtedly lay a little more open to the sea in that far day, before the Outer Beach had had time to make down from Pochet and close it in. The sea-worn headlands and boulder-strewn shores of the Islands, which even now practically barricade its eastern side, offer ample testimony to their ancient battle with the open ocean. The Inlet, which even within historical times opened directly into The Bay opposite my Nick-Shack, has been pushed hither and yon at the caprice of storm and tide, but the great Bay itself undoubtedly remains essentially as the melting ice pack left it.

The waters which fill it are nomads from the seven seas. Twice in every twenty-four hours they merrily meet outside the jutting elbow of Cape Cod. Frigid Arctic current rubs its cold shoulder with tepid Gulf Stream and then squeezes in between the North and South Breakers. It may well be that the waters which lap the sands below my Nick-Shack once washed the

shores of bloody Iwo Jima or basked in the limpid blue of some Italian grotto. I only know that for a few short hours they come together to fill The Bay, and then are gone again with the changing tide to the four corners of the earth, no one knows whither.

In their mad rush to hit high water mark and fill every creek, guzzle and saltwater

Warren Sears Nickerson, 1904.

pond between the Outer Bar and the Head of The Bay, the ocean tides roar in over the Roaring Bull, tear themselves into rips through the tortuous slues of the Cow Yard and twist into whirlpools as they hit the barrier of Ram Island Flat and the Mussel Beds. Once past the Flat, the main current swings northwest up channel to hawse up the boats moored under High Scatteree, while a split-off branch follows the Beach Channel up back of the Islands.

Still rushing toward The Bay, the flood turns aside to fill Ryder's Cove and Crow's Pond before it strikes Jesse's Folly and spits in angry foam on the lower end of The Spit. Over-running The Spit, it joins forces south of The Hummock with part of the current from Beach Channel coming in around the East End of Strong Island, and together they crowd out between Dogfish Bar and Great Point into The Bay.

From the front porch of my Nick-Shack on a calm day I can trace the bore of the flood as it pushes out into The Bay straight toward its northwest corner. At about half flood, it gradually swings toward the south until it finally is heading southwesterly along shore toward The Head of The Bay. With The Bay filling up, it pours through The Narrows into Little Bay, joining the flood surging up over the Flats back of The Islands, over-running the marshes of Sampson's and Hog islands, spilling over into Pochet Island Channel and then pressing in around Namequoit Point and on up The River to the headwaters of Meeting House Pond.

But even before it is high tide in The Bay, it is ebb tide on The Bar; and as I watch it creeping up the shore below my Nick-Shack, suddenly it has nipped, and a telltale border of wet sand below my highwater mark tells me that it is on the ebb again. The seaweeds and mosses brought in by the flood will trace their delicate patterns on the yellow sands, and soon The Bay will be waiting in hushed expectancy for a new tide to fill it with new water again.

How like the great mystery of life are the tides of The Bay. We drift into being out of the vast sea of life which seems to pervade the universe. The flood tide of youth with its whirlpools and undercurrents rushes us along for a little while, just as the waters from the seven seas meet at the Harbor Bars and swirl up channel into The Bay. Then, before we realize it, life's tide has nipped and is going out again, perhaps to scatter like the waters of The Bay to replenish that everlasting surge from whence it came, so that life in its myriad forms may still go on undiminished.

Warren Sears Nickerson,
From *The Bay as I See It*, written some 50 years ago

The Path

When our pioneer forefathers pushed down the Cape to make their homes, the only means of communication by land was over the old footpaths of the Indians. Route 28 between Chatham and Orleans follows very closely what once was the Wading Place Path of the Indians. Packed hard by countless generations of moccasined feet, this ancient single-file trail was the Indian highway from the land of the Monomoyicks down the Cape into Nawset country. It came out of the Indians Cotch-pin-ecote, Chatham's Old Harbor of today, and crossed the little creek which they called Pamuet, the Step Stones, from the fact that they had rolled big boulders into it so they could step across dry-shod from stone to stone. Route 28 crosses at exactly the same spot.

From the Step Stones, it followed along the Ryder's Cove shore to the lodge of Mattaquason, the Old Sagamore of the Monomoyicks, which stood near where the Christopher Ryder House stands today. Nearby was the grave of the Pilgrim's famous Indian friend, Squanto, who died here after he had piloted Governor Bradford in over the Bars and up to the village. Just across The Path, the immigrants William Nickerson and his goodwife Anne raised their cabin, the first settlers in the Town of Chatham, and on the knoll their graves still overlook the homestead they hacked out of a wilderness.

The Path continued on over the hill and down to the shore, where the Monomoyick River of the Indians empties into Pleasant Bay. A short distance upstream on the Harwich bank of the river stood the "English-built" house of Micah Rafe, the last full-blood in these parts, who my grandfather could remember well. Just below the present causeway, the Indians on the trail could wade the river on the clean yellow sands at its mouth. This was Aske-onkton, their Wading Place, and it gave its name not only to The Path but to the whole locality roundabout.

Leaving the Wading Place behind, The Path wound along the Bay shore to Wequassett, where, on the west side of Round Cove, stood the "Indian-built" wigwam of Isaac Jeems, known as the last wigwam Indian in this vicinity, and his mother, Wahenanon, the granddaughter of the Old Sagamore. After his death, my great-grandfather bought the wigwam site from Micah Rafe, and I was born and grew up nearby, while yet the spot was still known as Isaac Jeem's Wigwam.

The Path swung inland from Round Cove into Indian Hollow to avoid the mucky cedar swamps which lay ahead in those days. Route 28 does not follow it here but picks it up again just beyond Baker's Tar Kiln Meadow in South Orleans. In my boyhood, a short stretch of the original Wading Place Path still remained intact in the Hollow, just as the Indians who made it left it. Worn deep into the hillside, it had never been plowed under by the white man nor overlaid with one of his roads. It was a little spooky, too, for a small boy, because it ran right between the Squaws' Grieving Stone and the group of fieldstones marking Indian graves, probably those of Isaac Jeems and his mother, Wahenanon, among them.

Tradition had it that the curious cup-like holes sunk into the top of the boulder had been chipped out by Indian women sitting there to mourn their dead. I often took The Path on my way to school in East Harwich and always held my breath until I was safely past this scary spot.

After leaving the Hollow, The Path swung around the cedar swamps, nearly cutting my father's dooryard in two, and from there made a beeline for Baker's Tar Kiln. I followed this well-worn path on foot all during my student days at Orleans High School and believe it was a relic of the old Wading Place Path although it had lost its name and its identity.

My path took me on a single log across the beautiful little brook which babbles down into the Meadow and through the open field marked only by the smallpox gravestone of Thomas Freeman, one of my nearly forgotten great-grandfathers.

On the high hill overlooking the Bay, Route 28 again picks up the trail which it left at Round Cove and follows it in a general way down to Arey's Pond, where once the remnant of the powerful Nawset Tribe clustered around the wigwam of their last sachem, John Sipson.

The old trail must have sent a branch from Arey's Pond down into Pochet, and certainly one to Namskaket, over which Governor Bradford tells us he toted supplies for the shipwrecked *Sparrowhawk*.

One day in the summer of 1960, my daughter Dorothy took me and her children into the Indian Hollow to see if any trace of the Wading Place Path could still be found. What used to be a pasture field was now overgrown with the underbrush and forest trees of nearly three-quarters of a century. Still, we had little difficulty in locating the old path which was plainly marked by a dip in the earth running north and south under the leaves.

There, too, stood the lonely old Grieving Stone, with the curious holes in its top, just as it did when I scurried past as a schoolboy.

A rabbit had made his home under the downhill side, and in The Path beside it, red Indian-pipes were growing.

Warren Sears Nickerson
1888-1966

Alongshore

For years the building sat empty and quiet, and to many who passed by it was only a landmark—a place that used to be something.

But once upon a time not very long ago, Chatham's Old Harbor Lifesaving Station was anything but quiet. And for the surfmen who lived there—who walked the Outer Beach, staring out to sea, in fog, nor'easter and blizzard—work was a matter of life and death.

Here, taken from the U.S. Life Saving Service Annual Reports, is an brief look at what went on at the Old Harbor Station—once upon a time.

1898

May 1—Station officially manned by Keeper Hezekiah Doane and 6 surfmen.

May 24—The fishing schooner *Lorna Doone* mistook lights on shore and stranded on Chatham bars shortly after midnight. The station crew boarded her, followed shortly by the Chatham station crew and a crew from shore. The master made a contract with the men from shore to float the vessel.

August 27—A dory anchored in the channel, its occupants (two women and one man) having become tired out by rowing against a strong current. When they tried to get their anchor, they found it was fouled on a piece of sunken wreckage and could not be raised. Two surfmen went to them in a dory, cleared their anchor and saw them safely to the landing.

September 17—Two men in a small catboat anchored off the station, having been prevented from entering Chatham harbor by the heavy surf on the bar. The station crew boarded the craft and brought the men to the station where they remained overnight.

November 29—Bodies of five people who perished in the great storm (the *Portland* gale) were washed up on the beach between this date and December 1. Surfmen took charge of them until removed by the proper local authorities.

December 5—The station lookout found a man's body on the beach near the station. Surfmen took it to North Chatham in a dory and delivered it to the coroner.

December 6—Two surfmen picked up the body of a colored man on the beach two miles North of the station.

1899

March 31—The surfmen on North patrol burned a Coston signal and warned a schooner off a dangerous course.

October 23—The schooner *Jenny Greenbank* was discovered aground on Chatham bars at 2 a.m. The station crew reached her in the surfboat at 2:45 and soon succeeded in hauling her afloat, but as she was inside the other shoals, she stranded again. They then threw some of her cargo of coal overboard, but failed to release her. At daylight, a wrecking crew came off from Chatham, with whom the master made a bargain to float his vessel.

1901

July 23—Telephone cable laid across the harbor.

1902

Captain Doane and crew brought ashore the crew of the schooner *Commerce*, which was blown to sea. The crew was rescued by the tug *Lackawanna*. Capt. Pearson of the *Commerce* abandoned the vessel when he found it was being driven to sea.

1902

February 13—The fishing schooner *Elsie M. Smith* of 12 tons burden, hauling from Gloucester and carrying 18 men stranded and became a total wreck, involving the loss of two lives, needlessly sacrificed in the attempt made by three of the crew to reach land in one of the dories.

The schooner arrived on the fishing ground the day after leaving Gloucester and during the following 48 hours succeeded in taking on board a catch of 10,000 pounds. But on the 13th the sea was so rough that fishing became impracticable and she was compelled to stand off and on and at times heave to. After darkness shut down, the wind came on heavy from the Northeast, with frequent snow squalls and almost continuous thick weather.

The bodies of the two men who drowned were subsequently found in the vicinity and reverently buried in the cemetery at Chatham.

Had the entire crew patiently remained on board the schooner until the arrival of the lifesavers, none would have been lost, and on the other hand, had there been no lifesaving stations in the vicinity, all must have frozen to death in the rigging or, if they had drifted ashore, miserably perished on the bleak mid-winter sands.

August 17—A small skiff was drifting rapidly out of the harbor, carrying a small boy who was helpless. Surfmen rescued the lad and towed the boat ashore.

1904

April 29—During a thick fog, the schooner *Future* stranded on Nauset Beach. The heavy surf making it impossible to launch the surfboat, the life-savers immediately started to her assistance with the beach apparatus. After a hard drag through the soft sand, the apparatus was set up abreast of the schooner, a line was fired across her and the crew of eight men were landed in the breeches buoy. The rescued men were taken to the station, furnished with dry clothing and succored at the station for 48 hours.

July 1—About midnight, the British barkentine *Albertina* collided with an obstruction in Pollock Rip Slue, staving a large hole in her bow, and as she was making water fast the master ran her aground on Chatham Bar, 2 miles South of the station, to save her from sinking. Three days later, in response to a signal, the Keeper, with Keeper Eldridge of Chatham station, again mustered a crew, went to the barkentine and brought on shore the wife of the master and a quantity of personal effects. The following day, a board of survey condemned the vessel and she was stripped and abandoned.

October 13—The British schooner *Wentworth* stranded on Chatham Bars and all hands perished. She had sailed from Nova Scotia on October 11, bound for Newark, N.J. with a cargo of plaster and a crew of 7. The master owned 1/4 interest in her and was accompanied on the voyage by his wife and 3 small children. The vessel was first discovered at 7:20 p.m. by the South patrol. It had been blowing hard all day from the Northeast, making up an unusually heavy sea by nightfall. The Surfman had reached the end of his beat when the faint sound of a fog horn reached him. He ran down to the surf, where he could barely make out the outline of a schooner. He at once burned a Coston signal to inform the crew that their situation had been observed and that help was at hand. He at once called up the Keeper on the phone. A Coston signal was flashed from the station, but no response came from the schooner.

Shortly before daylight, the Keeper of Chatham Station reported that a name board with *Wentworth* on it had been found on the Chatham beach. This was the first knowledge the Old Harbor station crew had of the vessel's name. When day dawned, a dismal picture was revealed. The vessel lay stern on, with her hull almost submerged, her bowsprit and jib boom were standing, as was also her foremast. The main-

Old Harbor Life Saving Station.

mast was broken off at the deck. The mizzenmast lay in the water alongside with a mass of other wreckage. Her stern was split open and the after-deck house gone.

At 6 a.m., the patrol saw an object floating near the south point of the beach below the wreck. He waded out and brought ashore the body of a woman. She appeared to be about 25 years of age, was fully clothed, with a blanket looseley knotted around her body, as though it had bound a child to her. A little later, the body of a man was picked up on the beach some distance from the wreck.

The body of the captain's wife was shipped to her home. The seaman was buried in Chatham.

1909

March 9—The steamer *H.F. Dimock* collided with the steamer *Horatio Hall* and was beached 1/2 mile SSE of Orleans station to avoid sinking. The steamer could not be seen, owing to dense fog, but her distress signals were heard at the Orleans station. The master informed the Keeper that the *Horatio Hall* had sunk,

but that he had her passengers and crew aboard. The work of rescue was continued, and 67 persons were landed.

1910

December 8—Central heating system installed at station.

1912

January 9—Went to the aid of sharpie *Odessa*.

1913

August 10—Went to the aid of British schooner *Parana*, 6 1/2 miles south of the station. Saved the 5-man crew, but the ship was lost.

1915

January 28—The Revenue Cutter Service and the Life Saving Service were merged and became known as the Coast Guard, by an act of Congress approved this date.

1916

November 21—An unnamed motorboat parted her moorings and became stranded. She was hauled up on the beach.

1919

August 28—Navy seaplane #2241 became stranded 4 miles North of the station. It was pulled clear by the station crew and towed to the Naval Air Station at Chatham.

December 11—A motorboat with person onboard was left dry on the meadow 1 1/2 miles Northeast of station. It was launched by the crew using planks and rollers.

1921

June 29—The motorboat *Laconia* with 2 persons on board was towed into the harbor and anchored in a safe place after her motor became disabled.

As the years passed, activity at the Old Harbor Station changed dramatically. Fewer and fewer sailing ships passed by. Commercial vessels were powered by engine, and more of them were going by way of the Cape Cod Canal. Now, the Old Harbor men found themselves hauling in loose skiffs and rescuing pleasure boaters whose motors had quit.

Since 1898, the station had been a haven for men and women pulled from the sea. But by 1976, with winter storm tides pounding at its foundation, the empty old building itself needed rescuing.

In November of 1977, the last of the Cape's original life-saving stations was hoisted onto a barge and moved out of harm's way. By spring of the following year, Old Harbor Station was, appropriately enough, safe ashore—at Race Point Beach in Provincetown.

Marcellus Eldredge was no fool when it came to business. Born and schooled in Chatham, the boy moved with his family to Portsmouth, New Hampshire where he and his father later bought what would become just about the biggest brewery in New England. Marcellus and his wife, Chatham native Mary Dill, had a lavish home on Watch Hill and a fortune in the bank. Mr. Eldredge gave the town its public library in 1896, and with his brother H. Fisher Eldredge, contributed 3,000 books.

Somewhere along the way, the man from Chatham met a man from Maine.

Eben Jordan had left his hometown of Danville when he was fourteen. He had $1.25 in his pocket. Just as so many Cape Cod boys of the 19th century did, Eben Jordan went to Boston to seek his fortune.

He found it.

In 1851, the 29-year-old Jordan joined forces with Benjamin Marsh and opened a small business on Milk Street. By the mid-1880s, when Marcellus Eldredge started having thoughts about building a hotel in Chatham, Eben Jordan had much more than $1.25.

Eldredge had his eye on Nickerson Neck—a large, open expanse of land with water wrapped around it. Together with his brother and the Jordan Marsh partner, he bought both that land and Strong Island for $5,000.

The three smart businessmen were about to build the biggest, grandest and most fabulous flop the town would ever see.

The Hotel Chatham opened its doors on June 30, 1890. The place was astonishing, its advertising booklet wildly flowery.

"Who has ever glanced at a map of the United States and not marveled at that wild prank of creation, Cape Cod!" the book began, wooing the well-to-do to the "ancient town" of Chatham and its quaint people. "Born of generations of mariners and in the very

Hotel Chatham.

spray of the ocean wave, the inhabitants of Chatham are, through and through, a seafaring people, but not of the kind that are told about in books. On the contrary, they are, like the rest of the denizens of the Cape, a modest and amiable race."

Not only were the local folks swell, but they lived to be very, very old, the hotel folks pointed out. "Longevity is a conspicuous and grateful phase of human life throughout Cape Cod...." Presumably, a two-week stay at the Hotel Chatham might extend the lifespan of the vacationer.

The three-story hotel was built "upon the very brim of the sea. The hotel property embraces not only the peninsula or neck of land on which the building stands, but a neighboring promontory as well. Indeed, there is in all between six and seven miles of continuous water-front owned by the company...."

Inside the hotel were parlors, a billiard room, dining rooms and more than 70 spacious bedrooms, all of which had a water view. Broad piazzas ran halfway around the building, and one of them was for men only, "a provision that cannot fail to appeal to men who like to enjoy the selfish pleasures of their kind without intruding or being intruded upon."

The management waxed eloquent about the hotel's "natural drainage" and plumbing. "The system of sewerage of the Hotel Chatham was designed by us and constructed under our supervision, with the object of securing an absolutely safe and inoffensive removal of all the liquid wastes."

While the waste removal was "inoffensive" to guests, it probably wasn't to fish in the Bay. "All sewage is quickly removed to a distance from the building, and at the proper time discharged into the swift current of the ebb tide and carried out to sea."

Black servants attended the guests, and the list of amenities included bathing, gunning, fishing, archery, horseback riding and frequent clambakes.

If all else failed, shopping trips to Boston could be taken between breakfast and dinner, by way of the railroad that had been brought to town. A major stockholder in The Chatham Railroad Company, chartered on February 25, 1887, was none other than Marcellus Eldredge. The new service connected with the Old Colony Railroad in Harwich, and the trip from Chatham to Boston was made in the amazing time of 2 1/2 hours.

The Hotel Chatham, on its magnificent site, was expansive, lavish and a total bust.

It closed after three seasons.

The hotel sat empty for 15 years. Then its contents were sold at auction and the building torn down.

What went wrong? Certainly the financial panic of 1893 had an impact on would-be guests. Perhaps the place was too far from those quaint old people and the village of Chatham. A round-trip buggy ride to town cost $5, more than the price of a hotel room. What's more, some of the clever local folks were beginning to open their own boarding houses, most of them family-run and cheaper to maintain: the Travellers' Home, Monomoy House, Baxter House and, later, the Hawthorne, Hawes House, Hammond House.

In 1913, Charles Hardy started buying up land on the water in Chatham. He had an idea of his own, but some local people thought he was crazy to be spending as much as $500 an acre for land where you couldn't grow anything. Mr. Hardy, however, knew what to plant. The Chatham Bars Inn opened in 1914.

One more fairly elaborate establishment went up close to town at the end of the century. The Dill House—later renamed the Mattaquason—was built by the man who had married Mary Dill—Marcellus Eldredge.

Mr. Eldredge had the right idea. The Cape would be an ideal resort some day. Maybe the Hotel Chatham was just ahead of its time.

No matter. Eventually, another use was found for the land. The ghost of the old place sits just about on the fourth green at Eastward Ho!

The passing of the glorious 4th of July has left to memory a delightful reflection of the Pleasant Bay Yacht Club's celebration, the largest and most successful affair of the kind ever attempted in these parts.

Every feature of the program was finely carried out and excited the greatest interest. Nearly 3,000 people from all parts of the country, including many distinguished personages who are summering upon the Cape, were present to participate in the carnival and add to the first grand rousing send-off of the wide awake Pleasant Bay Yacht Club. The new club house was admired for its commodious and well-arranged rooms. The natural scenery surrounding the picturesque Bay was a charming view under the bright sky. No lovelier spot could be desired for a 4th of July outing.

Noise and fun were rife and unlimited. The Club has had an auspicious public debut, the club house has had a goodly warming and the organization is launched to the world with flying colors as a social organization second to none in the state.

The day opened clear and bright. The Stars and Stripes were hoisted on the new flagstaff at the signal gun, fired by veteran Webster Rogers, G.A.R. The Chatham and Orleans base ball teams were among the first comers on the ground, and there were yachts and boats of all sizes and descriptions—from the Commodore's (S.W. Winslow) steam yacht, Rear Commodore George Brown's knockabout, the auxiliary fishing boats to the little sharpies and skiffs.

About noon, Col. Caleb Chase of West Harwich arrived with Mr. Erastus Chase, Mr. Herbert Johnson and ladies.

A little later, Comm. Winslow arrived with General Blackmar, candidate for Congress, the orator of the day. Rear Admiral Rockwell was early on the ground, and like the jolly son of Neptune that he is, was the life of many little groups and knots.

We noticed at lunch table Senator Nye, Rep.

Cummings of Orleans, ex-Senator John Kenrick of Orleans, Marshall Adams of Provincetown, Osborn Nickerson of Chatham and John H. Drum of Harwich.

Commodore Winslow introduced Gen. William Blackmar in a neat little speech.

The words of the General were inspiring, and coming from the Dept. Commander of the G.A.R., had the force that is felt when delivered by one who has passed through the fire that tried men's souls during the Civil War. He spoke of the early settlers, their struggles for life and liberty, both on land and sea; the great sacrifices made from '61-'65 to save that which the fathers had planted with their prayers, watered with their tears and cemented with their blood. The veterans of the Grand Army present showed in their faces the love and pride and honor they felt, and all present were impressed with the same spirit of devotion to home and country that so filled the boys of '61.

The General spoke feelingly of the heroes of the Life Saving Service in both war and peace, and how much the country owed them. He also, with the large commodious Bay before him, encouraged the people in their efforts for a harbor of refuge here, where in the stress of weather, ships could make a harbor and not be driven down among the shoals, so dreaded by mariners since the days of "Eric the Red."

Admiral Rockwell eulogized the U.S. Navy, the deeds of the boys of the water, and explained in a humorous manner that although they might not be well up in the styles of land society, even if they eat pie with a knife (when they got pie), yet they had a knack of cleaning out anything that came in their way. He also thought the women of Cape Cod were not only handsome, but their sons were among the bravest and their daughters were the prettiest and best our land afforded.

The dancing in the hall, the boat races and sailing parties occupied the afternoon. The fireworks in the evening were the delight of the children.

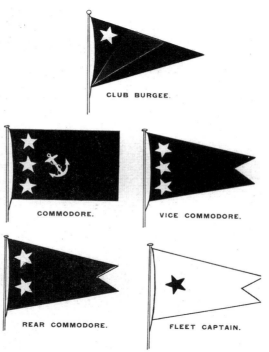

A Grand Affair

CLUB BURGEE.

COMMODORE.

VICE COMMODORE.

REAR COMMODORE.

FLEET CAPTAIN.

Pleasant Bay Yacht Club.

The dance hall was filled until the small hours, and celebration on Wequassett Hill in East Harwich was pronounced by all, both great and small, to be one grand success.

The yacht race was held back nearly one hour by the judges from the time set, by reason of lack of wind.

The race was on a triangular 3-mile course from a flying start. Winners in various classes were T. Carroll Nickerson, C.Y. Mayo, H.K. Cummings, Lawrence Brooks, R. Nickerson, N. Eldridge, Capt. Poor, A.B. Chase and J.R. Rogers.

By actual count, there was 83 boats, yachts, steamers and other crafts anchored off the new club house, which made a very pretty picture, and several inquiries have been made to learn if anyone had the good fortune to obtain a snap shot of the scene.

from *The Harwich Independent*
July, 1902

Pleasant Bay Yacht Club.

"It has become apparent since the war that the Lower Cape, apostrophized by Henry Thoreau as the future playground of America, has lacked facilties for the full enjoyment of outdoor life."

While it seems unlikely that Mr. Thoreau had imagined a "playground" with bowling, trap-shooting, lobster-broils, tennis and an "18-hole golf course second to none in the country," his name was used in 1919 to launch the sale of bonds for the new Chatham Country Club.

Four years earlier, G. Herbert Windeler and Charles A. Hardy had found some land they thought would make a fine golf course, the game having been introduced to America about 30 years before.

Nickerson's Neck in Chatham seemed to fit all the requirements for soil, grasses, contour, climate and wind. That all-important wind would guarantee that no hole would be the same two days running.

Scottish golf course architect Willie Park was asked to visit the site and report back to Mr. Windeler. "After going carefully over the land, I am of the opinion that it is admirably suited for this purpose. I should say it is one of the very best locations I have seen.... I would say a course equal to, if not better than, any on this (USA) or the other side (Britain) could be made at a very moderate cost."

Some 250 acres were purchased, and English architect Herbert Fowler was brought in to lay out the

Henry Thoreau & Eastward Ho!

The course.

Great Point Golf Club. Mr. Fowler, who had designed England's Westward Ho! course, had a simple philosophy; "God builds golf links, and the less man meddles the better for all concerned."

World War I meddled almost immediately, and the project was put on hold.

That "condition of status quo" ended a few years later, when the Location Committee of the Chatham Country Club voted to acquire the property, charter and organization of the as-yet-unbuilt golf club.

Now, with ambitious plans to create a "common meeting-place for the young and old of both sexes; to offer the best possible facilities for the enjoyment of outdoor sports on land, water and in the air...." the committee set out to sell bonds, with subscriptions from $1000 to $5,000.

Committee members were Joseph Lincoln, Joseph Crocker, D.E. Manson, Wallace P. Donham, S.W. Bridges, Herbert F. Winslow, C.F. Wing, Oscar C. Nickerson, R.W. Page, Everett Yeaw, Henry Fuller, N.S. Bartow, R.W. Sayles, Loring Underwood and Charles A. Hardy.

The formal opening of the Eastward Ho! golf links of the Chatham Country Club was held on July 3, 1922. *The Boston Herald* covered the event and called Eastward Ho! "Cape Cod's Wonder Links."

Two years later, the Country Club was in financial hot water. Members had supported three loans, and now were asked to do so again. More money was needed to finish work on the course.

The Club entered into an agreement with Charles Hardy, who already had second and third mortgages on the place. For the next two years, he advanced still more money to keep it going.

As the Country Club teetered on the edge of failure, the yachting committee organized as the Chatham Yacht Club and moved across the Bay to the shore of Edward F. McClennen's property.

Foreclosure was looming large in 1928, when Roy Tomlinson came forward. Mr. Tomlinson, who lived on the Bay and was president of the National Biscuit Company, bought the golf club—lock, stock and fairways—for $75,000. He then offered to sell the club back to its former members for exactly what he had paid.

On November 13 of that year, the Eastward Ho! Country Club, Inc. was established. Mr. Tomlinson had saved the day. The Chatham Yacht Club was invited back to the Eastward Ho! shore, where it remains today, as a tenant.

In his final report nearly 80 years ago, Herbert Fowler wrote, "I am quite certain that this course will compare favorably with the leading courses in the United Kingdon, and will be second to none of them."

Boat Racing on Pleasant Bay

The Chatham Country Club proposes to start small boat racing on Pleasant Bay in the season of 1921 with boats of the "Bay bird" Class. This class was designed by Burgess, and the boats will be built by William H. Chamberlain of Marblehead.

Boats of this type, 18' overall, 5'6" beam, jib and mainsail with centerboard, are in successful competition in Marblehead Harbor at the present time. In the opinion of the Yachting Committee of the Chatham Country Club, they represent the best type for local conditions.

The price is $300, f.o.b. Marblehead in groups of 15 or more. Fifty per cent is payable with the order, and the balance as called by the Treasurer of the Club.

Orders must be received prior to September 15th, 1920, for delivery at the opening of the Season of 1921. The Club will arrange for delivery at Chatham at the expense of the purchaser.

These boats will be cared for at the opening and close of each season by the Club, and storage provided during the winter months, at a moderate charge, if so arranged for by the owner.

Order blanks are attached hereto. The minimum number of 15 is already practically assured.

Further details may be secured from Messrs. O.C. Nickerson or Wallace B. Donham, of Chatham.

Well over one hundred years ago, small, odd buildings began appearing alongshore around the Bay. Almost always, they were built by a Cape Codder. Almost always, they were owned by a group of men from Away, that is, anyplace other than Cape Cod. And for a long time, they were part of the landscape.

The Club at Cole's Creek

These were gunning camps, where men of means would gather to eat, drink, dig clams, fry up scallops, swap stories, fish, make repairs, hike, take pictures and—as was the intent to start with—shoot almost anything that flew overhead. They built duck blinds out of slush, ice or seaweed. They shot and sometimes ate sheldrake, brant, geese and whistlers. They walked the flats, rowed the Bay and some were known to swim naked. They made popcorn, sang songs, played cards and, on rare occasions, invited along a wife or two.

Gunners from Away always had a local man in their midst. While he might not have been a club member, he was its guide, bird expert and, quite possibly, the only one who knew something about tides.

Rufus Nickerson of North Chatham had even more to do with the Cole's Creek Clubhouse. He built it—in the fall of 1913. And no matter the season, it was Rufus who ferried the men from the mainland to their camp.

The Cole's Creek Club was in the Broad Creek and Hog Island area of the Bay. Willie Gould and "One-Armed" (Fred) Higgins had camps in the same neighborhood, on the ocean side of North Beach. Principals in the sporting venture were Edward Allen Bullard, Emerson Morse Bullard, Ralph Emerson Bullard, Willard Everett, Dr. Arthur Hartwell, John Hartwell and Dr. Eben Norton.

A diary of activities was kept faithfully, Ralph Emerson Bullard being the chief scribe. The diary contains, too, a map of the Bay, noting places of particular interest near the camp: Blueberry Rock, Jeremiah's Gutter, Pocket (sic) Creek, Stinking Hummock, Oldfield's Flat, Lucy's Crotch, Hog Island Horseshoe and Uncle Jim's Slough.

Here follows a slice of life at the Cole's Creek Club.

December 16, 1915—What a night we put in from 8:30 to 5 this morning! Cold and blowy. Our steak and smothered onions dinner gave Hartwell a nightmare. He waked up all hands but himself. Physician, heal thyself. Morning cocktail all around of Sal. hepatica. Fine bright day. Ducks and geese in the bay seem fairly plentiful. Squires and Bullard bailed out box at the hummock, but not a duck passed in 2 hours. Rufus to take us where we can get a duck in the morning on "the first of the ebb." After supper Rufus smoked a

cigarette. Bad company begins to have its effects.

December 17—Up early. Took up stand in boxes across Broad Creek. Tide drove us out after Dr. H. had shot one "Whistler." Squires and Bullard relieved the ennui of their waiting program by shooting at single Whistlers at impossible distances. Rescued from the tide by Rufus in his shallop, we felt our way through the ice, moving in with the tide up to Rocky Point. Toured the hills for a time and enjoyed the scenery. Threatens a storm. Very pleasant song fest in the evening.

December 18—Blowing hard from S. west. Made ice blind near half-way house. Rain and wind melted it in short order. Shot 4 blacks from seaweed blind before 10 o'clock. Squires in One-armed Higgins' box to the south. Quiet afternoon at camp. Rufus made a bake of one black, the sheldrake and 2 whistlers. Splendid dinner. A fine vacation. Clearing and colder. Wind from the west. Rufus getting to be a cigarette fiend.

December 19—Everyone shaving and getting ready to go home. Leaving on floodtide about 10 o'clock. Total 4 days—7 blacks, 1 sheldrake, 2 whistlers.

May 20, 1916—Dr. Hartwell and R.E. Bullard left Norwood at 10:25 in Bullard's car. Lunched from a box where we stopped to look at the Cape Cod Canal. After a half-hour at Buzzard's Bay, we pushed on to Dr. H's house at 2:25. Put in the afternoon looking around, walking to the beach, where we bought lobsters and fish, and after a dinner of steak and onions went to bed at 8:15. Up at 6 o'clock. Took Mr. and Mrs. Rufus for a ride. Went to So. Orleans and looked over several acres of Scotch broom on a hill, with swamp at the back liberally sprinkled with blue cranes that rose up in a swarm when they saw us. Left a little after one o'clock for the camp, with Rufus in the power boat. Ran up to mouth of creek, though bumped propeller through sand for the last few hundred yards.

We do not place too much stress on what we eat, but for the benefit of future parties where eats may be less rated, we record with very comfortable feelings the menu of the evening's dinner: oysters fried in deep fat (egg and corn-meal kimonos), French-fried potatoes, macaroni-tomato-cheese cooked together (a glorious mess), lobster salad, asparagus on real toast, sliced peaches, spice cookies, tea, followed by cries for help, cigars, cigarettes and chewing gum—and a good drink to begin with. Did dishes, washed all the nasty towels, which left none for morning unless some dry in the night. A beautiful sunset. Prayers for a pleasant day tomorrow.

May 21st—The doctor threw another nightmare at one by the dollar alarm clock this A.M. Ye scribe was slumbering peacefully when he was startled wide-eyed by a series of yells from the doctor's boudoir. Wild cries of "Bill! Bill!" interspersed with groans and imprecations boomed through the camp, and peace was restored only by replying with similar yells and queries as to "Who in H—- is Bill!" The doctor informed his audience this morning that he was dreaming he had two wives. Having one, we are full of sympathy for his state of mind while dreaming of <u>bills</u>.

Up at 5 o'clock. Cold and blowy. Built a wood fire in the big stove after removing a tip-cart load of ashes. Made a blind by Higgins' camp and succeeded in photographing a few beetle-heads. The Dr. invented the piece-de-resistance for our dinner and named it "Cole's Creek Chowder." He swears the recipe shall die with him. It certainly was bully. R.E.B. had a fine swim in the surf just before dinner. Bathing suits are nix in this neck of the woods.

November 23—One-Armed Higgins showed up about 2 o'clock at his camp with 2 visitors. Up to now we have had no competition. Bailed out and located and waited. A motor boat making a H—- of a racket out in the bay somewhere drove in toward us two or three hundred ducks at least. We tried in desperation to stop some, but they were too high and coming before the wind like bullets. Then it rained and kept on raining. We stuck around and had the pleasure of of seeing more ducks & one that lit in with our sea weed decoys. Tried a pot-shot, but we had put the decoys out so far that the shot bounced off his bean. Rufus cleaned all the guns, while B. got supper and Dr. H. made candy. A quiet evening.

November 25—Fat chance to get a shot at a goose, the way they have been acting, sticking out over the bay halfway to Chatham. Reaching camp, the Dr. started in to make a duck-bake, picking a black and the beetlehead shot this morning. The one shot by Rufus the first day appeared to have gone into a decline before he was introduced to Rufus, so was passed on to the skunk-pile.

Took pictures of our ducks, and ourselves, by rigging the camera with a string out by the south door and standing by the piazza and pulling the shutter when everyone looked pleasant.

April 6, 1917—At it again. Left Norwood at 4 A.M. in a driving So'easter. Arrived at 8 o'clock—raining great guns and blowing a young hurricane. Too stormy to try to cross to camp, so we visited in Rufus' shop then had dinner at the Old Harbor Inn.

September 7—Hartwell, the whole damn family of Bullards, including Grandpa Morse, left Norwood at 4:45 in Bullard's Hudson. Moon shining when we pulled out, but this was quickly absorbed by the glorious sunrise over as beautiful a morning as ever proved the despair of a poet. A great ride down, with one stop at the height on the Canal, and then we rippled along at a steady 35 per hour. Dinner at Old Harbor Inn, which was unusually fine. (This for Rufus' eye later; he was cook at large.)

October 11—Warm as summer. Flies by the thousands. Arthur and several mosquitoes slept last night beneath a mosquito netting. At low tide we traveled miles and miles and miles and miles to get some scallops. It sure is worth it though. The stove pipe rusted off, so we had a nice cold lunch. Then we walked up the beach to the Life Saving Station. Fried scallops over two-burner oil stove. Figured out that we spent in getting, preparing and cooking evening meal about 5 1/2 hours. Hurrah for the simple life.

December 29, 1919—Cole's Creek full of slushy ice, and could not row the boat. Drew it along from the shore. Set decoys at box at mouth of Broad Creek and waited 2 hours. Picked up 5 buckets of scallops on Hog Island flats. Very plentiful. Dr. H. made some fine candy. Had the most delicious scallops for our supper, fried in a spider in lard by Rufus.

April 16, 1922—Easter Sunday morning, and as clear and beautiful as one could wish. What's good for a laugh must be good for the soul, so I guess the angels looking over the ramparts must have smiled in approval of the text for our morning's devotions, namely, "Play ball!" Dug a pail of clams and picked up 2 of scallops. Got the clams at Mikey's Hummock.

April 17—A grand morning with South wind. Left at 9 for a hike. Took skiff to Hog Island meadow, and from there hiked to Sampson's Island, took pictures and toured the place. Then across to Hog Island where we dug clams and steamed some in a pail. Great! Saw a lot of shelduck flying, and Jack and Em stalked a bunch of Higgins' geese decoys on the northerly side of Sampson's. They felt chagrined enough at their most natural mistake. Had the usual first-day dinner of steak and onions.

The first entry in the Cole's Creek Club diary was written on November 19, 1913. The book ends in December of 1929. Mr. Bullard noted, "Higgins had seven men gunning with him. This place is so exclusive now. Rufus shot a duck and apologized for so doing."

I grew up in West Chatham, near White Pond. We were dirt-poor, but it was a great place to live. My great-grandfather, Josiah Hardy, was keeper of the Chatham Light for twenty-eight years, beginning in 1872.

My aunt, Grace Hardy, was born in eighteen-something-or-other. Albert Read, pilot of the NC-4, was in her fifth-grade class at grade school in 1897. His father was a minister in town at the time.

Willard Nickerson and I were best men for each other fifty-five years ago. I worked for his father and grandfather down at Old Harbor Inn for a few summers. His father was the cook—a great cook. The help got the same food as the guests. If they had bass, we had bass. If they had lobster, we had lobster. It was beautifully prepared.

As kids, we used to ride over here on our bicycles and sneak into the blimp hangar through the window. There were ten thousand starlings in there! When they tore the place down, the starling droppings were a foot deep.

I can tell you, that hangar was right across there in front of us.

I went to work for American Airlines one month after I turned twenty-one. I was flying Captain when I was twenty-three, and I was with American all my career. We'd been living back here since '68, and I was commuting to Kennedy Airport. I guess it was just a natural thing for me to be interested in the Naval Air Station.

The base was built out there on Nickerson Neck because it had what they needed—a flat area and a place on the water for blimps and seaplanes.

Blimps had a greater range than planes. They'd scout for submarines. The gondola was nothing but an airplane fuselage. They lost quite a few people there—in the planes, not the blimps.

The Air Station was built on forty-four acres. Thirty-six acres were the farm, and another eight were leased from Great Point Golf Course—the predecessor of Eastward Ho!

Construction began in August of 1917, and the station was commissioned in January, 1918. The total cost of the whole thing was $7 million.

The station had two large and one small seaplane hangars, a blimp hangar, mess halls, barracks, a hospital and radio station, a munitions building, hydrogen tank, boat sheds, maintenance buildings, YMCA and Knights of Columbus buildings and a pigeon house, no less.

The blimp hangar was 252 feet long, 125 feet wide

and 75 feet high. The Class B blimp was 167 feet long, 30 feet in diameter and contained 80,000 cubic feet of hydrogen. The Class C blimp was 197 feet long, 42 feet in diameter and had 180,000 cubic feet of hydrogen.

Assigned to the base were twenty four seaplanes, two airships, six kite balloons, thirteen officers and one hundred and forty-five enlisted men.

The first flight was on June 6, 1918. The war ended on November 11, 1918, so you can see it wasn't in operation for a long time. It closed in 1923. In 1924, the buildings were demolished, except for the hangars. The blimp hangar was torn down in 1933.

The site was sold to a New York man in 1948—for $13,738. Then Fred Crowell bought it. I don't know what he paid for it, but he probably got his money back just from the lead pipe and cable in the ground.

It's hard to imagine the station was right over there where all those houses are. It was so inactive for so long after the war. It took money and an active economy to change that. Now, with prices they're getting, it's just plain scary.

Robert Hardy
North Chatham

Top: Bob Hardy and Willard Nickerson, 1938. Above: main gate to the base.

When war against Germany was declared in April of 1917, aviation was just getting off the ground. Planes were being designed, pilots were in training and the two east coast aviation bases—at Pensacola and Norfolk—were considered inadequate protection against possible attacks by enemy submarines.

The Navy designated sites for new stations, starting at Key West and moving north to Hampton Roads, Cape May, Rockaway Beach, Montauk Point—and Chathamport.

Construction at the Nickerson's Neck site began on August 29 of that year, and Chatham Naval Air Station was commissioned on January 6, 1918.

The mission of its men was to patrol the waters from Nantucket to Boston, escort and protect shipping and look out for U-boats. On hand for that work

The Base & The Flying Boat

were seaplanes, flying boats, kite balloons and dirigibles.

When the war began, plane-to-shore communication was for the birds—carrier pigeons, in fact. They were on board every time a plane went up, and if a submarine was spotted a pigeon was sent home with the message. By the summer of 1918, two towers were in place at the station, and planes were equipped with radios. But carrier pigeons still went along—in case of emergency.

On November 11, 1918—less than a year after Chatham NAS was commissioned—the war ended. Two years later, it was announced the station would close, and the following appeared in the NAS *Fly Paper*: "The Chatham Station, through its commanding officer, Lieut. Brewer, extends many thanks to the

Nickerson's Farm, site of the Naval Air Station.

residents of the vicinity for the courtesy that has been shown to the men.... They may deprive a person of almost anything imaginable, but they will never be able to deprive us of fond recollections, which we will always hold for you, 'Miss Chatham.' Good-bye and good luck to you...."

But before the station shut down, before the men left town and the buildings were demolished, Chatham Naval Air Station would play a part in one more remarkable event.

The Navy, wanting a plane that could cross the Atlantic and be as seaworthy as it was airworthy, had collaborated with seaplane designer Glenn Curtiss and developed a flying boat known as "Navy Curtiss" or "NC." In May of 1919, three of the "Nancies" took off from Long Island's Rockaway Beach. They were headed east.

Two of the small planes had trouble and went down before they reached the Azores.

NC-4 was forced down by engine trouble 100 miles off Cape Cod. She rode the sea all night, was spotted by a Coast Guard ship and towed to the Naval Air Station where—over the next six days—a new engine was installed.

On May 14, NC-4 took off, piloted by Lieutenant Albert Cushing Read. She made a scheduled stop in Trepassey, Newfoundland and went on to Lisbon, averaging 82 miles per hour. That was the flight's official end, but Lieut. Read flew on to Plymouth, England.

NC-4 was the first airplane to cross the Atlantic. She went from Cape Cod to England, just the reverse of the trip taken by some other folks nearly 300 years earlier.

In 1922, it was announced that materials at the Naval Air Station would be inventoried and sold to the highest bidder. Six years later, there was a small item in *The Chatham Monitor*; "Lumber from the airship building has been carted to Wellfleet, where it is being used for bulkheads and repairs to bath houses and cottages at Chequessett. Inn."

Chatham Naval Air Station.

NC-4, the first plane to cross the Atlantic.

Victory Day in Chatham, November, 1918.

July 21 fell on a Sunday in 1918. Things were quiet that morning along a hazy coastline. Folks sat on porches of summer homes that had begun sprouting on bluffs and islands and near beaches.

A few hundred yards off-shore, the tugboat *Perth Amboy* headed south on its way from Gloucester to New York, pulling a string of four barges. The first, loaded with granite, rode low in the water. The others were empty. One of those, a 180-foot long three-masted schooner, was the *Lansford*. Aboard were Captain Charles Ainsleigh and his crew, which consisted of Mrs. Ainsleigh and their two sons.

Down the road a few miles, things were Sunday-morning-quiet at the six-month-old Chatham Naval Air Station. Most of the men had gone off to play baseball.

But something ominous was swimming offshore that morning, and it was about to ruin a good ball-game and send folks as far away as Harwich flying off their rocking chairs.

The German submarine U-156 was up to no good on July 21. Its mission was to cut the trans-Atlantic cable that went from Orleans to Brest, France, thereby striking a massive blow to wartime communications between the United States and Europe.

First, the U-boat had to find the cable, which proved difficult. Then, once its location was pinpoint-ed, the cable had to be severed. That task proved to be at first challenging, then frustrating and, in the end, impossible.

The cable was buried too deep.

All of this took place while local folks were having their morning coffee, oblivious to the fact that within shouting distance was a submarine full of furious Germans who had decided to not leave without shooting something—*anything*!

The U-boat surfaced, and there—straight ahead—was the little tugboat with four sitting ducks follow-ing in a row.

The submarine opened fire at 10:30 in the morning.

What happened over the next two hours would prove annoying to the Germans, frustrating to Chatham pilots and vastly entertaining to those who gathered on the bluff to watch.

The first plane loaded with bombs couldn't take off from the Chatham Naval Air Station because of spark plug problems. The second plane got to the site and dropped a bomb, but it didn't go off. A third plane dropped two more duds. The first plane, presumably

with new spark plugs, arrived with another bomb that didn't work.

The planes were less than 400 feet above the water during this ineffective assault. One of the pilots got so angry he threw a wrench at the submarine. It hit the deck.

Meanwhile, the tug and its barges were still under fire. The *Perth Amboy* was damaged, and three of the four barges sunk—for being in the wrong place at the wrong time.

A few days later, *The Harwich Independent* reported the event:

"About 10:30, within a few miles of the shore, the U-boat began shelling the tug and a string of barges. Many of the shells went wide of their mark and struck the beach. The sound of guns caused the residents of that section of the Cape to flee to their cellars. When the firing continued and it was seen that no shells struck any houses, however, the people flocked to the bluffs to witness the strange sight. All accounts agreed that the submarine's shooting was very bad."

Dr. Danforth Taylor was of the same opinion. He was on his porch, about 100 yards from the bluff when the ruckus began. Dr. Taylor ran to the telephone and placed a call to *The Boston Globe*. From that point on, he ran back and forth from the bluff to the phone, giv-ing the newspaper a running commentary that was printed the next day.

"The fight is only a short distance from the shore and is plainly visible to all the cottagers here," Dr. Danforth reported. "There is a big German U-boat fir-ing at a tow-boat and four barges, but you should see that firing! It's the worst!

"The first shot landed in the surf just below this cottage. At first we thought the Hun was going to shell the houses along the beach, and a number of neighbors came here to take shelter in my place, as I have a good cellar.

"The first shot was fired at 10:30, and by this time everybody here with an American flag has it flying from their houses. Wait a minute, and I'll take anoth-er look and tell you how the fight is going!"

Later, Dr. Danforth said that 41 crew members, including three women and five children, had come safely ashore and were being cared for at the Orleans Coast Guard Station and in neighboring cottages. "Captain Charles Ainsleigh was wounded in both forearms by a bit of shell, probably shrapnel. I have attended to his wounds, but they are not serious.

One man who didn't hide in the cellar was Gilbert Russell Payson. Mr. Payson watched the event from his house on Pochet Island, and later wrote about it to Major Francis Palfrey, who was at the Base Hospital at Camp Greene, North Carolina.

Dear Frank,

I have not written to you in some time as I had very little to tell you, but we had some little excitement on the island a week ago yesterday, which you may be interested to hear about.

I was up at the new house in the middle of the morning when I heard a sharp report out at sea. I stepped out on the piazza just in time to see the flash of a gun on the edge of a fog bank, and immediately afterwards the explosion of a shell near a tow of four barges which were being hauled south, nearly opposite the island.

I immediately called to the family that a U-boat seemed to be smashing the tow which was passing, and all hands hurried up from the Old House to watch the entire operation.

The first barge was very low in the water, and we afterwards learned that it was loaded with granite. The other three were perfectly light. The U-boat fired quite rapidly and we could see each flash and the explosion of the shell on or near or sometimes halfway between the boats at which it

The photo Gilbert Russell Payson took on July 21, 1918, shows the **Perth Amboy** *crew being brought to shore by the crew of the Life Saving Station.*

27

seemed to be aiming. The loaded barge was sunk very soon and one of the light ones. Another one rolled over on its side and finally disappeared. The fourth went down by the bow, but the stern remained afloat and continued so throughout the week. When I left the island yesterday, the Wrecking Company was at work trying to salvage it.

The tug was struck four times and finally burst into flames, but remained afloat and was towed away Tuesday.

While this was going on, we could see the crew over at the station getting their surf boat out through the dunes, and shortly after watched them pulling rapidly toward the fire zone. The crew of the tug in the meantime had launched their boat and were rowing southerly to get out of the range of the U-boat, which was still shelling the barges and had now come so near that we could see her deck with the naked eye. She lay some south of the tow and further out to sea, so that the general direction of the shots was towards the Nauset Inlet. The crews from the barges launched their boats and were now rowing towards the north end of the beach.

Inside of the dunes, we could see a great many automobiles, where the sightseers had driven down from the mainland.

There is, as you probably know, a Naval Aviation Base over at Chatham on the point of land which was formerly part of the old Chatham Hotel property, and finally the planes, most of which seemed to have been out on patrol duty, began to fly over toward the scene of the trouble. The first plane got almost as far as the tug, and then veered and went northerly. The second plane, however, made a beeline for the U-boat, and we imagined must have dropped bombs, but she disappeared into the haze and fog about the same time that the U-boat also disappeared.

Just before the submarine vanished from view we heard a shot and almost simultaneously the whizz of some kind of a shell or shrapnel over our heads, so it is evident that her last shot was at one of the planes.

"One-arm" tells me that he saw this charge strike the water in the river over at Barley Neck. Asa, who was at the house when all this was going on, took me in his old wagon and we drove over to the station and were on the beach when the lifeboat and the crew of the tug arrived. I took a couple of pictures which were too small to be very valuable. I will send you a print later when I have some more struck off.

One of the members of the crew of the tug was hurt quite badly, a large piece of shrapnel having gone through his arm by the shoulder. The crews of the barges who landed up the beach were carried to Barley Neck by various Good Samaritans, but we ferried them to the island and they all spent the night at the station, with the exception of the wounded man and the captain of one of the barges. They were all taken off in various ways the next day.

I think I have told you the whole story, and believe that we had as good a view and as complete a view as anybody, although there was a great deal of peculiar drift in the papers from the summer boarders at Nauset, most of whom, as nearly as I can learn, took to the cellar and peeked through the piazza gratings.

In a little more than an hour that morning, 147 shells had been fired. Three boats were sunk, and three men injured. That no one died may have had a lot to do with poor shooting and bad bombs.

The submarine disappeared, the pilots flew back to Chatham and local folks left the bluff and went home for Sunday dinner, having just witnessed the only World War I attack on American soil.

Thirteen year-old Henry Payson, wearing a lifejacket from the Perth Amboy.

There may be a place somewhere in the United States that at one time or other had more summer camps per square inch than did the shores of Pleasant Bay.

But it seems unlikely.

Over a period of 90 years, seven camps on the Bay were home to thousands and thousands of children. Two of those camps came and went quickly, but a handful of others lasted a very long time indeed.

Portanimicut Camp for Boys, the first camp on Cape Cod, opened in 1900 on the west shore of Little Pleasant Bay. It ran for about a decade.

In 1925, Alice Murdoch opened a small camp at her house on the west side of Arey's River. Although the girls had lessons in swimming, rowing, sailing, leatherwork and basketry, French was the major subject at Camp Cheri. Mrs. Murdoch worked with her girls daily. They spoke French at all meals and during evening entertainments. Camp Cheri closed in 1934.

But in 1905, Mary L. Hammatt opened a camp that would continue for more than 70 years, with ownership passed down through the family, from Mrs. Hammatt to her son, "Poppa," then to his son and daughter-in law, Bruce and Ann Hammatt. Quanset Sailing Camp was the first of the Big Five on Pleasant Bay.

Camp Namequoit, on a 40-acre site happily wedged between Pilgrim Lake and the Bay, was the second. It was opened in 1925 by C.J. and Lou Anne Thayer, and upon their deaths, was taken over by their son, Brooks, his wife, Louise (a former sailing director at Avalon), and Arthur Farnham.

Down the Bay, at Crow's Pond in Chathamport, Ruth Gilmore started Avalon, a camp for girls, in 1929. In 1947, Avalon was bought by Gertrude and Bill Winkler. Twenty-two years later, Betty (Winkler) Laffey and her husband, George, took over.

Also in 1929, Camp Viking set sail at the Head of Little Pleasant Bay. Launched by M. Katherine Bryan,

Middies & Memories

Viking later was owned by Cedric and Beatrice Hagenbuckle and, at the last, directed by Tom Lincoln.

Alice Melcher, Mrs. Hammatt's daughter, opened Pleasant Bay Camp a few years later. It began as a day camp for 12-year-old boys and girls, but by 1943 was a resident camp with a staff of 23 counselors and 70 campers from six to 13 years old.

Together, the five sailing camps were a large and happy presence on the Bay for a long time. A lot of kids were in a lot of boats, having a lot of fun. Some of those campers came back year after year, growing into counselorhood. Some still come back—to visit the place where they learned to swim, learned to tie knots, learned how to get along.

They can come back and look at the Bay. But the camps are gone.

It didn't happen overnight. The camps prospered for years, but by the 1970s the world started to intrude.

Tax bills on waterfront property began climbing. Insurance premiums soared. Federal, state and local health and building regulations began piling up, and some of them were absurd. Conforming to those absurdities was costly, so enrolment fees went up. Campers of the '70s began to challenge rules and authority. Counselors wanted to do less and get more money.

And those who had been been in camping families for most or all of their lives started to wonder if it was worth the trouble.

Ultimately, they decided it wasn't.

Quanset closed in 1976. PBC closed in 1979. Camp Viking closed in 1984. And for Camp Namequoit and Avalon, the summer of 1988 was the last.

Still, people talk of a time when songs echoed across the water and the white sails of camp boats filled the Bay.

At present an acute problem of finances confronts the directors of Cape Cod camps. It is not profitable, nor is it economically sound, to try to run a camp which, from its very nature, should be more or less isolated, located on extensive tracts of otherwise vacant ground, on land that is worth from five hundred to three thousand dollars an acre. If the "boom" in Cape Cod real estate continues for even a short time longer, there are camps that ought to move and that probably will do so.

From a newspaper article, July 3, 1926

PBC cookout on the beach, 1949.

The camp family. Front: Jim Melcher, Mary Hammatt, Jean Melcher. Back: Anna Hammatt, Alice Melcher, Francis, Bruce and Ned Hammatt and Mary Lou (M'Lou) Melcher.

My grandmother, Mary L. Hammatt, started Camp Quanset in 1905. She and her husband had bought a house on Quanset Road in the late 1800s, and that building was the nucleus of the camp. She started it so my mother would have playmates; there were only a few kids at the beginning. They used to walk along the same road you came down to go to the beach.

I don't know how my grandmother knew how to run a camp. She had no experience. She didn't get to go to college. My grandfather wrote to owners of land and a lot of heirs; that's how they accumulated this camp land.

My mother worked with her mother, helping to run the camp. In 1936, my mother, Alice Melcher, left Quanset and her brother took over. In 1938, she started Pleasant Bay Camp, next to Quanset. Oh boy, did I love it. What a wonderful way to live. When Mother started PBC, it was a day camp. They had an old

woodie, and she hired specific counselors to drive the wagon and pick up kids. She had a route in Orleans and one in Chatham.

Most of them were summer kids. They had the money. But there were some local kids, too: Bill Snow and Freddy Livingston and Jan Nickerson and Joey Manson went there.

Some came for a month, some for the whole summer. There was a schedule for every day, because of the tide change. You tried to have swimming at high tide. We taught pottery, archery, tennis. Of course, the sailing program was the main thing.

A lot of people met their mates there. They came back year after year, I guess until they had children. Then their children came.

I have very fond memories of Quanset, especially, probably because I was little and didn't have any responsibilities.

When I was old enough, I was a camper. I lived in the bunkhouse, and I didn't get any special treatment. We'd race at Chatham Yacht Club. Of course, PBC raced there, too, but by then I was a counselor. When you're a counselor you don't do the sailing—just the instructing.

Every year they had a treasure hunt, and they'd plant clues on Hog Island or Sipson's Island. You had to sail to get them. My mother told about one time when someone found the treasure. They didn't want anyone else to come along and find it, so they took it and mailed it to themselves at the post office.

My father, Jim Melcher, worked at a bank in Newton, so it was the usual thing people did. He came down on the train for the weekend, and we picked him up. We were here for the summer; he wasn't.

I think my mother was a liberated woman, and I think my father knew and understood that she needed something to do—a career. The summer after she left Quanset, she built the biggest iris garden I've ever seen. She dug the earth, planted the flowers. It was gorgeous. I just love irises because of that. The next year she started PBC.

Here's a memory; Quanset had a boat—a big boat called *Tioga*. I'd call it a sloop, but it was large. We used to walk out on the bowsprit and dive off. We had all-day sails, take a cabinful of kids and most of the time sail to Chatham and the outside beach. Sometimes we'd camp overnight, build a fire on the beach and cook out. Nobody worried about that then. There were no permits. If it was raining, we'd walk up to Quilty's on Main Street in Chatham, get ice cream and sit there reading magazines until the rain stopped.

My grandmother taught me a lot. She read a lot, studied, spoke several languages. She would encourage children to follow their interests. One time she gave me a microscope—a real microscope. She hired someone to come to the camp and teach French and have a French table. We had an orchestra, too. My grandmother hired Mr. Nassi to come teach and conduct. I played the cello, and his daughter played the cello. Whoever could play something got into it. My grandmother was very progressive, I think.

At Quanset, they used to put on plays—this was before my time—at Town Hall, now the Academy of Performing Arts. Sometimes they did operettas. Those must have been wonderful. I think the camps interacted with the town more back then.

We also had a wonderful man who taught shop. Quanset was a girls' camp, but he taught us how to make boat models. We'd do the shaping and sanding and painting, and we'd make the mast and boom and sail.

You know, Ann Hammatt still has her boat. I wish I'd kept mine.

Mary Lou (Melcher) Brier
South Orleans

Alice and Jim Melcher.

Outfit

The outfit necessary for each camper consists of 4 single sheets, 3 pillowslips, 4 face towels, 3 bath towels, one pair of heavy weight, one pair of light weight blankets (gray preferred), 2 laundry bags, umbrella, rubbers, raincoat or oilskins, hot water bottle, sneakers or tennis shoes, 1 pair wool bloomers (navy blue), 3 pairs cotton bloomers (Quanset blue), 2 pairs white bloomers for Sunday, 6 middies, 1 black square tie, 1 Quanset blue square tie and a few simple light dresses. All articles must be plainly marked by the full name in woven name tapes. The order should be sent in with the application.

The fee for the season—June 30-August 25—is $350.00. July only, $180.00. August only, $185.00. Sisters have a 5% reduction.

Allowance for spending is deposited with the camp. This is limited to $5.00 per month for girls under 13 and from $10-$15 per month for older girls.

Camp Quanset, 1923

Cape Cod in February

The wind is rustling through the pine trees,
The surf is rolling on the shore.
The sun is shining brightly,
The sky is very blue.
Hear the cawing of the crows high in the air.
I am snowshoeing up the hill.
See the deer tracks in the snow.
See the boat on the Bay.
See the steamboat on the sea.
Don't you love Cape Cod?
I do.

Mary Lou Melcher
8 1/2 years old

Campers in Quanset middies, in the late '30s. Mary Lou Melcher is sitting in the back, maybe writing a poem.

Quanset girls at the Lodge, about 1910.

You get me started, and I can't stop. I feel I've been connected with camping more than anyone. I began in 1928. Grandma Hammatt—Mary L.—was quite a character. She had lost a sixteen year-old son, Robert, who was a playmate of her daughter Alice. So she said, "We'll have our own camp." She invited six or eight of Alice's friends to come down for the summer as paying guests. They were at the lodge up the road here until about 1912, when Grandma bought the land down on the Bay.

For those first few years, they had crafts along the Indian line, with headresses and all. They'd walk up to the post office—which then was at Sparrows' house at the end of Namequoit—in the hopes of meeting some boys along the way. In the evenings they'd make fudge, for entertainment. They kept logbooks back then. So did our campers. You know, girls haven't changed a lot in seventy years. They still talk about the same things.

I was a camper in 1928. I was here all summer and loved it. I remember we went down around Monomoy Point and out into the ocean right to Stonehorse Lightship. We were invited to come aboard. I was fourteen and thought I was very grown up. I was thrilled to be on a real ship.

When I was there in '28, first you sailed in sharpies, flat-bottom boats. While you were learning, you sailed a definite course. I always thought that was great. You didn't just get in the boat and sail wherever the wind took you. You stayed the course.

When you passed the test for sailing sharpies, you

36

raced Baybirds. They raced in Chatham, and there was great rivalry.

Bruce came to camp in '29 to work in the garden. If he worked two or three hours in the garden, he had sailing time coming to him. In a couple of years, he was teaching sailing. He was a great sailor.

I didn't come back to camp until 1935. I was at Mt. Holyoke, and I wrote for a job as a counselor. Alice Melcher interviewed me.

When Grandma Hammatt gave the camp to Poppa, she gave Alice a few acres to build a house. Then Alice did the same thing Grandma had done; she started with a few campers, then had Pleasant Bay Camp.

Bruce and I met in 1935 and were married in the fall of '36. We moved here in 1943. He fished with Howard Walker out of Rock Harbor for awhile, then bought his own boat—the *Annie H.*

Poppa Hammatt ran Quanset until 1962. His daughter Dorothy ran it through 1965, and we ran it from 1966 to 1976.

One little camper lived on Squaw Island off Hyannis. She was sent to camp for a month and didn't want to leave. Her parents were away someplace, and she got ahold of some money and took a taxi back to camp. She stayed in an empty bunkhouse and got one of the girls to bring her some food. She's the only one we ever had who ran away from home to come to camp.

One summer we had one hundred and fifty campers in July. That's a lot to take care of, especially when you've got twenty-two counselors who are more trouble than the campers. In the '60s that age was rebelling. One year they got together, came to us and demanded something or other. We settled it, but that was a difficult time. The last five years, we had great counselors.

Bruce had more charge of the physical plant, the bunkhouses, buildings, boats. He knew where the cesspools were when something got stuck or when roots got in the lines. We had a program director who took care of those things. I guess you might say I handled some of the personnel problems. I had done all the winter work, all the writing to parents. I knew who the children were, what the parents did. I was the mother, really, and I had my fingers in a good many pies.

When we took over, we didn't know where to begin, how many napkins to order. All four of our boys were with us then. Park was our program director. Merv was teaching sailing. Tommy worked on

Poppa Hammatt and daughter, Betsy.

maintenance. Bruce probably taught sailing then. That was a help for us that first summer.

We didn't know anything about the food. Our cook did the ordering, and the salesmen from the different companies, like S.S. Pierce, helped us. We also went to the American Camping Association meetings in Boston. That was a big help. We got in the swing of it.

One of the cooks served the girls lamb chops, at a cost of I don't know what. And kids hate 'em!

Then the rules started to change. The A.C.A. had their regulations. And the Town put in these rules. One was, we had to have exit lights over the doors of the bunkhouses. We didn't even have electricity in the bunkhouses. So here's the thing; they wanted us to put in electricity, so the exit signs would come on when the electricity went out!

When we met with the group from the State Building Inspector's office, one of the men said, "You have street lights around the camp, don't you?" Well, of course we didn't. The girls used flashlights.

That's enough to stop you. It drove me crazy. They changed the rules about how many you could have in the dining room. If we'd done that, we'd have had to have two sittings. We couldn't do it.

In the infirmary, we had to keep a special book. It couldn't have any pages ripped out, and we had to keep all the records for twenty years. We had one girl who brought some dope into camp. I took them out sailing on the Tioga,

37

and I could tell something was wrong with her. I could see she wasn't just right, but when you have girls thirteen or fourteen years old, you're never sure what's wrong with them.

We took her to the hospital, and she was full of dope. They sent a hospital bill. We had loads of insurance, but they wouldn't cover it because they said we weren't sure if she was trying to commit suicide! You didn't have a leg to stand on, no matter which way you went.

I said, this is foolish. We can sell the land and make more money than we can running a camp. Why the hell are we working ourselves to death?

We used to go horseback riding to Cliff Pond. We'd go for a swim, maybe have a picnic supper. And we'd do a breakfast ride. But things changed. Roads changed, and we had to take different routes. Eventually, the breakfast ride ended up at the town dump.

Civilization was closing in on us. We'd run a good old-fashioned camp, but times were changing.

About a third of our campers came from the Boston area, a third from New York and New Jersey and the rest from all over the world, from Belgium, South America, Japan. We had a nine-year-old from Japan, and they sent her on the plane by herself. We went to Boston to pick her up. The next year she came back with her little sister.

The Bay is so safe. There's nowhere where there's a current enough to bother you. No matter which way the tide is, it's always a slow, easy current.

It's been almost twenty-five years since we closed camp, and we still have campers come to visit. All of them associate the Bay with the joy of living. When we sold the land, some of them didn't want to come back anymore. They didn't want to see the change. I told them, "Come back. The Bay hasn't changed. It's just the way it was when you were here."

In my mind, I can see it back when the girls walked from the lodge to the beach, when they sat around in the evening and made fudge.

I still can see it.

Ann and *Bruce* Hammatt
South Orleans

Bay-diving, about 1910.

Cheer then, for Quanset!
Hail her bright name.
Far through the land her girls
Shall bear her bright name forever.
Down through the ages
Renowned shall she be
Fairest in all the land
Ever her name shall stand
Ever her girls sing to thee.

Quanset Driftwood, 1919

Ruth Gilmore was the original person. She lived in Squaretop, the house across the way there. They'd row over here and camp out. This was before 1929. Her kids kept bringing friends, and she decided this was something she could do. She started Camp Avalon.

Primarily, they did crafty things then. One of the big activities was making hammocks. Mrs. Gilmore ran the camp right through the war, with those ration books and all.

My aunt was Poppa Hammatt's second wife,

My aunt and uncle were divorced in 1947. My parents looked around to see if they could find their own camp. They stopped by to see Mrs. Gilmore—just to see her. She said, "What would you say if I said I wanted to sell this place." My father said, "Talk to me!"

Their first summer at Avalon was 1948. There were twenty-two campers and probably fifteen or sixteen counselors who came from Quanset with my parents.

They moved here in 1953 and ran the camp through the summer of 1969. We had come up for one summer, in 1961, and George headed the waterfront. In the fall of '68, my folks asked us, "What should we do with the camp?" We decided we'd come up and

Camp Avalon girls, 1934.

Elizabeth Hatch Hammatt. She married him somewhere in the early '40s. In 1938, my aunt called my mother and asked if I could come to camp—to Quanset—for a month. I was seven. They put me on a train; it came right into Orleans in those days. I came up for, I guess, six summers. Then, in 1943, Poppa Hammatt asked my folks, Gertrude and Bill Winkler, if they would come help out. My father was a pharmacist, and he figured that he could come up for the summer and go back to the pharmacy in the fall. He and my mother came for four years.

help, so we ran it together in 1969. Then we took over and ran it until 1988.

When I came here before Betty and I were married, I was trying to impress the future in-laws. I helped put in the pier. In those days, you didn't pump them in, you rocked them in!

There were kids here from all over the world. We got up to a total of one hundred and twenty-four campers and a staff of forty. We ended up feeding about one hundred and sixty.

Avalon, 1950s.

We were in California recently and visited one girl who was with us for fourteen years. A lot of the girls came as little campers and stayed to become counselors.

When we took over, we added a number of boats: Baybirds, Mercuries, Turnabouts. When Pleasant Bay Camp closed, we bought a Baybird and their big sailing whaleboat, a thirty footer. We had six Baybirds, nine Mercuries, five Turnabouts, the sailing whaleboat, a catamaran, a Marshall cat, plus four boats with motors. We had Boston Whalers for patrolling races. We all—all the camps—were very, very careful with our kids on the water.

When the 1988 season ended, we painted the floors of all the cabins, polyurethaned the dining room floor, got the boats put away and set for the next summer—did the things we always did. We were all ready to open again.

It all started when some people came down and asked us about selling the camp. We said, "We're not going to sell."

The State was beginning to talk more about handicapped people being allowed in all buildings. We would have to have ramps to all the cabins. We'd have to have bigger bathrooms. The bathrooms were inside, so to make them bigger would have meant losing cabin space. Exit signs over doors would have to be electrified. Our kids could get out the windows faster than they got out the doors!

All of a sudden there were worries about AID.S. In those days, people were afraid that if someone breathed on you, you'd get AIDS.

And people had begun to sue, left and right. "Oh, I stubbed my toe!" It never happened to us, but it was a concern.

Insurance prices went out of sight. We had a trampoline; we had to get rid of it. We'd never had a sailing acci-dent, but our insurance had gone up relatively quickly, sometimes double and triple.

We had no children who were interested in taking over. That was true at some of the other camps, too. Also, I never wanted to have a last season.

Neither of us wanted a "last season." It's bad enough when the kids leave, because they cry like the devil. But we didn't want them to spend the summer saying, "This is the last time we'll ever" do this or do that.

And we were getting older. We'd always been "Betty and Laff." We didn't want to be grandparents to the girls.

It was very, very tough when we wrote the letter saying we were closing.

The Bay was a wonderful place for a sailing camp. It has ten miles of inland water, and that's ideal for small boats. They'd sail from here at Crows Pond to Big Pleasant Bay and all the way up to Little Bay.

There are lobster pots in the channel now, between Strong Island and Eastward Point. They make navigating somewhat difficult. And the tides are different; low tide is lower and high tide is higher.

Being a camp director was one of the finest things I could ever have done. I wish I'd done it right out of college, rather than waiting. We had no disrespectful kids. They all were good people.

In the fall, we were tired and needed some rest. But we had wonderful, wonderful summers.

Betty (Winkler) and *George* Laffey
Chathamport

Camp Avalon is having a Splash Party and Luncheon at the Y.W.C.A., 120 Clarendon Street, Boston, at 9:45 to 2:30, on Thursday, February 21st. For those already signed up for the coming season, there will be no charge. For others, the charge is $2.00. Please reply to Mrs. Ruth Gilmore, 51 Rockledge Road, Newton Highlands. Bring bathing cap if you can.

February, 1946

Camp Namequoit
Atlantic Ocean Water Shore Line.
Cape Cod · 1944 Mass.

In 1925, the Cambridge YMCA started a caddie program at Eastward Ho! Caddies came from the Boston area. I was from Lexington, and I came down in 1939—my junior year in high school. We must have had sixty to seventy boys, anywhere from fifteen to nineteen years old.

This was just prior to World War II, and the Depression wasn't long over so it wasn't hard to find nineteen-year-old boys who didn't have jobs.

We had bunkhouses; we lived right there, and we had to pay room and board of $6.75 a week. What we got for caddying eighteen holes was one dollar! So you had to caddie every day just to make room and board, or your parents had to pay at the end of the summer.

C.J. and Lou Anne Thayer were the directors. Their son Brooks was about eight.

I caddied for two summers. I didn't have enough money to go to college then, so I began working. Then I came down on my two-week vacation and worked as a counselor. The caddies were allowed to swim in the Bay, and we had campfires and cookouts there. To caddie and be able to walk around the holes and see the Bay from every angle was wonderful.

In 1941, we began doing an awful lot of marching—drilling, I probably should say. It really meant something to us. In another year, of course, we were gone. I went into the Marine Corps in 1942.

One time, C.J. asked me to have lunch with a fellow who had been a caddie years before I was. It was Harold Russell. If you remember, he lost both arms in the war.

I believe C.J. and Lou Anne bought Namequoit in 1943. They weren't allowed to operate that first year, because the war was on and there were threats along this shore.

I went to work at Namequoit and was there for thirty-seven years. I was track and field coach and cross-country coach at M.I.T. for sixteen years, but I gave that up in 1973, came here and invested in the camp with Brooks. We were in partnership in the camp, but Brooks owned the land, of course, which he'd inherited from his father. This was the only camp on the east coast—maybe in the country—that was bounded by fresh water on one side and salt water on the other.

Namequoit started out with from forty to fifty campers. They'd come for the full season, eight weeks. Over the years we grew and grew. At the highest level, probably in the '70s, a total of two hundred and twenty attended. Then we settled down and realized we were overcrowded. We dropped down to one hundred and fifty and stayed with that right to the end. Our last season was 1988.

There were, over the years, fourteen or fifteen camps right here in Orleans, including a French camp for girls on Arey's Pond. I don't think there's a boy or girl who went to any of them who could ever forget their experiences on Pleasant Bay.

Most of our daily lessons—for all of us—were in the Little Bay. We had regattas on Wednesdays. Pleasant Bay Camp had an annual Tin Cup Regatta. We raced every Saturday at Chatham Yacht Club, camp against camp. We had a Cape Cod Intercamp Regatta with camps from the western part of the Cape. When they closed, we had the Pleasant Bay Intercamp Regatta.

When Camp Quanset closed, Viking, Namequoit and Avalon bought pretty much all of their Baybirds and some rowboats. It was sort of an auction. The camps used Cape Cod Knockabouts, Turnabouts, Widgeons, Mercuries, Baybirds, O'Day Sailors and catboats.

We had waterskiing, windsurfing, canoeing and all-day sails. We had social sails—you know, sail over and meet the girls at Avalon.

We had an outpost on the Outer Beach and would have camp-outs. We'd drive down the beach—it was eight miles from Nauset Beach—with supplies for them. They couldn't take much in the boats.

Most of our campers came by way of a *New York Times* ad. That was the big thing for us. And a lot of the boys might have been with us for ten years or more, as campers, then counselors.

One summer I think we had as many as fifteen boys from eight different countries—from all over the world. There were a lot from South America. The Spanish-speaking people wanted their sons to come here, but they didn't want them in cabins with other Spanish-speaking boys. They wanted them to learn English.

We had two brothers who attended. The older one was going to be seventeen, so we made him a Junior Counselor. He didn't get paid. The next year he *was* going to be paid. They were stopped at the airport in Dallas and asked where they were going. The older boy told them he had a job on Cape Cod. I got a call from the Immigration office in Boston. The man said,

"Do you know you're breaking the law by hiring an alien? I could come down there and have you arrested."

We kept him on without pay. He called his father to tell him what had happened. His father was the Mexican Ambassador to the United States.

I remember a little boy from New Jersey. On closing day, everybody had gone home. We shipped them off by bus, by plane....We had one kid left, and he didn't know why his mother wasn't there. I called New Jersey, and she said, "Oh, you're closing today? I forgot all about it." She just plain forgot to come get her son.

We got so many letters every year. That was wonderful. But I'd get a letter that said, for instance, "We can't believe the change in Jonathan; he's become so mature." The kid had been here for seven weeks and was "so mature." He was ten!

My wife, Jerrie, was a great supporter all those years. She'd do all kinds of things, help in the infirmary, go shopping. At the end of the summer, the kids from other countries would have about six hundred dollars, and they wanted to buy American clothes—Levi's, sneakers. Jerrie took them to Watson's. Then she'd come in a few days after camp closed, and we'd go over all the clothes that had been left behind. We'd send everything back—everything but socks and underwear.

We've been on the Bay for so many years and watched so many kids grow up. We've sailed there, gone swimming there. That familiarity has brought a great deal of satisfaction.

The Bay is majestic.

Arthur E. Farnham, Jr.
South Orleans

Namequoit waterfront.

Stripes and squints at Pleasant Bay Camp, 1946. Where are they now?

The Best of Boat Worlds

Talk to longtime Pleasant Bay people for five minutes, and you begin to hear the same words over and over: sharpie, Rookie, Mercury, Baybird, cat, knockabout. When they throw in "gaff rig," you throw in the towel and begin to ask questions. There's no shame in that, after all, not if you didn't grow up with one sailboat or another parked in the front "yard."

Alan McClennen, who's been sailing since he passed the swimming test given by his parents, explained the basics of a few boats that have been part of life on the Bay.

The Baybird is a round-bottom sailboat, 18-feet long, with a centerboard, a jib and gaff-rig mainsail. We had as many as 44 of them in the Bay. They lasted from 1921 to '39 or '40 as a racing class.

A Mercury is a 15-foot, round-bottom boat with a centerboard and a Marconi rig mainsail—a tall, thin, three-sided sail— the kind you usually see today. The gaff-rigged boat is an antique.

A sharpie is a flat-bottom, straight-sided, open or slightly decked sailboat. It could have either a Marconi rig or a gaff-rig mainsail. It usually didn't have a jib. It's a simple boat.

Does that clear it all up?

Maybe a few pictures are worth five thousand or so words. The following drawings are by Merv Hammatt, formerly a boy of the Bay, now the man at Compass Classic Yachts in Orleans.

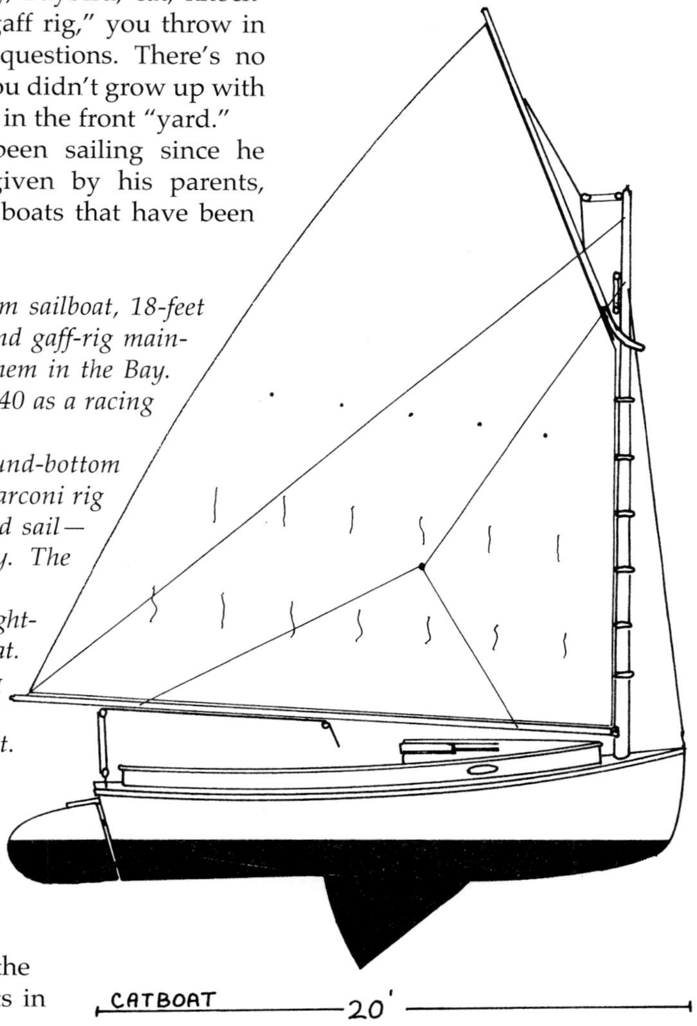

CATBOAT ———— 20' ————

MERCURY _____ 15'

KNOCKABOUT _____ 18'

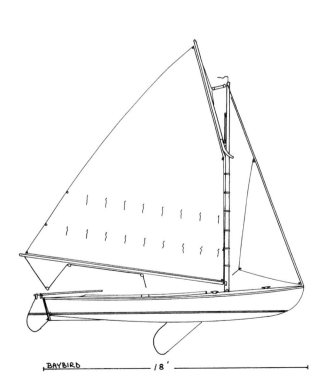

BAYBIRD _____ 18'

DAYSAILER _____ 17'

BEETLECAT — 12'

WHISTLER — 16'

ROOKIE — 8'

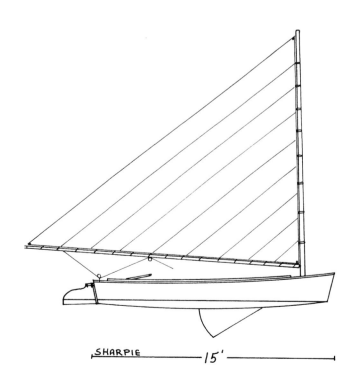

SHARPIE — 15'

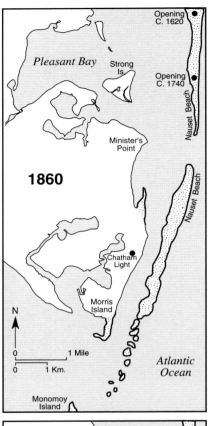

Pleasant Bay
Strong Is
Opening C. 1620
Opening C. 1740
Minister's Point
1860
Nauset Beach
N
0 — 1 Mile
0 — 1 Km.
Chatham Light
Morris Island
Atlantic Ocean
Monomoy Island

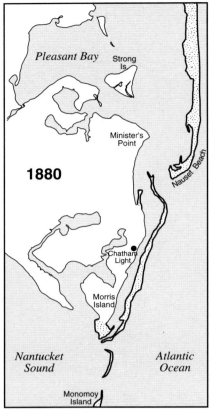

Pleasant Bay
Strong Is
Minister's Point
1880
Nauset Beach
Chatham Light
Morris Island
Nantucket Sound
Atlantic Ocean
Monomoy Island

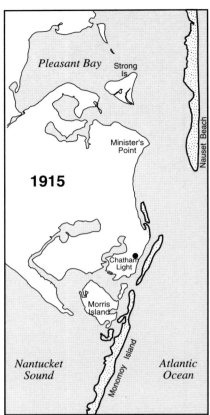

Pleasant Bay
Strong Is
Minister's Point
1915
Nauset Beach
Chatham Light
Morris Island
Nantucket Sound
Atlantic Ocean
Monomoy Island

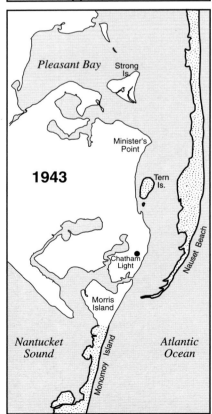

Pleasant Bay
Strong Is
Minister's Point
1943
Tern Is.
Nauset Beach
Chatham Light
Morris Island
Nantucket Sound
Atlantic Ocean
Monomoy Island

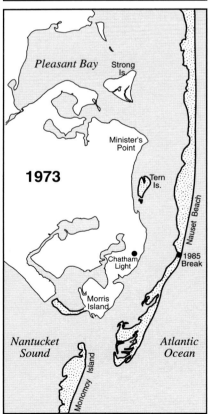

Pleasant Bay
Strong Is
Minister's Point
1973
Tern Is.
Nauset Beach
Chatham Light
1985 Break
Morris Island
Nantucket Sound
Atlantic Ocean
Monomoy Island

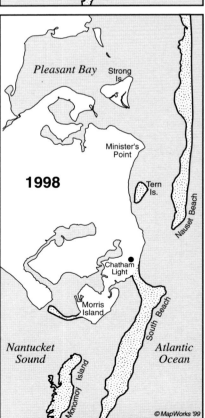

Pleasant Bay
Strong Is
Minister's Point
1998
Tern Is.
Nauset Beach
Chatham Light
Morris Island
South Beach
Nantucket Sound
Atlantic Ocean
Monomoy Island

© MapWorks '99

What's It All Aboat?

Now that the reader is able to distinguish (sort of) between a Rookie and a Baybird, perhaps these pages will be of further help. They contain definitions (in no particular order) of some common boating terms.

Hull—the basic body of a boat

Bow—the front end of a boat.

Stem—the furthest forward solid timber in a boat's frame.

Stern—the other end, hence the phrase "from stem to stern."

Keel—the main timber running lengthwise along the bottom of a boat.

Keel over—everyone gets wet.

Heel—to tip a sailboat sideways at an angle (not to be confused with "keel over").

Rudder—a flat piece of wood or metal attached to the stern and used to turn the boat left or right.

Tiller—a piece of wood used to control the rudder.

Port—the left side of a boat when facing forward.

Starboard—the right side.

Leeward—the sheltered side of a boat, away from the wind's direction.

Windward—the other side.

Skeg—a small, keel-like board below the structural keel, connecting the keel with the bottom of the rudder post.

Mast—a long, thin piece of wood or metal up which sails are raised.

Stay—a length of wire from the deck giving fore and aft support to a mast.

Guy—a line used to steady a spar, holding it in the fore and aft plane.

Boom—a long, thin piece of wood or metal extended aft from the mast to hold the foot of a sail.

Aft—toward the stern of the boat.

Fore—toward the front or bow.

Ballast—weight (iron, lead, etc.) in the bottom of a boat to give it stability.

Batten—a thin wooden strip placed in the pocket in the leech of a sail to help hold its form.

Leech—the after edge of a fore and aft sail.

Batten down—to secure.

Cast off—to let go a line.

Aloft—overhead, above decks.

Foot—the bottom of the sail.

Halyards—lines used to hoist sails.

Cleat—a piece of metal or wood with two arms, used for making fast ropes.

Belay—to make fast or secure a rope on a cleat or pin.

Block—a pulley.

Centerboard—a movable plate of metal or wood that is lowered through the keel to prevent the boat from being blown sideways by the wind.

Cabin—the spaces under the deck.

Thole or **Thole Pin**—a wooden peg driven into a hole in the gunwale of an oared boat, against which the oar bears when pulled.

Carvel-built—a boat built with flush planking, as opposed to clinker-built or lapstrake, where the top strake overlaps the one below it like the clapboards on a house.

Cockpit—the area with no deck, where the crew can sit.

Thwart—a bracing member used as a seat in small boats.

Coaming—a splashboard on the deck at the edge of the cockpit

Gunwale/Gunnel—the point where the deck and the sides of the boat meet. In earlier times, this was the wall above the deck through which guns were fired, an activity rarely seen on Pleasant Bay these days.

Anchor—the hooked instrument that is dropped overboard—ideally with a line attached—to keep the boat in position and prevent it from going to someplace in Europe.

Flukes—the triangular pieces of iron at the ends of an anchor.

Flake—to coil rope, often by forming a series of loose figure eights.

Furl—to roll up sails and secure them.

Heave—to throw one's weight into pulling a rope.

Pay out—to ease off or let out a chain or rope.

Gaff—a piece of wood or metal carried high up the mast, to which a four-sided sail is attached.

Mainsail—the major sail attached to the mast boom and gaff.

Jib—a sail carried in front of the mast.

Spar—any mast, gaff or boom to which a sail is attached.

Spinnaker—a triangular sail flown relatively free from the mast and attached to a spinnaker pole and guy rope and spinnaker sheet.

Sheet—lines attached to the foot of sails, or what people who don't sail call "rope."

Reaching—sailing across the wind.

Running—sailing with the wind coming from the stern.

Tacking—proceeding to windward by continously altering course and sail, from starboard tack to port tack and vice versa.

Jibe—to change tacks by swinging the stern of a vessel across the wind.

Beating—sailing toward the direction of the wind.

Bilge—the lowest inside point in the boat.

Bilge pump—important to have when there's water in the bilge.

Bilge water—weak coffee.

Head—water closet.

Chart—a nautical map showing depths in fathoms and underwater contours.

Fathom—nautical measurement of depth equalling six feet.

Draft—the vertical distance between the keel and the waterline on the hull, or the depth of water necessary to float a boat.

Rigging—general name for all working ropes and lines on a sailboat.

Sound—to measure the depth of water beneath a boat, formerly done by lead and line, now by electronic device.

Capsize—when the boat tips over.

Three Sheets to the Wind—a boat running free without restraints from the sheets, therefore barely able to navigate.

People

View from the Tomlinsons' boathouse, North Chatham. Outside are Milton Baker, Howie, Carrie and Roy Van Vleck, their cousin, Sally Tomlinson and, in the doorway, Aunt Nancy Tomlinson. Afloat are the family's Baybird and sharpie.

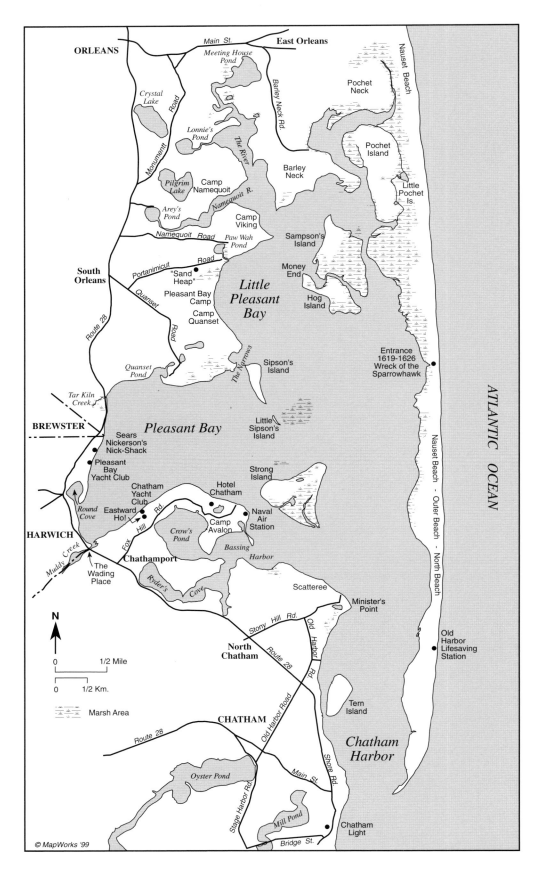

Among the many stories which my grandfather Nickerson told me as a boy, the one I remember most distinctly was about an old Indian named Micah Rafe, who lived nearby and whom he remembered well. He pointed out to me the spot where Micah's house once stood, and said he was the last full-blooded Indian in the town of Harwich. Since that time I have spent years of research into the lives of hundred of Indians between Bass River and Race Point, and it is my considered opinion that he was not only the last full-blood in Harwich, but on the whole Lower Cape as well.

At his death in 1816, there were not over a half-dozen Indians anywhere on the Lower Cape and these all of mixed blood. Even at Mashpee, I doubt if more than six or eight of pure Indian blood could have been found at that date.

Documents in my possession show he never signed his name Micah Rafe (pronounced to rhyme with safe) as he was commonly known, but always as Micah Ralph in a good clear hand. Sometimes he added "Indian Man" as if to let the world know that he was no half-breed. Although he lived and died in the heart of the Monomoyick Country, he was no Monomoyick. His blood ties stretched straight across the Cape to the North Shore sachems who welcomed the Pilgrims.

His great-grandfather, named Ralph, was the son of Sachem Ma-chantampaine of Nobscusset, but I have never found his Indian name anywhere in the records. From first to last it stands simply as Ralph, and is perhaps the only instance on the Lower Cape at that period of an Indian carrying an English name not taken from the Bible. Micah's great grand-mother, Mana-toto-mus-ke, Ralph's wife, was one of the daughters of Sachem Na-poy-tan who was probably the son of Sachem Iyanno of Cummaquid, of whom a Pilgrim wrote, "he was gentle, courteous and indeed not a savage at all except in his attire."

In the year 1694, "Jeremy Ralph, Indian," Micah's grand-father, registered the ear-mark of his cattle with the Town Clerk of Eastham. According to existing documents, his wigwam stood on the south side of the outlet to Arey's Pond in South Orleans, next to that of John Sipson, son of Quan-tockamon, the last hereditary sachem of the Nawset tribe. This area was at the time under the jurisdiction of the original township of Eastham, and was fast becoming the haven of the dwindling Lower Cape Indians. I believe Jeremy married into the Sipson family, because he soon became a Head Man in the Potenumicut Tribe, as this group became known, and was given hundreds of acres of land by the old Chief "because of love and good will." Some of this land bordered on my father's cow pasture and was known as "Injin land" when I was a boy. This tract was finally sold by act of the Massachusetts Legislature in 1891 when I was eleven years old.

When Jeremy Ralph died about 1738, he left a number of small children, among whom was a Micah, the father of our Micah Rafe. I have never learned the name of this Micah's wife, but I know their lodge stood near the little pond in South Orleans which emptied into the northwest corner of Baker's Tar Kiln Meadow. He became a soldier and a buddy of a great-grandfather of mine in Gorham's Rangers, and was either killed or died of disease in combat service in the French and Indian War in 1748. Samuel Linnell was named by the court to collect and distribute his back pay, along with that of seven other Potenumicut Indian casualties. The records show that Mr. Linnell charged five pounds apiece for "getting the wages" of each dead Indian, allowed the Court Registrar three pounds five each for jotting down the amounts, and the Honorable Judge a pound apiece for hearing the returns. What little was left of the "balance due the estate" was at last paid over to the "wido to support hirself and family and Small Children."

Micah Rafe, one of the widow's children, was undoubtedly born in his father's wigwam in South Orleans. In 1753 he married Hosey Steven, the great-great-granddaughter of Mattaquason, the Old Sagamore of the Monomoyicks, and their little "English built house with a smoke-hole in the roof," as my grandfather described it, stood on the north bank of the Monomoyick River in East Harwich, a few hundred yards upstream from the present Chatham-Harwich causeway on Route 28. This locality was their As-ka-onkton, the Wading Place, where, before a bridge was ever thought of, the age-old Indian trail from Monomoyick to the Nawset Country crossed the River on the clean sands at its mouth.

In the homemade account book of my great-great-grandfather, Elnathan Eldredge, the Miller, which has come down to me, are jottings of some of his dealings with Micah Rafe. Besides grinding his corn and making shoes for him and his family, he fashioned "leathern bands," halters, and harnesses for his cattle and oxen. Sometimes the bill against the old Indian ran quite high, but it was always paid. Little cash passed between them, and credits such as "reping an acre of rie" were common. One bill was squared by "squawing hay from the flats"—squawing being Grandfather's way of spelling scowing—while others were paid off with "One se-duck which waid three pounds and a half," or "100 pomkings."

If Micah and Hosey had any children of their own, they died young, but they were deeply attached to little Isaac Moses, who they say was born in their house and which became home for him and his mother, Hannah. He undoubtedly was close kin to one or both of them, but what their relationship was I have never found out, although I do know that his Moses Indian blood was already crossed with Negro.

His wife's name was Nancy, and he was known as Isaac Mike, a fiddler of local repute and an exceptionally fine penman as shown by existing documents. He outlived Micah, and his grave, near those of his foster parents, was, within my memory, still marked by a headstone.

Hosey, Micah's wife, was a short, stocky, kindly old soul. As the last surviving heir of the old Sagamore, all his remaining unsold lands were hers by right of reversion. She left all this to her "beloved husband Micah Ralph" in her will of October 12, 1798, with the proviso that after his death all and every part was to go to "our well-beloved friend, born in our house, Isaac Moses." She died not long before the 29th of March, 1800, when her will was filed for probate.

Micah himself was now a very old man, with no one in the world but Hannah Moses and Isaac to keep his home fires burning. On July 7, 1814, he made his own will, bequeathing "all real and personal estate" to Isaac Moses, with the request that Hannah be supported out of it as long as she lived. From time to time for the next few months, he disposed of a piece of land as his needs required, most of it to my people. His last sale, the lot known as Mike's Hummock, near the spot where the shipwrecked *Sparrowhawk* lay, was to Ensign Nickerson on the 19th May, 1815.

Micah Rafe died a short time before the 18th of March, 1816, on which date Isaac Moses presented his will for probate. He was laid to rest beside Hosey, on the west slope of the hill on the north side of Bay Road going west from the Wading Place. My brother Carroll's wife, who was born and grew up almost across the road from their burial place, told me she could remember when their graves were mounded with fieldstones, among which the spring violets always grew larger and bluer.

It must be a solemn thought for a childless man to know that when his eyes close in death, a chain of generations which began when man began is broken. How profoundly more so must it to be know, as Micah Rafe knew, that with him a race is dying.

W. Sears Nickerson

Muddy Creek, by the Wading Place. Photo by Richard C. Hiscock.

The first member of the family to come here and rent a house was my father, in 1903. He had at that time a tubercular wife and two daughters. The person who later became my mother was a young girl who lived with them. Mother had been born and brought up in Brookline, in an area called Pill Hill because all the doctors lived there. She went to Wheelock College and learned teaching, I presume. I don't think she ever taught. By 1900, she was living with my father and his first wife. My step-sisters called her "Sister."

In 1910 or so, my father's first wife departed—with another party—and left him with these two girls. My mother, Mary Crane, stayed on to take care of the children, and my father, who was an up and coming young lawyer in Boston, moved out of the house until things settled down a little. Apparently, they settled down by the middle of August in 1911, when my father married Mary Crane.

Nobody has ever really explained all that to me. It was a difficult situation for my father and for my mother. Her family was very straight.

In due course, Mother had five children.

The train got down to Orleans before 1890 and to Chatham around 1887, I guess. Once the Cape became accessible for seasonal use, a lot of men about Father's age or thereabouts came down here. Sometime in the 1890s, I believe, Father came down with a bunch of bachelors to an inn on the Bay, north of Camp Quanset and south of Paw Wah Pond. This whole mess of young men Father was associating with in Boston did that kind of thing.

The first summer cottage on Big Pleasant Bay was built in 1887 or so by John Graham Brooks. He was a newspaper man, I think. The first property Father rented was built in 1889.

In December of 1907, he bought the place he had

Mary and Edward F. McClennen, 1929.

rented for three years. By the time I was born, I'm sure they were down for all summer. My father was thirty-three, a ten-year member of the Boston Bar, not rich but certainly successful. I was the youngest of all the children, the younger of twins.

The Winslows had all bought land on the Bay. Sidney Sr. was closely enough related to the Old Colony Railroad at that period—around 1910—that a parlor car came down to Orleans. You'd get good service with that kind of connection.

We had two maids and a nursemaid. The maids took care of the kitchen. We took the laundry out to a neighbor. The nursemaid sat with us on the beach to keep us out of trouble. The maids came with us from Cambridge, where we lived. At that time there was a great deal of immigration from Barbados and other West Indies islands. These were good, solid, churchgoing people. Our cook, Edith Ince, from Barbados, was a young girl when she came to work for us in 1912. She was with us until the end of World War II. Our maid, Mignonette Clarissa Mappe, was Edith's niece. Well, I was in shorts most of the summer, and I'd get pretty darned brown. Mignon said to me, "Alan, if you get any blacker, you'll be blacker than I am." She worked for us for twenty years.

What I first remember about the mail is that we'd go to South Orleans for it some years and to East Harwich for it other years. The South Orleans Post Office was in John Kenrick's General Store. He was a substantial neighborhood man. A Mr. and Mrs. Moore ran the Post Office on Church Street in East Harwich. It was a little box of a building north of Bay Road. We had a car from 1920 or so, but I never got the impression that Mother liked to drive. Sometime in the late '20s, Father got in touch with our Representative, Congressman Gifford. He persuaded the congressman to persuade the Post Office Department to extend a rural delivery line for a mile-and-a-half to our property, so Mother wouldn't have to drive to get the mail.

That led to a delightful confusion; all the people who wanted RFD had Chatham delivery, as new houses were built along that mile and a-half. When

The wreck. "We boys climbed to the top."

Father did this maneuver, there were five year-round dwellings close to the road.

Finally, just this year, the Post Office got to changing the line, and I'm still trying to get it straightened out. We're not Chatham anymore. We're now officially in Harwich, although we actually live in Brewster.

As long as I can remember, Route 28 has been paved. But nothing else was. There were dirt roads with two ruts. It also was common to put shells on roads. Route 28 didn't get a good surface until 1925 or so.

There wasn't any police record of it, but I do recall throwing rotten apples at a passing car. The car kept going, but it came back a short time later and we took off.

Mother didn't really go shopping. There was a meat truck, a fish truck and fruit and vegetable truck. Those businesses were run by Southern Europeans—Greeks and Italians. Local people ran the stores.

When we were young, we were on a telephone line with eighteen parties. Our number was twenty-one ring five. It was lots of fun, because we could listen in on everyone's conversation—except the French guys who were here working on the Cable Station. We

couldn't keep up with them. The women would gossip in French.

Initially, Father tried to get away without a phone. But it didn't take long for people in his office to find out that if you called Eddie Chase across the street, Father would get a message and have to call back.

We were taught to not be afraid of thunder or lightning. We sure could see it there, but we weren't afraid. But I was on the phone one time when the house got hit by lightning; it came through the wiring, hit the soapstone sink and knocked a piece out of it. That piece flew across the room and hit the cook in the knee.

We lived by kerosene light and candlelight until 1925 or so. Here were all these little kids, living in this tinderbox of a house, taking candles upstairs to bed. There was never a fire; no one got burned. Mother cleaned the lamps herself, trimming the wicks, cleaning the glass chimneys. She didn't let the help do that.

As children, we played on the beach a lot. We built dams around the springs to make ponds. We'd go rowing. We never had any lifejackets, but the rule was, if you could swim from the pier to the raft, you could go out in a boat. We picked up scallops off the bottom and ate them raw. We'd go sailing to the Outer Beach; we called it the Outer Beach. Some called it "Outer," some called it "North Beach." The name will change from time to time. It's shown on the maps as Nauset Beach.

Anyway, we'd sail to the Outer Beach to climb on shipwrecks. One was tipped over, with lots of timbers showing. There was no Occupational Safety Board then, but nobody ever got hurt. We'd also climb all over the roof of the family house. That house was a circus. Those upstairs wings were added, up and out, and people would say, "Oh, Mrs. McClennen must be having another baby."

We knew the Winslow boys, the Dicksons, the Brookses and the Davises. We played with all those kids to a certain degree, but it was pretty lonely until the sixteen year-old stage. When you got your license you got some freedom. Once we became mobile, we were dealing heavily with the Chatham Yacht Club. My older brother used to drive me to the Chatham Beach Club's Saturday night dances. I learned to dance with the older girls.

The Pleasant Bay Yacht Club was organized in 1902—they had been racing in the Bay in the '90s—when big Sid Winslow came down and old John Kenrick was an official. The Cape was beginning to summer-grow. The club ran, probably, until 1910, and the building remained until 1935 or so.

The Chatham Country Club started, apparently, in 1915, and there was a plan to build what they called the Great Point Golf Club. I assume the idea died in World War I, then started up again. Sailing began there in 1921, and golf, in 1922. The Country Club went broke in '26, but the sailors remained as an association. For one summer we were the Pleasant Bay Yacht Club. Then Father changed the name to Chatham Yacht Club. The feeling was, there had been a PBYC that was dormant, so the name couldn't be used. It's too bad they didn't talk with the oldtimers who had been there and get to use that name. An element of continuity would have been rather nice.

Father was a lawyers' lawyer, and he did his job. He took a great deal of interest in the golf club, except for one thing; I never saw him play golf. I believe he had some clubs, which I remember carrying. But what he wanted to do was make sure nobody built any damned houses on that point.

The Country Club was reorganized in 1928 as Eastward Ho! Father's legal efforts in setting up the club that year tied up land ownership there so tightly that nobody could untie the thing! He died in 1948, and it took ten years for some younger people to corral the one hundred bonds that had been issued and get them back into new, active ownership. All those bonds had gone into family trusts and estates, and it took awhile to round them up.

Tommy Fuller, Alan McClennen and Mel Webster.

Alan, May 6, 1934.

get you a four-burner stove. They have a three-burner one." I said, "Order it," and she said, "I already did."

Our house was built by E. C. Nickerson, of Church Street. He had been a variety of things in his lifetime—typical of Cape Codders. But if Father hadn't seen that little piece in the paper, I'd never have gotten any of what we needed to build.

I just grew up attached to the Bay. We were so attached to it, in fact, that we called it "our Bay." I never thought of going anywhere else. I think we sailed more than most, because we were brought up by a sailor—Mother. Father raced a little, and the Yacht Club records showed that Edward F. McClennen was sailing. But Mother had sailed as a girl.

"Weezy," 1936.

I was down here every year of my life, including the two years I was in the service. Finally, I wanted a house. I didn't want to build between my brother Josh's house and my brother Louis'; that was no place to live. But I was irrevocably attached to the water.

In 1941, Father saw a very tiny notice in the newspaper. It said something about the war and about supplies being hard to get. He said to me, "Can you finish your house plans so we can get E.C. to order the lumber?" E.C. Nickerson was our caretaker. Father said, "Get Zenus Kenrick to come dig the foundation ASAP." We went to Emery's Plumbing Store in Harwich and ordered all our supplies, two sinks, a shower, a tub, two jons and two set-tubs. On Thursday of that week, all the lumber and plumbing supplies were delivered. Father's secretary called me at work at M.I.T. and said, "Cape and Vineyard can't

I never considered whether my mother was pretty or not. She was just "Mother." But when Weezy was a young girl, damn, *she* was pretty. We met at a dance my freshman year at Harvard. I was there with someone else. So was Weezy. She thought I was the loudest, noisiest thing she'd ever met. I may have been loud and noisy, but I straightened out eventually.

Alan McClennen
Brewster

Josh and I met at a coming-out party or dance. I don't remember just which one. Then we lived in Ann Arbor, where he was a professor of English and journalism.

Well, the Bay was just fine then. We didn't have so many motorboats. Josh and I used to sail and sail and sail. It was beautiful. It still is, if there weren't so many motorboats. People are just in such a hurry out there.

We knew the Winslows and a lot of other people around the Bay, but everybody's dead except me. Well, not really everybody. The Winslows were on one side of the Bay, and the McClennens were on the other, but there were more Winslows than McClennens.

When Josh retired we moved here permanently. Now don't ask me when he retired. I don't remember dates anymore.

I remember most the sailing and the sunrises. They were spectacular sometimes. We used to go over to Strong Island, to Sipson's and Little Sipson's. We'd sail over, maybe picnic.

Those motorboats are terrible. They bump into big fish and leave scars on them.

Josh knew about sailing. I didn't know an awful lot about it. But he knew how to get into the little places. Well, he was practically born there.

The old house is a funny one. It was added onto for children and grandchildren. I can remember when Father McClennen—Edward F.—put on the dining room. I think we had twenty-four at the table. It's not a beautiful house, but it was wonderful because of the people. We always had Sunday dinner there, and on Wednesdays we'd go over for steaks. Oh, yes, I liked my in-laws. I think we were a very good family, and that was largely due to Father and Mother McClennen. Father died before Mother, and it was a terrible time for the family.

Sometime, I wish you'd come and see me at my house—South Cottage. I have a nice deck and a wonderful view—except for the motorboats. Anytime after October is beautiful. Those boats are gone.

People have sold property, which they shouldn't have done. My Bay house is still there. And it's going to be.

Eleanor McClennen
Brewster

Bayberry Bluff.

The first summer homes on the Bay in South Orleans were those of John Graham Brooks (1846-1938) and his wife Helen Lawrence Brooks (1846-1938). The pair of plain, sturdy cottages—wrapped in porches—remains there still, as do descendents of JGB and HLB. In 1975, John and Helen's son, Lawrence Graham Brooks, wrote of the family's early days on the bluff. Those recollections were included in Judge Brooks's memoirs, printed privately in 1981. Here, with permission of grandson and editor Lawrence A. Carter, is a much-too-brief look at a time, a place, a family.

South Orleans makes up one of the important threads of my life. My parents' first trip there was made at the suggestion of one of my father's parishioners in Brockton, a Mr. Blake, who summered in South Orleans. They took the train one autumn day in 1887 from Brockton to Orleans. Trains ran in those days from Boston to Provincetown. The roadbed was terribly dusty, and the last few miles between East Brewster and Orleans were twisting. It was not difficult to be car sick.

From Orleans they were driven four miles by carriage over sandy roads to a point on the shore of Pleasant Bay which was for sale. There were two adjoining parcels of land containing in all nearly forty acres, part of which was swamp land.

It had been raining when they arrived, and the fog was so thick that, standing on the bluff about 25 to 30 feet above the Bay, they could hardly see the water. Then, almost miraculously as they stood there the fog lifted, the sun came out and they were able to look out across the whole lovely expanse of Big and Little Pleasant Bay. Without hesitation, they decided to buy the land.

The property and surrounding area had no trees on it then, outside of a few cherry trees which had grown from stones dropped by birds as they perched along the cedar fence rails. One fence ran from the top of the bluff due north to a swamp. Another, judging by the position of the cherry trees, must formerly have crossed it at right angles.

The nearest house, belonging to Thomas Eldredge, was located in a hollow a little way back from the water about a quarter mile due west of our bluff. Eldredge lived with his invalid daughter Fannie, a housekeeper, Mrs. Arnaud, and her daughter Flora. Beyond to the west on a high bluff, fully 50 or 60 feet above the water, was the Blake cottage, a small, light-frame structure over which ran a cable attached to posts on each side to keep it from blowing away.

The only other house in the vicinity belonged to Captain Uriah Rogers and his wife Bethiah, universally known as Uncle Uriah and Aunt Bethiah. Uriah was a retired sea captain just under seventy years of age, one of those invaluable, handy Yankees who could do almost anything, from sailing and repairing a boat to carpentry and plumbing work. He wore white whiskers in a fringe around the bottom of his chin. Uncle Uriah never could quite understand why other people did not get up at 5 a.m. Part of his daily life, when the weather was fitting, was to leave Pleasant Bay before dawn in his catboat *Webfoot* and go out fishing on the ocean. This was his main livelihood. He returned, depending on the tide, sometime

Uncle Uriah.

between 2 and 4 p.m. The fish were mostly cod, some pollock and haddock, which he sold fresh at 10 cents a pound, or cleaned, salted and barreled.

To build a cottage on our bluff, Father hired Ezra Knowles, a local carpenter. It was a very simple structure requiring no architect: a large combined living and dining room and a kitchen on the ground floor and four bedrooms upstairs. Attached was a shed with a pump for drinking water and beyond that a two-hole outhouse.... The house was built with a piazza on three sides, the bay side 15 or 20 feet from the edge of the bluff; the bluff itself was grown over with beach grass and a few wild plum bushes. The house was finished in the spring of 1888.

China basins and pitchers had to do for washing facilities. The only other toilet arrangement was the outhouse, from which a zinc-lined box was periodically removed by Uncle Uriah (or, in the last few years of its existence, by me). The basins, in fact all other receptacles, came in for additional use on rainy days that first summer when the house was not tight. There were times when the rain came in in such quantity—both through the roof and through the walls, particularly in driving southerly storms—that rubber blankets had to be strung under the ceiling in the living room to catch the overflow from upstairs.

[A few years later] my father found it desirable to build a second and smaller cottage where he could get away from the family noises in order to do his writing and preparation for lectures. This house was erected by Winnie Nickerson in the same style as the other, except that it has only bedrooms and has what the larger cottage does not: a cellar.

The isolated position of the cottages in the early days precluded much social intercourse. My mother grew very fond of Fannie. Uncle Uriah and his wife, our most sociable neighbors, we visited constantly. There was also Uncle Uriah's brother, Alexander Rogers, who lived with his wife on the river beyond Charlie Rogers' house.... Mrs. Rogers used to make yeast, and at various times during the summer my mother used to walk there from our house and back, a trip very close to four miles, then almost all open land, now completely wooded. Alexander Rogers was a very subdued man who, I have the impression, had something happen to his head. I can only vaguely recall it.

Not far from the Brewster line on the Chatham Road, lived Webster Rogers with his wife and his daughter, Emma Augusta. Webster was a veteran of the Civil War, a very swarthy, black-bearded man who was rather the joke of the natives because of the care that he received from his family. He had apparently never got over the effects of the War. One of the jokes at his expense was to apply to his case a song popular about 1900, which went:

"Everybody works but Father; he sits 'round all day,
Sitting in front of the fire, smoking his pipe of clay.
Mother takes in washing; so does Sister Ann.
Everybody works but Father, my Old Man — the damned old loafer!"

Every year my mother, with some member of the family, would either walk or row over in the cedar boat to call. Emma, who was just my age and lived to be 97, occupied the old homestead for many years.

In the autumn of 1905, my parents bought property in Jackson, New Hampshire, and gave up South Orleans as a summer residence until 1930. First to occupy the place in our absence were Dr. William Davis and family, of St. Paul, Minnesota. That summer after the Davises' arrival, it blew hard from the southwest, and for a full week there was fog. The doctor and his wife were on the point of returning to St. Paul, having become thoroughly weary of the Cape at its worst. Then the wind changed; lovely weather ensued, and they stayed on for the rest of the summer. They ended by purchasing land adjoining ours at the Narrows, where they built a lovely house which they first occupied in 1907.

The friendship between our families, which began when Dr. Davis' daughter Helen lived next door to us in Cambridge...now includes a fifth generation. Helen, who married perhaps my best friend, Charles W. Locke, and her sister Margaret, who married Moncrieff Cochran, had between them 48 grandchildren. And so it goes on like the big and little fleas ad infinitum.

Another family who came to the Cape in the early days and whose children, grandchildren and great-grandchildren have become part of our lives are the Brenton H. Dickson, Jr. family. Dr. Davis persuaded Brent to purchase the bluff belonging to my father between his own property and our house. Brent's son William, the sailor of the family and a doctor formerly of Milton, now lives year-round in South Orleans, where he and his wife Harriet are invaluable and beloved neighbors.

When I began to sail (in the mid-1890s), the main channel connecting Pleasant Bay with the ocean was about opposite the Chatham Bars Inn; that is, one sailed out due east from the Inn. Usually, one felt the effect of the ocean swell inside the Bay up as far as Minister's Point. Uncle Uriah, who, like Queen Victoria, was born in 1819, remembered well when, in 1851, a great storm broke through the outer beach due east of Strong Island, creating a channel well to the north. By 1930, however, any northern channels had long since closed up and the main access was working its way rapidly southward. The southernmost part of the beach that summer lay due east from a spot perhaps 100 yards north of Chatham Light.

It is a very interesting matter to speculate how this process will continue. If the entrance moves far enough south, tidal wash will become too weak to keep a channel open, in which case Pleasant Bay may end up becoming a fresh water lagoon.

It has been argued that the ocean will again break through at some low point of the outer beach, perhaps back of Strong Island as it did in 1851. In the hurricane of 1944, the ocean did break through there and flow in and out of the Bay. The channel, however, soon filled up, and by the time we returned the next summer there was no trace of it.

It is unlikely that such a channel could become permanent now, for opposite all the low points shoals have developed, the result of, along with other things, sand being carried into the Bay when the ocean has washed over the beach on exceptionally high tides. Consequently, there would not be enough water power to keep the channel scoured.

At high water, the part of Pleasant Bay seen from our house does not seem to have changed at all, except that the bluffs have moved back in the course of years. At low tide, however, it is very apparent that the shores are far more shelving than they were in my youth. This part of the Bay is gradually shoaling and silting in. This is due, in part, to the sand which washes up constantly from the shoals to the east and partly to the constant erosion from the bluffs.

A major factor in the shoaling of the Bay was the disappearance of eelgrass during the winter of 1929-1930. We had visited Pleasant Bay in the fall of 1929, and eelgrass then was plentiful—almost everywhere; it always had been as far as I know. Though it obstructed boating by fouling propellers and made bathing much less enjoyable, it did have the crucial advantage that it impeded the spread of sand by the tide. On our return in 1930, we were astonished to find eelgrass entirely gone. How suddenly and completely nature had reversed herself. Studies to try to find the cause concluded that some rapidly spreading parasite had attacked the plant throughout the Atlantic but not the Pacific. With nothing to hold them, the sand flats in the Bay began spreading everywhere. I wrote in 1947, "Unless the eelgrass comes back in sufficient quantities to cover the flats, I see nothing to prevent Pleasant Bay from eventually becoming like Plymouth Harbor—God forbid!"

Lawrence Graham Brooks
South Orleans

Judge Brooks saw the return of eelgrass in the Bay, but he wasn't here on January 2, 1987, when the ocean once again broke through the Outer Beach. This time, the breach was due east of Chatham Light. This time, it didn't close up again. What began as a tiny rip in the barrier beach was—by the end of that year—a mile wide.

Lawrence Graham Brooks died in 1981, halfway through his 101st year. He was described then as "one of the last of a distinguished breed of Boston-born, Harvard-educated liberal men of principle."

The Judge wrote only of the early years in South Orleans. His purpose was to "make it harder to forget the beginnings," and he remarked that it would be up to his children and grandchildren "to write their own memoirs."

Susan and Lawrence Brooks, 1975.

In my early days, until 1930, the family was not here, except to open and close the house. My grandfather had contracted asthma, and they decided to try the mountain air. They bought the place in Jackson, New Hampshire in 1905.

In 1930, they concluded it was too remote up there, that they'd be closer to Cambridge and medical assistance down here. Mother came down and settled in for the summer. Grandfather died in 1938.

On the knoll over there is a whale bone—part of the backbone. Father and I went to the beach in the Model T in about 1920 and brought back two of them. They were here until a couple of years ago, when some teenagers broke in and stole one. That was a drastic insult to the community.

When the sailing ships came here years ago, the Bay was just barely big enough for schooners to tack in. The water was a lot deeper than it is now.

The major difference around here is the vegetation. I can remember the line of cherry trees my father mentioned in his book. They marked the fence line. But around 1900, there was not a sign of anything growing around these houses.

But maybe the shoaling up of the Bay is the biggest change—that and the fact that I haven't seen a quahog here for many years.

And does anyone catch puffers anymore? Blowfish. Scratch their bellies, and they puff up.

There's a great difference in bird life. Terns used to be all over the place. They were nesting on Little Sipson's. Guess they got squeezed out by the gulls. I haven't seen any Least Terns on the Outer Beach. There used to be a bunch of them—little guys screaming away.

I used to wear a Wirthmore Feed hat with three or four layers of newspaper inside, because the terns would come down and peck you—go right through any hat.

Another change is that we now have a resident cardinal, a resident Carolina wren and a mockingbird. They didn't exist in these parts twenty or thirty years ago. The mockingbird has continually divebombed a cat and dog who were here last year and this. The the-

John Brooks and his father, Lawrence, at Bayberry Bluff.

Photo by Richard C. Hiscock

ory is that the bird is trying to pull that soft hair out of the dog for a nest.

I was in college by the time the family came down regularly. I'd sail over to the Rogers place three times a week—or drive in a Model A Ford Roadster—to tutor the Rogers children. I learned far more from Dr. Rogers than his children ever did from me. I think Sam was eleven, Midge was five, and I was in law school.

Midge never stopped talking, and her father wondered, "Is this a phase or a disease?" She was a cute kid, but she did have a busy mouth.

We did a lot with the Locke and Davis clan—picnics, overnights. We never had a Baybird—mostly Beetlecats. And we had a sharpie.

We used to race that in the Chowder Race. There was one every summer. The idea was to get from start to finish, no holds barred—using umbrellas as spinnakers, poling with the oar. It was a great deal of fun.

I don't know why it was called the Chowder Race, whether that was the prize or the outcome. My future wife, a friend of hers and I were racing in it one year and capsized. They didn't like that very much. But we got married, and the friend still is a friend, so I guess it was all right.

We've known the Dicksons forever. My mother grew up with Bill's mother. We concluded that you should never underestimate the intelligence of a Dickson.

Two times during the '40s, I walked from here to the Outer Beach, swimming across the Narrows and across the channel just inside the Outer Beach. The rest was walking. There was much more dry land than there is now. Just two short swims. At low tide you could almost ford it.

The tides are higher, clearly, and the water a little colder since the Cut in 1987. The Bay is shoaling faster. I came through at North Chatham yesterday, and that's shoaled up an awful lot. Channels have an uncanny habit of being a beautiful channel and then shoaling up. You'd think they'd scour themselves, but they don't.

We've had five generations here. We're wrestling with the same thing as everyone else. How are we going to set it up?

When Mother died, we divvied up the family real estate. Now the Carters and Brookses share July, and the Reads have August. We had twenty of us at table Memorial Day weekend. We've now got three seniors, and there are eleven grandchildren.

The big issue is, what's going to happen? Do we have the guts to say it's never going to be developed and do a conservation easement? Or do we just follow the stewardship principle? We're going along on a very loose basis so far.

We all love the place.

John Graham Brooks, II
South Orleans

My Orleans roots began with the Payson family of Belmont. During the latter half of the nineteenth century, Gilbert Russell Payson Sr. purchased Pochet Island along with Sampson's and Hog islands. This purchase included the "Old House" on Pochet, which still stands unchanged.

My father, Brenton H. Dickson, Jr. and the oldest Payson son, Russell, were the very best of friends. They were classmates in Boston and graduates of Harvard in the class of 1890. While in college, and until my father married in 1901, they had many vacations on Pochet Island along with numerous mutual friends.

There were no telephones and no electricity in those days, and all communication was by half-cent postcard. Asa Mayo of East Orleans was the wise know-all, do-all aide to the Paysons and to everyone else in East Orleans. Asa would figure the tides and the trains so Russell and his friends could go from the Orleans Depot to Pochet when the flats were less than horse belly deep. Once there, the group lived off the land. There were no hunting laws then, and a lot of Russell's friends, including my father, were good shots. The bag must have included lots of yellowlegs, plover and ducks. All of these were cooked rare and were laced with a certain amount of rum.

Uncle Russell and Pochet Island bring to mind many fond memories. It was a welcome excursion when Father, my siblings and our dogs drove to the landing on Barley Neck and rowed across to Pochet. More than once, the mosquitoes and bugs were so thick we had trouble finding the "Old House," then in the middle of a large field. Our arrival prompted a hail from Uncle Russell, whereupon our jolly host squirted the screen door with Flit, then handed us the Flit gun. After we had squirted each other, we were let in one by one with quick openings of the door.

The settling of the Dicksons in South Orleans also came about because of my mother, Ruth Wilbur Bennett. During the late 1800s, the Bennetts were neighbors of the Turners and Hallowells in West Medford. They had a bunch of girls—and boys, all good-looking guys. The girls, all in their teens, called themselves "Farmers." They were early rebels; they wore bloomers, played cards, rode horses astride, played basketball and indulged in all sorts of unladylike behavior. They became lifetime friends. Margaret Davis (Cochran), Susan Hallowell (Brooks) and Ruth Bennett (Dickson) were three of the wild "Farmers."

Well, old Mr. John Graham Brooks—Sue Brooks's father-in-law—had built these two extraordinary houses. Margaret Davis got wind–through friendship–that they had a house they rented. Somewhere around 1903, the Davises rented the house and came down. It was miserable. Rain came through the shiplap. It was cold. They ran around with chamber pots trying to catch the drips. They stayed indoors, played bridge and said, "Never again."

The last day they were here was a typical Cape Cod day—the good kind. It was clear, the sun was shining. They took a walk, and Margaret fell in love with the place. She talked her father, Dr. William Davis—Margaret was still "Davis"—into buying land, and they built a house about 1905. They built it right, so it was cool in the summertime and the sun came in during the winter.

Along about this time, Susan Hallowell Brooks and Ruth Bennett Dickson came down to visit. By then my parents had six children, and I was on the way. Father spotted this two-acre island. In 1915, he persuaded Mr. Brooks to sell it for $200—a tremendous price for a useless piece of land.

Our original old house was built by Mr. Charles Hopkins of East Orleans. Finished in 1916, it was dubbed "The Dump," perhaps because of all the money that was dumped into it, or perhaps because of its appearance. It was finished just in time for our family to come down for Margaret Davis' wedding to Moncrief Cochran. Our house was occupied as a summer home from that year until 1983, when it burned down.

We came from Weston for the summer in an eight-cylinder Peerless that burned oil, so a great deal of smoke went out behind, and there were dogs and everybody sitting in everybody's lap, and between blowouts and punctures and stopping to get watered, it was a good six-hour trip. Somehow, Nellie Sullivan—she was the factotum—got the stove going and fed us a really good supper. It was a miracle.

Nellie was our Irish cook who loved to cook and didn't care when we came in to eat.

None of us went to camp; we just camped out here. There was a great deal of playing of games, cards, charades. Everybody was musical. We had no electric lights, but we had a telephone with eight of us on a party line. We could call each other without bringing the operator in.

My family and the Davises and the Brookses were all characters. Every one of them had great strengths and a few weaknesses. Margaret Cochran—

The Dicksons at "The Dump," 1926. Left to right: Theodore, Ruth ("Babe"), Grandfather Brenton, Edward, William A. II, Uncle William and Brenton III ("Bumpsy").

Granny—not only had the gift of gab, but was as sharp as a pin up until the day she died. She lived to be over a hundred. So did Judge Brooks and Susan. Those people lived a good healthy life, a good lively life. They didn't smoke, didn't drink. They swam and walked a lot.

Back then you couldn't go to the store for milk or eggs, and you couldn't get ice. The person who supplied us was Charlie Rogers. He made a path through the woods. He had an ice house, and he milked his cows and got eggs from his chickens. Charlie was kind of a lonely guy; he liked to come talk with us. He prefaced everything he said with, "I see now, looka here now." In the late '20s, he said to my father, "I see now, looka here now, Mr. Dickson, you ought to buy some General Motors stock." He'd bought some on margin. My father said, "Charlie, I'm not going to let you leave this room until you promise to sell that." Charlie lost his shirt and went into bankruptcy. We thought, "My God, if he goes bankrupt, there'll be no more milk or eggs!" So we bailed him out. I forget how much it was.

The Davis family were the first occupants of The Narrows, and they were very gracious hosts. Every Sunday they had a generous dinner. Charlie would come crank up and make ice cream. The Davises ate at two or three in the afternoon. We weren't that luxurious. We had our meal at one o'clock.

Lunch was at one. My father would then have his nap and then what he called his "wash." He wore a flesh-colored swimming suit—one of those one-piece wool things. The Davises would look out to watch him swimming without any clothes on. That was a one-man show. In those days, we hardly ever took a bath. We had a tub, but we just swam. Mama and Dada were ardent but not expert swimmers.

Judge Brooks's father, John Graham Brooks, was a philosopher, a Unitarian minister and a man of letters, and he was rather stuffy about it. Well, Mrs. Davis—Margaret's mother—was sort of a boss. She'd say to

Granny Cochran's house (left) at The Narrows.

Using a sunfish sail and his feet, Bill Dickson kept moving when the Bay froze in 1977.

her husband, "Now, Bill, you've got to go talk to Mr. Brooks." Dr. Davis would say, "What do I want to see him about? He wants me to read 'The New Republic' and 'The New York Times,' and all I know is what's in 'The Saturday Evening Post.'" So he'd go talk to Mr. Brooks for about five minutes, then come by here and talk with my father for hours. They got along well.

When we went for the mail, we sailed down in our sharpie, up Namequoit River to Arey's Pond and then walked to the post office. It wouldn't have been a helluva lot longer if we'd just walked from here. It was an excuse to go sailing.

I have vivid memories of the Naval Air Station in North Chatham. It was very active during World War I, and they had those noisy, pusher-prop airboats that went about forty or fifty miles an hour. They were very unreliable; one of them crashed into the bluff on Strong Island. They often flew low, and it was exciting to wave our white midi hats to salute our heroes. The pilots would lean out of their cockpits and wave back. If a plane broke down or crashed, it was rescued by a "speed boat." They were very heavy twenty-to-thirty-footers, notorious for their loud noise and their ability to charge along at fifteen knots with huge rooster tails and wakes.

They were awfully jittery about spies then. One of my father's friends, John Paine, was a butterfly catcher. Soldiers pounced on him in the woods someplace here. They thought he was a spy.

My brother, Brent III, loved to look at the Sears and Roebuck catalogue and dream. He talked my father into buying him a searchlight, so to speak. It was 1918, and he was about fifteen or sixteen. He couldn't wait for it to get dark, so he could show my aunt how strong the light was. He went out and pointed it at the pine woods.

Everybody went to bed. About midnight, someone knocked on the door, and my father opened it. Soldiers grabbed him and said, "You're under arrest." Father got out the Sears flashlight and the receipt. I think they believed him, but they stationed someone to keep an eye on us for awhile.

There must have been some sort of spying though, because when the German submarine came up to annoy a barge almost all the Navy men were playing baseball with Provincetown down in Chatham.

I learned to row when I was about five. I learned to sail—sail by myself—when I was ten. This was a joyous place to be. Still is. We'd go fishing; we'd get flounder, particularly in the dredged part—the artificial basins—at the Naval Air Station. You could sail around here unobstructed by motorboats. Well, there were motorboats, but they mostly wouldn't go. They were very unreliable.

In my day, one of the biggest industries was quahogging. The men used to row or skull over to between Jean Primavera's and Alan McClennen's. Almost all the quahogs were taken over there. They didn't use outboards, because they didn't work very well.

Lonnie Chase—you know, Lonnie's Pond—was one of those quahoggers. He was almost as round as he was tall; that's why he was called "Chubby." He was a very good-natured man. And there was One-Arm Higgins. I can't recall his first name, but he shot his arm off. He was sneaking for ducks, and he bent over. This gun was there and was cocked. But he could do anything, including row like crazy.

When we raced in Baybirds, there was rarely any annoyance. Now the place is a mess of motorboats, and it's almost impossible to race fairly out of Chatham Yacht Club unless the wind is really strong. One motorboat can pass by and push one sailboat ahead or put another one behind, particularly if the sailor isn't really experienced.

We had various boats, beginning with the *Appendix*, a clumsy lapstrake dory with a seventy-five pound one-cylinder Evinrude outboard. My brother Teddy was the only one who could make it go, and that was a constant battle. Dada was very kind and forbearing as he watched his sons struggle with various pieces of machinery.

The sharpie was next, and later, when we acquired a blue sail, she was dubbed the *Blue Bottle*. We always had to hold the main sheet in our hand, because we would ship water with the slightest heel. Next we got two excellent rowboats from the Cape Cod Shipbuilding Company in Wareham. They were twelve-foot boats, easy to row and light enough to pull up on the beach. In 1919, we acquired *The Motor Boat*, a lapstrake eighteen-foot dory with a one-lung Palmer motor. We named it *The Motor Boat*; we were a very unimaginative family. The motor was always very balky and in shallow water would twist great globs of eelgrass around its propeller, causing long delays.

In 1922, we got the Baybird. A whole fleet was ordered from Chamberlain, the wooden boatbuilder in Marblehead. They were towed down here by tugboat, I think. Baybird #20 was the source of lots of entertainment for many years. My brother Brent raced in white flannels and a blazer, the usual apparel of the 1920s. By the end of the summer, his pants were pretty well shrunk, you know.

Later, the Baybird was raced by my sister, Anna. She did well in light winds and earned her share of silverware.

Eventually *The Motor Boat* was given to Skip Norgeot, and the Baybird to Bruce Hammatt, who still sails her. What a beautiful sight!

I get out off Monomoy, and these big motor things come along and take pictures of me. There must be a dozen pictures of me shaking my fist at them. You know, I go out in my little catboat, God's in His heaven, and then one of these big damned things comes and circles you and wants to take a picture because you're the only sailboat!

Too many people know about the Bay now. There are too many boats. The water quality bothers me, and although I've had a revetment here all my life, they bother me. If we didn't have one, both these buildings would go into the sea. But I have mixed feelings about them.

Mama was a sand castle expert. She was a very good mother and came up with things to amuse us. Her castles had chutes which allowed marbles to run down under bridges and over moats. Then the tide would wash away the castles. Now there's no sand down there—just rocks. There are no bluffs anymore to nourish the beach.

I love it out there in the early morning. You can barely hold me back from going out with the current and coming back with the current. You really have to play the Bay by the currents. I have a tide chart. All winter long, I refer to it every day—to figure out what I can do.

William A. Dickson
South Orleans

72

Memories of the Cape

Images and emotions, dreams and realities
Shining seeds sowed
Planted in me when my tiny infant lungs first filled
with angry salt air,
when my baby hands first held smooth grains of sand
when my soft tiny feet first trod upon the crunchy black
of dried seaweed.
Fed by the laughter of the breeze
the lullaby of the waves
the warmth of the sun,
the seeds grew as I did, steadily year by year.
The House;
Built of sunsets and corn on the cob,
thunderstorms and lemonade
sunburns and sandy feet.
The House;
where history hung in the air
where memories stuck to the walls
where my heritage clung like dust
in the folds of musty curtains;
my stubbornness sticking like pennies
lost in the floorboards.
my loud laughter heard in every slamming
of the screen door,
my intellect nailed to the rafters
like sixty years of Yacht Club winnings.
Born, planted in 1973,
fed by love and warmth and history
the vine of my memory grows thick in my mind,
lush and green in my heart
But grows limp, brownish and sad
at the edges of my soul
where secret wishes lie.

Josanna Bennett Dickson
(granddaughter of William and Harriet Dickson)
June 5, 1993

Sally Holyoke Davis and Dr. William Davis--"Gaga and Gampa"--at The Narrows on their 50th wedding anniversary.

Granny Cochran knew the Brooks family when she was young. She was about the same age as Lawrence, and she loved the Mousetraps over there—those little wooden houses. She'd come to visit. They'd walk around, and they rode horses all the time. She saw this point of land and told her father, Dr. William Davis. They bought it.

The Cochrans created a culture of their own. I learned about extended families from them. They all got along—didn't cross swords too often. I didn't have an extended family worth mentioning.

Granny got married in her thirties and was married for only fourteen years before her husband died. She had a rich brother-in-law. That helped. Thomas Cochran was a Morgan partner. He lived in New York and had silk sheets, according to Monnie. Doesn't that sound repulsive?

Granny had six children, Monnie being the first. Her husband died when Monnie was only fourteen or fifteen. It made such a difference to him; I think that's why he was always so good with teenage boys. He took over the Sea Scouts when Albion Besse retired, and kept doing it for thirty years, I think.

We were married in 1941, and the war came. We dealt with it. In around 1946, Monnie came down and got a job at a new newspaper being started—*The Cape Codder*. He worked for Jack Johnson as advertising manager for a year. But he hadn't graduated from any college, although he had three and a-half years at Harvard. So we went to Granny's Concord house for four years while he went to Boston University.

The next four summers we went out west. It was important for me to get away. I didn't want to live with Granny all the time. I thought she was pretty hard to take. She had twenty-three grandchildren and lots of cousins, too. I couldn't see living off her with all those other people wanting to come down.

But that first summer here, in 1937, was a culture shock for me, coming from Boston where I'd lived in rather austere fashion. I spoke to my siblings, and they to me, and we had a pleasant time. But it wasn't this sort of clannishness. They almost had their own language, and I didn't get it, whatever they were saying. They talked about things I didn't understand, and I felt like an insignificant other. I really did, when I first came down.

It was a fiefdom, and the head honcho was Dr. Davis, "Gampa" to family members. His three daughters were powers behind the throne, and Monnie's mother, later my mother-in-law—Granny—was to be the successor. She was a very athletic, talented woman who helped run the show then. She made soap out of kitchen drippings, filled the shelves with beachplum and wild grape jelly and could deliver a flawless rendition of "Casey at the Bat." She could still whack a tennis ball over the net when she was in her nineties. Up until two weeks before she died—at a hundred and two—she still was going outside every day to saw wood for her fireplace.

Her sisters, Helen and Mamie, were equally powerful in their own spheres when I first came here. Aunt Helen was an intellectual and wonderful cook. Mamie was a planner, family historian, prime conversationalist and key bridge player.

Monnie promised me we'd play tennis. I'd learned proper tennis form at Windsor School in Boston. Monnie never had proper form, but he'd slam that damned ball so hard you couldn't touch it. But before we could play, we had to weed the tennis court. We each had a square to weed.

There were little cubicle bedrooms upstairs, with clothes pegs in the corners. Hanging on the peg in each girl's room was an India print dress. That's what you were supposed to wear for dinner. So I did. All the boys wore sailor suits—white middies and pants.

They'd swim their horses over to Sipson's Island. It was something. Later, our family got leftover horses—left over from Sea Pines School or someplace. We didn't have fancy-dancy horses.

When I came to the Cape, there were two Uncle Charlies and two cousins named Bill. Uncle Charlie Holyoke had what Monnie called "a corporation;" that is, he was portly. He had a rigid routine. He'd have his nap on a little sofa under the stairs—a cozy little place. He'd take his walk on the porch; he never ran anywhere.

The Fourth of July was a big deal for them. They got fireworks from wherever they were allowed when they were allowed, and these were apportioned out to the kids. They'd shoot them off as soon as they got them, but one of the nephews, Andy, put some of his away—in a box under that sofa. There was a piece of punk in the box—still lighted. During Uncle Charlie's nap, "Pop, pop, pop!" Charlie had to hasten out, and Andy was crying. "Uncle Charlie just shot off my fireworks!"

The big deal as far as the Bay went in my memory was to go out for a picnic on the ocean beach. They all could go skinnydipping then. I didn't. Later, you couldn't because there were beach buggies. The kids would dig big holes in the sand so the buggies would fall in. My kids did that, too.

Years ago—my sister put it best—the Bay was like a tub that you'd taken the plug out of. The water was going down so. Then the Chatham cut happened. The water came back, and it was such a relief to everyone.

When I was young, my father heard how people here put eelgrass around their houses for insulation. He was Samuel Cabot. They all were Samuel Cabots all along—paint, stains, that sort of thing. He started making the Cabot Sheathing Quilt. They put all this eelgrass between pieces of cardboard, then sewed it all around and put it between walls for insulation. They were dependent on eelgrass, of course, and there was a tremendous eelgrass blight here in the '30s. That's when father began getting his eelgrass from Nova Scotia.

Monnie loved the Cape. His family was into sailing. This area was a farm once, apparently. Granny bought it and gave a big hunk to the Conservation Trust.

Our kids learned to do the various things kids learn to do on the water. I sailed, but never was a great sailor. But Monnie was one, so that's O.K. One in the family is enough.

Granny had Radcliffe girls. I'm not sure that's where they all came from, but they were her "Radcliffe girls." They stayed in what was called "the castle," a little shack with a beautiful beech tree in front. They wanted summer jobs. They did cooking and stuff like that. But Granny loved to clean. I did *not* love to clean, and if I *tried* to clean I didn't do it right. So I went into the kitchen with Aunt Helen—Helen Locke— and learned to cook. That's where I made my contribution.

In her old age, Granny lived on the Cape. In those days I felt different about her, because the power base had changed. We were more balanced. She also wasn't as mean.

She sure as hell had stories. She knew a lot. I'm sorry you can't hear her stories.

Betsy (Cabot) Cochran
South Orleans

Margaret (Davis) and Moncrieff Cochran, with their daughter,"Sitter," and son, Mon, Jr.

Basically, I was brought up on the Bay. That's why I got into all these projects. When I was about nineteen, I worked in Woods Hole for a marine contractor, Dan Clark. He hired me out to do zillions of projects for the Marine Biological Laboratory. Back in the '60s, I was Cultured Clam's first employee, and I was Shellfish Warden and Harbormaster here in the '70s.

I have no degrees, whatsoever.

I was pretty much fulltime on the Bay since I was eight, I guess. It was all rowing—rowing and learning—rowing around Little Pleasant Bay, Hog Island, Sampson's, Sipson's—rowing—and watching the bottom.

I'll show you where the Orleans/Chatham town boundary rock is. It's underwater at the north end of Strong Island. I mention this only because fish and birds and tides and horseshoe crabs have no boundaries. Humans had none either. They made boundaries because they wanted to own something. Greed is an awful thing. The Indians had the right idea. Nobody owns the land.

My great-grandfather fished out of St. Pierre, off Newfoundland. He was mayor of St. Pierre and owned about half the fishing fleet. The whole fleet was destroyed in one hurricane or another on the Grand Banks. The cemetery there is full of stones with no bodies under them.

In the early 1900s, my grandfather, Gaston Pierre Norgeot, was a teletype operator at the French Cable Station in Orleans.

I learned from my mother's father. He trapped, fished and quahogged in the New Bedford area. He told me to talk with the oldest people I could find. That's the only way I would learn.

One of my favorite sayings of his was, "I saw, but I did not observe."

The first thing I learned was, "Don't get lost on the Bay. Learn the direction of the eelgrass." Where the eelgrass splits off, so does the tide. After a period of time, you'll get to know the eelgrass like the roads we drive or the paths we walk in the woods.

Once you learn the roads on the bottom, you can't get lost in the fog.

When I was Harbormaster and looking for someone who was lost at night, it didn't do me any good to have a compass. I'd just shine a light on the bottom and drive the road.

In 1626, the inlet was east of the north end of Strong Island. This was called Old Ship Harbor. It also was called Monomoyick Bay and the Port of Namequoit. That's where Portanimicut came from.

There's a story that in the middle 1600s—after a hurricane or some big storm—the tide was so high that the Indians were in trees to stay alive.

All the shellfish in concentrated areas of the Bay are near freshwater leaching places. That keeps the algae in the water agitated. The ponds are important as spawning areas. The water temperature year-round is in the fifties on the bottom. That's why fish come in to lay their eggs there, so they won't freeze.

All of these ponds that are deep have freshwater springs. They should never be dredged: Arey's, Lonnie's, Meetinghouse, Paw Wah, Round Cove, Crow's Pond, Ryder's Cove, Stage Harbor—all of them are loaded with freshwater springs. When you open the sea into that pond, you're releasing the fresh water out of it, letting salt water in and changing the salinity. All the water quality testing they're doing is for naught, because it's not the way nature meant it— as a nursery, feeding the whole ecosystem. For the most part, dredging is to allow bigger and bigger boats in.

Little Sipson's Island meadow was given to the Town of Orleans for one dollar in 1976 to be used for the purpose of shellfish reproduction. Ever since then, I've been trying to get the town to close that area, to make it a habitat and sanctuary, so the greatest predator on earth—man—doesn't get in there and upset Mother Nature's real balance. Closing the place would allow the natural reproduction of fish and

shellfish. If you don't put money in the bank, you don't get interest.

You've got to have people with hands-on experience. That's what I tell the kids. A scientist can come study something until he dies. He writes a report, and it's all over. The scientists look at one thing or another thing. They base their study on a book. Well, you've got to ask the local yokel. It's like the Master of a ship; you learn something and teach those who are aboard. Kids should get hands-on in the boat, hands-on in the water. There are no apprenticeships anymore. The world's too fast. Wait 'til someone shuts off the electricity someday.

I tell the kids, "You've got to write the books. Don't just read them. Come up with something new."

Sand nourishment of the Bay is very important. Now—because of land values—they're stabilizing the banks with rock walls. It's stopped that nourishment.

There should be areas in the Bay, in the Sound and in the ocean that are just closed off for sanctuaries— not to infringe on the fishermen's bounty or on taxpayers—but to protect Mother Nature's womb. It's not only here; it's everywhere. The Bay is stripped.

Willard Nickerson.

There's nothing for birds to come here for.

A lot of birds were gunned out of here by 1850. Cape Codders ate seagulls and crows. That business with the gulls on Monomoy? The Indians knew that when a place got overpopulated by birds, they'd just take the eggs. They didn't shoot the birds.

In my time, Little Sipson's Island was a rookery. The north end of Big Sipson's was a rookery, and fifty per cent of the south side of Strong Island was a rookery. They were all here eating something! Man drove them out to build.

They sprayed DDT bigtime out here in the late 1960s until the '80s, for greenhead flies, deerflies and what we know as gnats or no-seeums. All the birds were nesting. The spray wiped out bluebirds, doves, egrets, hawks. Who knows what damage it did.

Fish migrate from the Carolinas and from the warm waters of the Sound. What used to come into the Bay came through the passage at Morris Island— alewife herring, fluke, blueback herring.... They're anadromous fish. They come from salt water inland to spawn in fresh water. One of the oldest laws in Massachusetts says you cannot obstruct any fishway of anadromous fish.

The Town of Chatham decided it was advantageous to put in a dike there, to receive tax revenue from building. Consideration of a drawbridge was out of the question.

The Terrapin Turtle used to go through there. Now, the scallop spawn from the Sound can't go through. They have to go from the Sound through cold Atlantic water, which I'm sure they hate to do.

I used to spend a lot of time on North Beach, on the Bay, on Monomoy in the winter, and I'd run into Willard Nickerson. There were very few people there, but the oldtimers used to walk. They sometimes had a surf rod, or a gun, or a dog—just out there walking. Willard and I were the best of friends. I was selling fluke and flounder to him when I was twelve. He told me, "Bring me every fish you can get."

Willard would say, "The people just don't listen. Don't spend money on dredging. Just wait. Mother Nature will take care of it. They just don't listen."

Willard was a prize. His son, Nicky, is a good fisherman. And he cares.

Something that's been detrimental to the marshes is that from the mid-19th century to the early part of this one, all the fur-bearing animals were trapped out: otter, mink, muskrat, also the saltwater rat—muskrat. They kept the creeks open. They'd navigate through the creeks up to the marsh, where they'd feed off the vegetation and shellfish.

A lot of these rivers have been plugged off. They're not flowing anymore, and underneath the marsh is always fresh water flowing.

The last heavy population of Terrapin Turtles was at Boatmeadow Creek in Eastham, at the entrance to Jeremiah's Gutter. The turtles were seined by chicken-wire and shipped to New York and Philadelphia. The last of that was done in the late '30s.

In the Bay, chicken-wire seines or nets were used to trap large schools of striped bass. If you couldn't afford a regular seine, you'd go down and buy a couple bales of chicken-wire.

Fyke nets were banned around the 1850s, maybe 1860. They were lethal. Indians used them. They were shaped like an ice cream cone, with hoops holding the net out. The first hoop was six feet tall, the second one maybe four feet tall and the next one two feet. The leaders off the open end could have been a thousand feet long. The fish would come along those leaders and be forced into the fyke net.

In all the rivers in the 1950s and '60s, we had huge runs of bass. At night, particularly on a moonlit night, the rivers would be solid with fish. You'd see just flashing fins.

According to the oldtimers, fish run in seventeen to twenty-year cycles. That includes bass, bluefish, blue crabs, eels. It's the same with crops of scallops. The cycle will run uphill for ten years, then down for ten years.

That's Money Head over there on Hog Island. There are many old stories about Captain Kidd burying his treasure there. However, in the late 1970s, one of the counselors from Camp Viking bought a gallon can of old French coins at an antique shop in Boston. He salted the front beach around Money Head so the kids could go on a treasure hunt. If you find a coin there, it might be Captain Kidd's. Or it might be from Camp Viking.

The British used to come in here. Sailors wore silver buttons on their uniforms, and those were prized by the Indians. They carried them around. Some people have found them. They'd be black now, of course, but they're solid silver.

There are a fair number of relics here. A lot of Indians lived on the Bay. I've found arrowheads up to ten thousand and twelve thousand years old. Some are pointed at both ends. Very smart. Break one end, and just turn it around.

Everywhere you go in the whole system are shell-fish middens. Some people call them "heaps." In those middens lies the secret of the Bay. What species of shellfish the Indians ate. The age of the shellfish. You know what's indigenous to the area. Everything that was here when the Indians were is proven— including oysters. They were in all the rivers and ponds and were fished out, I'll say, by 1955.

The middens tell about the Indians, too. Their teeth were perfect, and the average height was six feet. They were very healthy people.

Through all of these marshes there were sink box blinds. They actually dug a hole, pumped out the sand. The tide would fill them, but when the tide went out you were down in the box. Some of the sink boxes here are ancient. The Indians probably built them.

We're going over the Hog Island flats now. Under them is an ancient clam bed. If you dig down about eighteen inches at low tide, you'll find the old bed. I think it probably was capped during some great storm around 1650. And there's fresh water under those old beds. There's fresh water underneath the whole Bay.

That's The Narrows and Granny Cochran's house over there. I was pretty much raised at Betsy and Mon's house. Young Mon and I were close. Either I was at his house, or he was at mine. They had boats and horses. I didn't have any of that.

We'd swim horses across the Narrows to Sipson's Island. We weren't supposed to. You'd slide off the horse's back when he was swimming, grab the tail and just hold on.

I think the beginning of my back problems came from riding bareback on Cochran horses.

You know, back then it wasn't anything to see a hundred-and-fifty sailboats out here, with all the camp boats. Those people were put out of business by regulations

As far as resources of the Bay are concerned, we can help them by good management and good enforcement. We've got to keep local control. This Bay should be a sanctuary, to a point anyhow. There's no place like it in the world.

Did you know that all the water in the Bay turns counter-clockwise?

Albert "Skip" Norgeot
South Orleans

My mother came down here and taught school in Harwich Center around 1915. She was from Wolfeboro, New Hampshire and had gone to Mt. Holyoke. She wanted to get away from home. Imagine coming this far alone. How courageous. She lived at Ma Moody's in the Center. She stayed in one house, and there was another one about half a lot away. That's where they ate, and the local men used to come there to eat. My father, Warren Sears Nickerson, met my mother there.

He had all kinds of jobs. He'd gone to sea as a young fellow, then came home and didn't know what to do. He was a builder, he did harness-making, and soon after he married my mother he got into the funeral business. There wasn't an undertaker anywhere down here, so his business took him all the way to Provincetown. He built the house where the funeral parlor was on Main Street in Harwich Port. That's where we lived. My sisters and I played in the caskets.

We also played in the cranberry bogs. All those people had bogs then. I wouldn't think of eating a raw cranberry today, but we thought they were good for us then and they probably were.

I don't know how the rich people lived, but I can tell you how the rest of us did. When we lived here, we had nothing to do with them. Not on purpose; it just worked that way.

We grew up in Florida. My father had a heart attack, and he was in bed practically when I was born.

Mary, Dorothy and, in front, Jean Nickerson, at the Nick-Shack, 1927.

Oscar C. and Warren Sears Nickerson, watching the races, about 1940.

They told him he had to quit running around in the funeral business, so we moved to Florida in 1930. Then we became summer people here, living in "Nick-Shack," the cottage he had built in 1922. He'd built the fireplace of stones from the beach.

Before that, in 1921, when they were getting ready to build Eastward Ho!, someone told him there were Indian remains there. He thought, "Who knows; that might have been Squanto." That's when he became so interested in writing the history of Lower Cape Indians. He knew he had to find something to do with his time, and writing was it.

We always had some kind of boat, and of course there never was a motor on a sailboat. Our favorite thing to do was take a picnic on a day-long trip down the channel and to the Outer Beach. We had Vienna sausages, sardines and crackers, and we'd build a little fire on the sand. My mother wouldn't let us eat regular hotdogs, but she thought Vienna sausages were just right for our little digestive systems. Often as not, we'd come home in a flat calm, paddling and being bitten by gnats.

I remember an all-day affair in the boat with my father. We had to go with the tide, because you had no motor. He'd wait for a certain day. We went to Meeting House Pond, and I'd run up the path to the general store and get an ice cream cone. We'd stop all along the way to look for arrowheads. I loved that trip—just moseying along. I'd have gone anywhere with him.

I remember once going with him out over the Bar. The opening was right across from the lighthouse, about where it is now. They'll tell you a break like that happens about every sixty years. It was unusual to do that in a small boat—probably a little seventeen foot boat. We never had a big boat—just whatever was cheap.

When we grew up we did the same things we'd done when we were little. We were always lured by the Outer Beach. We'd go to my half-sister Betty Eldridge's place, called "Time Out." Our nephew Dana was there, and he always knew where the clams were.

Geneva Eldredge was my father's favorite sister. She was an "e" Eldredge. Betty is an "i" Eldridge, and never the twain will meet on that business.

There were twelve children in my father's family; of course, maybe five of them died in childhood. On sailing days when I was little, my father, Uncle Oscar—Joshua's father—and Uncle Carroll loved to sit on the bank and get a front-row seat for the races. They'd argue and calculate who had the best chance of winning.

Uncle Oscar had a housekeeper who was Catholic. Some nuns came to visit her, and they brought the Mother Superior. They all came to Uncle Oscar's Lean-To, and he took the Mother Superior out rowing in all her trappings.

He also had Babe Ruth there for gunning. We'd go over to the Lean-To and hunt up the logbooks, looking for his name. We didn't usually have any celebrities here. Oscar built his Lean-To for gunning; my father never got into that.

Uncle Carroll lived at Wequassett, which wasn't Wequassett then. He kept his catboat *Gladys* out here at a mooring, because he had this fish shanty. He put up his cutting table right at the edge of the water, and he cleaned, gutted, salted and packed the fish in barrels. His was a one-man operation, 5 a.m. to 5 p.m. He'd go out four or five miles with no motor. He was the real loner in the family.

My sisters Mary and Dorothy and I would squeeze the eyeballs out of the fish. We played with them. I remember making "eyeball soup." We didn't have many resources, you know.

The camps on the Bay taught the children a lot. This business of learning to sail and being responsible and independent. Like my Uncle Carroll—he'd go off in that boat, and whatever happened, he was responsible.

Our traditions—like looking for arrowheads and quahogging—have to be passed on from generation to generation. The Bay is always there. Fundamentally, it's the same, from one generation to the next. Nothing else in life is. Talking about it today is very emotional for me.

Jean (Nickerson) Primavera
East Harwich

The Nickerson men and their sister. From left, Joshua A., W. Sears, Ernest C., Geneva, Albert E., T. Carroll and Oscar C.

The Lights

When the darkness gathers 'round us
And the whisp'ring evening falls,
As the gull, with outspread pinions
To her mate below her calls,
While the breakers on the beach
Sound forth their booming roar,
We stand there all enraptured
On the wreck-strewn sandy shore.
When the glowing moon arises
On the sunset following close,
And the mermaids from the waters
Drive forth their shadowy host
Of the hundreds they have strangled
On the treacherous Chatham Bars,
We turn our eyes in gladness
To those two, mute shining stars
That men up there have builded
To warn their brothers of the sea
Away from the siren's beckoning host
That here holds wild revelry.

Joshua A. Nickerson
1901-1990
written in January, 1917

The twins.

My earliest recollections of striped bass fishing are of a day when, as a boy, I happened to be on the North Beach in Chatham with my father. There was a "power dory" with a rowing dory in tow just off-shore of the surf. In the rowing dory was a seine, and there were three or four men in the two boats, among them, as I recall, Rufus Nickerson and his brother Joe. Dad said they were about to seine a school of bass which they had spotted near us in the surf.

First they rowed ashore and landed a man with one end of the seine on the slope of the beach. He attached the bottom corner of the net to his foot and held the upper corner in his hands, while the other men rowed off paying out the seine as they went around the school of fish. When it was all out they rowed in and brought their end of the net to shore. Then, carefully, the men began to purse up the seine from both ends. As soon as the fish became aware of the net, they tried frantically to escape, and some of them did, but not by going over or around the net. As it was drawn to shore, there were moments when the bottom of the seine was not securely down on the sand, in spite of the leads. Those bass would put their noses down and try to burrow through sand and water, in the undertow, under the bottom edge of the net. Some escaped this way. But most of the school were brought flipping and flopping up onto the dry sand. For more than fifty years, now, this method of catching bass has been outlawed. But up until then it was a common method used by local fishermen when the Autumn run of bass was on.

As I grew up, I heard men talk of "heaving and hauling" for bass, so I decided to try it. The equipment consisted of a good length of heavy cod line wrapped around a straight stick something over a foot long. At the end of the hard-tarred cod line, we bent on two or three yards of softer and slightly heavier line, and at the end of this a lead drail, fairly heavy, in which—when the lead had been molten—a stout hook had been imbedded. The softer line at the heaving end was to save some of the wear and tear on your fingers. The fishing method was to uncoil as much line from the stick as you thought you could heave, then take the end nearest the drail, whirl it around your head a few times and heave the drail out over the surf. As you retrieved the line, hand over hand,

you hoped for a strike, and sometimes you got one. The lead tended to turn black from the chemical action of the salt water. So it had to be scraped bright from time to time with a knife. Some of the old-timers became very proficient with this method of fishing and could heave a lead drail as far as fifty yards over the breakers. Needless to say, the bass had to be close in to be caught this way; but they often are when chasing bait in the fall.

It was not until sometime in the 1920s that I first saw anyone fishing with a rod in the surf. At the time, I remember thinking it was a pretty effete way to fish, influenced in part, no doubt, because it was a summer resident from New Jersey who was doing it. Before long, however, surf fishing with rod and reel became very popular locally. The rig consisted of a split-bamboo rod about five or six feet in length plus a detachable wooden butt about two and a-half feet long, to which was fastened a heavy spool-type reel filled with twelve or sixteen pound test linen line. Also strapped around your waist by a leather belt was a "butt socket" into which the butt of the rod was inserted when retrieving. These were usually of leather. But some used a beer can for a butt socket.

The lure was almost invariably a tin drail with a hook imbedded in it, shaped with a slight bend to resemble a squid and to give it more action. Sometimes we pointed the hook with a strip of pork rind to give it even more action. The tin remained bright in the water (as lead would not) and required only an occasional rubbing in the sand to keep it shining. The linen line had very little give to it, and as a result, a back-lash, when casting, almost invariably resulted in a sound like a pistol shot and a drail sailing out to sea. To lose half a dozen drails in this manner in a few hours of fishing was not unusual. But in those days, they cost only 35 cents (and cheaper by the dozen) at the local hardware store. Each day after fishing, the line had to be strung out in the air and dried, because if it were left wet on the reel it tended to rot and lose its strength.

During the '30s, we organized the Lower Cape Surfcasters Association which awarded arm patches for proficiency in casting the "tin clad" jig. The neophyte first achieved his twenty-five yard patch, then fifty, then seventy-five, and finally he might make the hundred yard patch. Both men and women were members, and some of the women were better casters than most of the men. In the summer we had a big clambake, and after the bass fishing season was over, an annual meeting and dinner. This club was very successful and lots of fun. It brought together people from all walks of life with a common interest in surf casting. And it also served as a mutual aid group, for it was during the 1930s, that "beach buggies" (mostly Model A or Model T Fords) first appeared on the beaches in numbers. They were all two-wheel drive and under-powered for use in sand. So getting stuck and having to be shoveled out and jacked up, and having driftwood boards or planks put under the wheels to get out was common operating procedure. Learning to drive on the beach with this equipment required quite a bit of doing and occasional help from others. The Surfcasters Association finally just died out and and disappeared with the advent of World War II and gasoline rationing.

During the war years, gasoline rationing prevented using motor vehicles on the beach for fishing. But I had a flat-bottomed, center-board sharpie with leg-of-mutton sail. As there were no motor boats racing around to disturb them, because of gasoline rationing (and even if there had been, the biggest outboards in common use then were only five or ten horsepower), I caught a lot of striped bass in Pleasant Bay. It was rare, indeed, to troll a line behind my sailing skiff between the islands and the beach and come home empty-handed. We also did some casting from shore with good catches at places like the mouth of Crow's Pond and at Pleasant Bay Narrows.

In the late '40s and early '50s, things began to change. Up until then, almost all surf casting had been with jigs—usually tin or tin with feathers or bucktails. Now it was discovered that striped bass would take surface plugs such as were used on the western lakes for pike. Gradually, plugs of every description began to take over as lures, replacing jigs. It was about this time, too, that glass rods in one piece, some as long as nine or ten feet, began to replace the rods with a split-bamboo tip and wooden butt. Even back in the '30s, some surf casters had used single pieces of "Burma cane" which were longer and whippier than the split-bamboo.

Also during July and August, when most of us never expected to catch bass in the surf, people started fishing with (of all things) sea worms. Then night fishing started! When drails (with accompanying backlashes) were more commonly used, our fishing stopped after sundown, except on the full of the moon. But with the advent of nylon braided line, and later monofilament, and especially the backlash-free spinning reel, which came into use in the '50s, night fishing became popular. I have never been able to see much sport in sitting in the dark on a stool waiting for a fish–usually a skate, sometimes a bass–to take my hook—when you can't see what's happening. But it is popular with many people today who put high value on the catch—higher than they do on the catching.

During the 1960s, other changes took place. Since Nauset (North) Beach is attached to the mainland in Orleans, this has resulted in a concentration of so-called "beach buggies" there. But the beach buggies have changed, too. Instead of being light or stripped-down vehicles, they have become heavy campers, converted milk delivery trucks, and the like, designed for overnight camping. They contain complete living facilities, and lumber along at low speeds until they reach their chosen location where they set up camp for as long as the regulations permit them to stay—a far cry from chasing signs of fish up and down the beach casting our tin-clads, this is. These are mostly bait fishermen, whose lines just set there in the surf gathering weeds, while the fisherman dozes over his can of beer.

The fishing in Pleasant Bay has changed, too. No longer is the day fishing reliable. By day powerful outboard motors of up to one hundred horsepower or more race about towing water skiers behind them and breaking up any schools of fish which might be on the surface chasing bait. Most of the fishing is at night now or early in the morning while the motorboat jockeys are still abed. And there is little fishing with jigs and plugs. Instead the fisherman uses live eels as bait or tows behind his boat a contraption which looks like an umbrella frame—a Christmas Tree—loaded with multi-colored lures, sometimes catching two or three fish at once. Hardly "sport," I'd say. But these "meat-fishermen" are no worse, I guess, than the seiners. Nor are they worse than some of us who set trawls at night on the flats when the low tide came at dusk and at dawn, hauling them out soon after sunrise, before the gulls could get to work on our catch. The difference is that these men called themselves sportsmen!

I have written this memorandum about bass fishing so my grandson, Peter, can know a little of how it used to be before the waters of Pleasant Bay were filled with high-powered outboard motor boats and the sands of Nauset Beach were occupied by heavy motor vehicles designed for camping.

Joshua A. Nickerson
(Written in 1971)

(Some years ago, Mr. Nickerson's North Beach camp was given by his family to the Chatham Historical Society. It now is on the grounds of the Atwood House Museum on Stage Harbor Road.)

My memories of the old butter paddle that Mother always said helped her to make men of her boys are rather vague in a way.

I was next to the last of the Nickerson family of twelve, and all the "butter paddle boys" except Sears, who was three years younger than me, were young men when I remember them.

Edison, the son who received the most chastisement, was married, with a daughter the age of Sears, when I remember.

But I do remember the old paddle hanging by a loop of string on the wooden partition that separated the buttery, as it was always called, and the cellar way.

I remember, too, the hand-made, wooden potato masher hanging on one side of the paddle and the long-handled tin skimmer on the other, which was used for dipping steamed clams from the big iron kettle.

On the wide pantry shelves set pans full of rich Jersey milk with thick yellow cream that Mother would skim with a pure white sea clam shell kept for just that purpose—one with a thin edge that wouldn't scoop up too much milk.

First she would take a table knife and run it around the milk pan to start the cream from the edge; then with the clam shell she would push the thick leathery cream that looked like rich folds of velvet to one side of the pan, where she would dip it up and drop the full shell into the waiting brown crock with the knob-like handles on the side, where it made a peculiar sort of plop when it landed.

When she had skimmed what pans were needed, she would pick up the crock, take the paddle from the wall, and step briskly off to the kitchen where she knew Father was sitting in his Morris chair by the East window, stealing a few minutes to read *The Last Days of Pompeii*, or *The Rise and Fall of the Roman Empire*. Or perhaps his thoughts led to poetry—and it would be Longfellow or Whittier he was perusing. Always his Bible lay handy—not that he was so religious, for he never attended church, but studied it as ancient history and knew it from cover to cover. Preachers from far and near came to converse with him and argue on his points of view, which today I realize were far ahead of theirs.

But to get back to the paddle.

The brown crock held just enough cream to stir without any splashing and would produce a good big pat of golden butter. Mother, seeing Father engaged in nothing special except harking back into history, both Biblical and otherwise, would advance upon him with the cream pot and the paddle, and before he could gather himself for a getaway, would say, "Stir this cream, Jenson, while you're sitting there, and that will give me a chance to do the beds." Father would lay aside his book and take the brown cream pot and old paddle in hand and begin to stir slowly and vigorously, sometimes singing a little ditty from his own childhood days to Sears and me, who would be standing nearby to watch the cream turn to butter, and maybe get a lap from the end of the old paddle just before the cream separated.

This we would spread with our tongues over a molasses cookie we were holding behind us, ready for the occasion. I can see that picture now, and hear the tune of that little ditty echoing down the years:

Riddle ti diddle and riddle ti ran,
Come butter, come, as fast as you can"

And soon the cream would separate, and blobs of golden butter would be floating in the buttermilk that Mother would pour off and set aside to make buttermilk biscuits for supper.

This done, she would work the rest of the buttermilk out with the paddle, pour it off, add salt, then with her hands, take the ball of butter out of the brown crock and mould it into a round pat which she laid on a plate, and with the paddle smoothed top and sides until they were like glass; then turning the paddle on the edge, mark deep lines across the top for decoration. Sometimes she marked single lines, sometimes crisscrossed them into squares.

I remember, too, how good that new butter tasted on the hot buttermilk biscuits that night for supper, with maybe fresh strawberries from Father's strawberry patch, below the house next to "Percy's bog," or later the wild blackberries that grew in the rye field back of the hill.

So you see my remembrances of the old butter paddle are pleasant ones.

But I remember my older brother joking with Mother about the "butter paddle days" and her saying, "but not one of you boys refused when I said 'Go get the butter paddle,' nor did you draw back when I said 'Hold out your hand'."

Mother was a short woman—"just heart high," Father said, when he—over six feet tall—stretched his long arm out for her to stand under. Mother's boys were all tall, too, but with her butter paddle she ruled like a queen and her boys respected and honored her for it.

They never resented the paddle. They knew they deserved the punishment, for Mother loved them dearly, but "they must follow the rules and obey orders." Besides, Mother's forebears were deep-sea captains, and she had told me that in her home the children all addressed their father as Sir. He was Captain Joshua Atkins of Chatham.

I was there the night Mother was presented with the paddle at the old North Hall as a Christmas gift— a gift that brought tears to her eyes and to the eyes of many others. Even Father blew his nose vigorously.

How proud I was to see Mother, on the platform, making a little speech of acceptance—the paddle in her hand that had helped make men of her boys.

It was always Father who did the speech-making for he was an excellent public speaker, well versed in all the doings of the day, town affairs, and particularly schools. But Mother proved herself a close second, once she gained control of her emotions. She had a charming personality and a deep sense of humor, a sweet disposition that helped to keep the household on an even keel; for Father, dearly as I loved and honored him, had a temper like a bold highwayman. I've seen him have a clam drainer almost done to the last slat, and, because the nail didn't drive just right, he'd take his hammer and smash it into forty thousand pieces Ten minutes later, he'd be as mild as a June breeze.

But he was a wonderful man for all that; both he and Mother were above the average in intellect, which they imparted to their children through the home environment of honesty and truth, fair play and respect for themselves as well as others.

Geneva (Nickerson) Eldredge

(Geneva Nickerson was born in 1877, within sight of the Bay. She was the next-to-youngest of 12 children born to Warren J. and Mary (Atkins) Nickerson and was Joshua Nickerson's aunt.)

Photos on the following pages were taken in the late 1960s and early '70s by Richard C. Hiscock, who has lived here since he was seven and is beginning "to feel like an oldtimer."

My father was named after his Uncle Joshua, so he was "Second." By the time I was born, his uncle had died, so I was "Junior." When he wrote his book, *Days to Remember*, he wrote as Joshua A. Nickerson II, because, he said, that's who he was at the time he was writing about. That was his reasoning anyway.

I grew up in the house at the top of the hill, right next to this one, and as far as Pleasant Bay goes, I've been on it and around it and over it all my life. We had the camp out on the beach. It was built in 1947, because that's when my father could get the materials—after the war. We lived out there all summer. My mother and I would motor back here once a week, to do laundry and get real showers.

My father had a 1930 Model A—a woodie station wagon—and we'd fish our way up the beach and fish our way home. There were so few cars on the beach after the war that you could tell by the tire tracks who was there. Some fished, some didn't. In those days you could raise hell on the beach.

During the war, we had to go down by sailboat. You couldn't go by motorboat or car because of gas rationing. We had a flat-bottom skiff—about sixteen feet—with a leg-o-mutton sail. It had a centerboard, and you used an oar for a tiller. Ours was the last camp down on the beach then; the end of the beach was right about across from Chatham Light.

The Coast Guard was out there—at the Old Harbor Station—patrolling the beach with dogs. They used Welsh terriers. We raised some for awhile. It was my job to feed the dogs. I don't remember who we were raising them for; I was only six or seven. But the idea was, if the Germans came ashore and shot a Coast Guardsman, the dog would run back and alert someone.

You know, during the war—in order to survive—Nickerson Lumber Company built doghouses for the Coast Guard along the entire East coast.

It was very scary on the beach at night. Just like on the mainland, we had to cover our windows, inside and out. The Germans *were* out there, because they kept sinking provision boats. I'd walk the beach and pick up all kinds of stuff: canteens, life preservers, cigarettes. I gave my mother the cigarettes. I'd find K-rations. Those were great for Sunday night suppers. They always had Spam in them.

Our house here on Bay Road was heated by oil, so for about three years during the war we had to live at that same Uncle Joshua's house on Old Harbor Road in Chatham. It burned coal.

My father had a deed that said he owned from five hundred feet south of the Old Harbor Coast Guard Station to the "point of the beach." He got that deed in 1926. Well, from 1926 to 1966, the beach grew two and-a-half miles! He could have gone wild selling land for camps out there. But when the National Seashore came along, he gave what is now South Beach to the Town of Chatham. He gave all but about fifty acres. He gave me the old camp and forty-some-odd acres, and he kept six. In the middle of his six acres was "the hospital." That's what they called it, because all the crippled birds came there. They were crippled by hunters; it was a great place for hunting. There was a beautiful marsh there with bayberries, cat-o-nine-tails, all the natural things that grow in those places. Beautiful.

I started hunting when I was fourteen—ducks and

Jan Nickerson's father, Josh, and one that didn't get away.

95

Walter and Edith Whitehead, with Barbara and Josh Nickerson and their son, Joshua, Jr. (Jan).

geese—not deer or anything else. The best fun was shooting them at midnight in the moonlight.

My father and his friends would have these 12th of October weekend parties at the camp every year. If the 12th came in the middle of a week, they'd argue about which weekend to have the party and they'd end up having two. They really had a time out there—my father and Frank Thompson, Carleton Francis, Oscar Cahoon.... One time, Frank drove a car off the beach at about sixty miles an hour. They got out of it, then the car rolled over in deep water. A friend of theirs flew over in his plane and spotted it, and it was hauled out. I think Frank had that car back down there the next weekend. It was a 1936 Ford, I think.

My grandfather, Oscar Nickerson, was one of the founders of Chatham Yacht Club. We had three races

a week, and sometimes there'd be a hundred and fifty sailboats out there. Almost every kid who lived around the Bay had a sailboat. I didn't. I sailed McClennen boats. Josh McClennen's son, Dougie, was a friend of mine, and if Dougie was working I could sail the boat. But I turned it over one day and got the mast stuck in the mud. Josh didn't let me use the boat after that.

We either lived on the Bay or went to parties or dances at Eastward Ho! All our parents were members, and it was a welcome place for teenagers. They encouraged us to be there. The other place we had parties was at Chatham Beach Club. We could have beach parties back then without checking with the police. All we had to do was clean up our mess. And there were no fire permits. When you're sixteen or seventeen, you don't need a fire. We just cuddled.

The weather has changed a lot over the years. It used to be that the Bay would freeze solid at least once a year. People would ski and snowshoe across it.

One winter, Mon Cochran took his mother out on the Bay in his Volkswagen Beetle. I think Granny was about ninety at the time. The police were trying to find out what damned fool was driving around the Bay. I knew, but wasn't about to tell. So they stationed someone at every town landing, figuring whoever it was would have to go ashore by one landing or another. Well, of course, he didn't. He just went home. He'd put planks down between the high water mark and the ice, and just drove onto the Bay.

It was a beautiful moonlit night. He didn't have the headlights on, so all you could see were his tail-lights, going all over the place. He was having a ball.

The biggest change I've seen since the breach in 1987 is the filling-in of the sand. This little creek over to the right is almost choked up.

What's so special about the Bay? I'm always watching it. It's a fantastically beautiful place, and there's always something going on. There are ducks and geese, swans, egrets, those goddammed cormorants—you know what they do to boats—and the tide is always rising or falling. The color of the water changes all the time with the tide and the light. In the middle of winter there are no boats and no people—just water and wildlife. Once in awhile we get a seal. I've seen deer swim across the Bay.

In about an hour, the seagulls will come in and fly up Muddy Creek for the night—to eat and sleep, I guess. They can't go to the dumps anymore.

What's special about the Bay?

Well, why are *you* watching it right now?

Joshua A. "Jan" Nickerson, Jr.
East Harwich

I've told people that I'm an Eldridge on one side and a Nickerson on the other, so you're dealing with thirteen generations of inbreeding.

I barely knew my grandfather, Sears Nickerson. But what a wonderful, wonderful grandfather I had on the Eldridge side—Levi Wilbur Delmar Eldridge. He and my grandmother lived about a half-mile down the road from us. I was the first grandchild and, for a long time, the only one.

When I was ten or twelve, my grandfather asked me if I'd like to go fishing. He introduced me to snapper blue fishing. He had a car and never seemed to worry about getting gas. He had massive cars, Buicks or something.

He was rotund. Sort of like Winston Churchill. The complete opposite of my build. Well, he used a bamboo fishing pole, with a line wrapped around it. No reel. Just dirt simple. We went to Jackknife Harbor, where Muddy Creek dumps into the Bay.

He bought probably the first outboard motor ever built. It must have weighed five hundred pounds. Of course it didn't, but it was a huge thing—sixteen horsepower. I think it was a Neptune.

I used to go out around Strong Island, both with my grandfather and, later, my parents. We did a lot of flounder fishing there. We did a tremendous amount of bass fishing. We'd go to Crow's Pond, Ryder's Cove.

You'd use a willow-leaf spinner and tow a sea worm. Theoretically, this was supposed to get the bass's attention. Then he'd come after the worm.

In the mid-'40s, when the war was on, my mother and father and I would go out in the boat. My father would row, and my mother sat in the stern. They had a wonderful time, but I was berserk. I thought it was so boring, I kept asking if I could go ashore. This was on Crow's Pond, on the other side of the Eastward Ho! landing.

I'd spend an hour or two just goofing around on the shore. I found a deserted house, and I got to think it was mine. I'd sit on the porch and watch my parents rowing around the pond.

Summer used to be eagerly awaited, unlike now. It would open a floodgate. Because they came from away, the summer kids had a little aura of good, whether they deserved it or not. Back then the summer people came down, the mother and children stayed and the father went back and forth on the train.

During the war, oil was washed up on the beach all the time. Dead and dying birds washed up on the Outer Beach, and it wasn't unusual to find bits and pieces of uniforms.

Monomoy, which had been a pretty benign place, all of a sudden sprouted a giant bullseye—a strafing target. It was a pretty active place to be; "rat-tat-tat!" It never dawned on us that they wouldn't have had to be too far off on their aim and we'd be a statistic.

I knew Carroll Nickerson. He was absolutely bald and had bleached-blue eyes. We used to go visit Uncle Carroll and Aunt Emmy. In those days everyone was "uncle" or "aunt." We'd have ice cream, which I rarely had at home.

When I was a very small child, Aunt Emmy said she wanted to show me something. She picked up a cat by the back legs, held it straight out in front of her and dropped it! The cat spun around and landed on its feet. I never knew it would do that. Here I am, almost seventy, and the memory of that is quite strong.

You didn't just go boating in those days. Outboards were unreliable, and you were too busy earning a living. My parents, who grew up in the Depression, felt they couldn't play much. We didn't. When I was a kid, if we went to the beach we'd try to get a bucket of quahogs. Today, play is an important part of living. I was the first generation to just play on the beach.

You know, Meeting House Pond used to be over there to the right. Warren Baker lived here. He'd sit in his house and watch the ducks fly in, but they'd fly to the right and he couldn't see them behind the trees. So he had someone come in, and they moved the pond to the left and the marsh to the right. In those days, marshes were nature's mistakes and you could do any damned thing you wanted with them.

I've got a hundred-thousand quahogs that I planted in there. It's kind of fun, although it's a drop in the bucket compared to the guys out in the Bay.

Life is really good.

We've got all the common shellfish—plenty of

clams and quahogs and a very healthy worm population. There used to be a good crop of scallops. Blue crabs are very cyclical—every three or four or five years. There are bass and bluefish, and every fall the snapper blues are up in here to hit the menhaden. Oysters have not been common in my time.

Blue mussels are invading the Bay. There used to be a big razor clam fishery down north of Strong Island and lots and lots of bass on the east side of Strong Island. I once counted sixty-two boats there.

Back when there used to be ice, we used to go eel-fishing. There's not enough ice now to carry the spear, let alone the spear-holder.

We had a Yellow-crowned Night Heron in here—a really sporty-looking thing—but way out of his normal range. And I've seen two or three Diamondback Terrapin in this pond—not a big population. There are Ospreys. Whoever put up those nests did a good thing. There are Snowy Egrets and Great Blue Heron in the pond. I've seen seals come in here, although there's nowhere for them to haul out. I'm not sure they're brave enough to crawl onto dry land. There are deer, opposums, coyotes, raccoons.

I almost feel guilty; there's so much good stuff here.

My grandfather Sears Nickerson saw much evidence of Indians everywhere around the Bay. It would be interesting to close your eyes and try to see what this was like when the oceans were two to three hundred feet lower. This pond was a cedar swamp.

The Bay is sort of like an aquatic pantry. There are some clams somewhere. There are some quahogs somewhere. My son goes down to catch a bass or a bluefish.

Mon Cochran once took my son—much to my horror when I heard about it after the fact—out on the Bay when it was frozen. He drove a van and pulled the Sea Scouts behind him on sleds.

When we lived on the end of Namequoit, we let our kids go out alone in boats when they demonstrated they could swim. They'd go over and camp on Sampson's Island.

When it came time for my son, Dana, to use the outboard, we told him, "Don't go any further than Strong Island." We stretched the boundary when we finally said, "OK. You can go to the end of Monomoy." From the end of Paw Wah Pond, that's a long trip. He went off with a friend to fish. He was probably sixteen, and we told him to be back by six o'clock. It got late, and I finally went down to see if I could find him washed up. There he was, towing somebody. Not only was he not in trouble, he was helping someone else. Tears came up in my eyes. Why had I doubted this boy?

My mother says, "Wib and I had the best of the Cape." I say, "Bull. I've got the best of it." And my kids will have the best of it.

You don't look back.

Dana Eldridge
East Orleans

My grandfather, Charles F. Poor, Sr., bought this house, I'd say, in 1890, from a man called Ziba Eldridge. I don't really know when South Orleans became separated from Harwich, but in 1739, this was Harwich.

The first part of the house was built in the 1700s, and the new part was built in 1865.

My grandfather was a captain in the Boston Fire Department. In the history of the department, my grandfather was listed as injured in some big fire. He had to retire early, so he came to live here permanently sometime in the 1890s. My grandmother would not come with him; my Aunt Gertrude was still in school, and my grandmother didn't want to uproot her from the Boston schools and bring her to this place.

Grandfather started a farm. He had chickens and pigs, a cow and a horse. He grew vegetables and sold eggs. I can remember vaguely, as a little girl, the chickens. One evening the family couldn't find me. I was three or four years old, and I was up on the hill saying goodnight to the chickens.

My grandfather also started a shellfish business across the road on the Bay. I've found records of the business, and we still have a handwritten sign he'd made. It said, "No trespassing! Shellfish bedded here." Maybe it was quahogs. At one time this area was quite active with the fishing industry and shellfishing. There was some sort of an area for boats—a marine outfitting place—over to the left there.

Back then, growing up, you didn't really hear stories. To tell the truth, I got most of my family information from Emma Augusta Rogers; we called her Gussie. Her father, Webster Rogers, was the oldest living Civil War veteran in Orleans. He died in the '30s.

Apparently, my grandfather was very well liked

Grandfather Charles F. Poor.

here. He had one of the first Model Ts, and Emma said he'd pick up the neighbors and take them for rides.

After living here awhile, he acquired what they called "a Cape Cod housekeeper." This went on for awhile, and there was to be a divorce. Emma said that her mother, who was a lovely person, learned that she was going be subpoenaed to testify. She said, "I will not testify against my friend Charlie." The night before she was to get that subpoena, she traipsed three miles through the woods to a friend's house, so she wouldn't be at home to be served.

There was no divorce. My grandfather died of a heart attack in the early '20s, running to a fire on the Winslow property.

One time, Mr. Winslow sent his chauffeur here. He said to him, "Tell Poor I want to talk to him." My grandfather said, "You tell Mr. Winslow if he wants to talk to me, he can come here." Winslow must have bought some of that land across the street from my grandfather. The Winslows owned the whole sweep of land. I can hear the bowling balls now, from Saturday nights at the Winslows.

My grandfather always said, "There's no reason for anyone on Cape Cod to starve. There's fishing, fowling, gardening, vegetables." There was always plenty to eat.

Webster Rogers and my grandfather were very friendly. I grew up with Emma. After Webster retired from the Civil War, he did nothing. I remember he was a very short man, and he seemed to be always lying down. He'd tell this story. He was in the infantry during the war. It was a very warm day, so he took off his army coat and rolled it up under his leg while he was riding his horse. Someone shot at him, and the bullet went through his coat. He showed the coat to me—with the bullet hole.

Emma and her mother had to earn money to support themselves. One thing they did was take in laundry. They did the Winslow laundry. They'd get in the skiff and row over to pick it up—then row it back.

Emma was a real Cape Codder. Webster's first wife died. He and his second wife had Emma, who was over six feet tall. They took in boarders. There was a barn behind the house. Years later, Emma fixed up the chicken coop and rented that, too. She'd keep track of the guests on a list. After some of the names, she'd write "N.A.," meaning "Never Again!"

She always wanted to go to school and become a nurse. But she had to stay—to take care of her mother, then her father. She worshipped him.

Some years ago, a couple of the selectmen had visions of making a big marina here on the Bay. What had Emma upset was that not only did they want her beach, but they wanted her house. They were going to tear it down and make a parking lot. Her house meant everything to her. They wanted our beach, too.

Well, someone had a connection, and they got her on television to talk about it. That story went all over the place.

They didn't take the land, obviously.

Emma had a dress that she and her mother had made for her senior dance. But her father wouldn't let her go, so she didn't get to wear the dress. She kept it all her life and was buried in it in 1977. She was ninety-six.

Emma was a real Yankee. She'd save her pennies, because they had to last all winter. And I mean pennies.

When my daughter Harriett got married, the second gift she received was from Emma. It was a full book of S&H Green Stamps. Well, she didn't have money; that was a real gift from her.

When I was little, I spent most of my time on the beach. My sister couldn't because she had very fair skin. I played, drew houses in the sand; this is the livingroom, that's the kitchen. I spent hours and hours there. No one was with me, but I never minded. I could always find something entertaining.

My aunt had a Model A Ford. Once a week, she'd get us and we'd go to town to do the shopping and get an ice cream cone. That was a big treat. There was another outing in August every year. We'd pack a picnic and go to Race Point, celebrating my birthday and my father's.

Originally, just down the road, there was a little wooden bridge by the marsh. At one time, somebody wanted to close that off and make a cranberry bog. But that's actually a tidal marsh. Emma told me that on a summer's evening young people would gather there. One of them would have a fiddle, and they'd play and dance on the old bridge.

I have a twelve foot skiff with a little motor. I love to get in and go out into the Bay—just go.

Gertrude (Poor) Cutler
South Orleans

Christopher Macort is a diver and rock musician, the grandson of Gertrude Cutler and great-great grandson of Charles F. Poor. He's 33 years old, which means he can't possibly talk about the old days around Pleasant Bay.

Or can he?

I wasn't born here, but the Cape has always been home. I'm fifth generation in this house. I've been here every summer since I was six weeks old. I started scuba-diving when I was twelve. I was always in the Bay. I worked off and on at Arey's Pond Boat Yard for about five years. My brother Brian manages it now.

I was a diver, and I sort of helped Barry Clifford run things on the *Whydah* project for two years. Then I went to Venezuela with him twice, to map and document a fleet of French war ships that were wrecked on a reef in 1678. We found nine out of thirteen of those ships. We did that with the Discovery Channel and the BBC. I had a lot of amazing experiences with Barry.

When I was really little, I found a lot of broken pottery pieces on our beach. About ten years ago, I started following the pottery trail up the creek and into the woods. I found an old dump there. The earliest thing I could date was from 1880. The latest was an old, enameled 1917 New Hampshire license plate.

I figure there was a farm there, and they had a boy and a girl—maybe two girls. I found boys' toys—like a tractor—and porcelain dolls' heads. There were

101

shoes, hats, farm implements, a piece of a very big farm tool and the workings of a Brewster clock—a mantel clock.

That's OK back up there, and it's fun. But then we had to dismantle the barn here. The roof had gone, so we took it down. It was built from wood they found here and there. There still was bark on some of the timbers.

John or Joseph Freeman was the original buyer of this land, and he built the house in the mid-1700s, when this was part of Harwich. He was in the Revolutionary War.

Over where my brother lives now was called the Old Indian Field. Freeman's wife was disturbed that he built the house so close to the Indians. Right here by the Bay was the Indians' summer camp. They'd go back into the woods for the winter.

big one and a smaller one that must have belonged to the man and woman. Can you imagine sticking this in your mouth?

I used a screen to sift things from there. These are fishing hooks. I don't know where you could find handmade fishhooks, probably from around the Civil War.

If I hadn't seen the cistern I don't think anyone would have lifted a finger to save it. Maybe these artifacts don't seem that old—150 to 200 years—but you won't see them again. These things are a time capsule. It's history, and if you don't catch it and keep it, it's going to disappear under the wheels of all the machinery that's killing the Cape.

At Kent's Point I found a spear point—about five inches long. It's in perfect condition. I found a flint for a rifle right on our beach, and I found these arrow-

Lucretia Romey

While we were taking down the barn, I found a powderhorn that's been dated to the Revolutionary War. Unfortunately, part of it's been eaten by mice. But on it is carved a woman standing on a platform, a huge bird of some kind, a meeting house and another design. Probably it belonged to Freeman.

Then I noticed a slight dip in the floor area, and I said, "OK, I'm going down." Under the barn was an area about ten by four feet, made of stone and mortar. I think it was a cistern where they'd catch water. In it were hundreds of antique bottles, shoes, forks and about a hundred pounds of pottery, some of which I pieced together.

I've found a lot of pipe stems. One is from the late 1700s. All of them were made in Glasgow.

In the cistern were bone-handled toothbrushes—a

heads right here in our yard. The Indians were all over the Bay.

I found a ship out there a few years ago. It's not quite to the Outer Beach. I imagine it probably was at least one hundred feet long; the beams were enormous. Judging by the nails, I'd say it went down just after the Civil War. It gets covered and uncovered. It's in the water.

I found it by just looking. I go out in my grandmother's skiff.

In the late '80s, my brother and I would fish right off our beach. There were massive schools of herring that were trying to get up the creek. We'd catch the bluefish that were feeding on the herring. There must have been a herring run there once, or they wouldn't have been trying to get there.

[*Emma 'Gustie Rogers said years ago that there was a run there. She used to catch herring in her hands. But a "man from Brockton" built a dike there to put in a cranberry bog, so the herring run was blocked.*]

What really worries me is the jet skis in the Bay. They use a jet drive that sucks up anything living in the sand. Hopefully, they won't last long. They don't belong here.

There are stories about whether Captain Kidd sailed into Pleasant Bay. He may have. We know that in 1699 he did sail from New York to Boston. We know, too, that he went to the Tower of London and was hanged in 1701. Black Sam Bellamy was known to sail through the Bay.

There's some serious history in this place.

Christopher Macort
South Orleans

It took Chris months to locate most of the pieces of a child's cup found below the old barn. On it are the following words: "Dr. Franklin's Maxims—Handle your tools without mittens. Remember, the cat in gloves catches no mice."

Bay bathing beauties: Trudy, Aunt Gertrude, Jeanne and Harriett Poor.

In the south part of South Orleans, Massachusetts there is a Cape Cod house built in 1831 for James Smith. In 1879, it was bought by Webster Rogers. In the early spring of 1881, a new member arrived in that family.

Now, after three score and ten and more years, all she can do is read and think and write about the changes that have taken place in all that time.

The first summer people to arrive and build a small cottage came from Brockton (the name Blake). It was built on a bluff near Quanset Pond. At that time no trees were on the bluff, and so to keep the cottage from blowing away, iron rods were fastened to the cottage and to boulders sunk in the ground.

Mrs. Blake rode seven miles horseback to the then-called East Orleans Beach to call on people in the Camp Cummings cottage who were interested in the rival cottage at Pleasant Bay. At one time a dozen or more cottages were on Nauset Beach.

Soon after the Blakes were located, others came to board at a Cape Cod house owned by Captain Uriah and Aunt Bethia Rogers. This house is now owned by the Ewings.

One boarder by the name of Fred was awakened one night by a thumping sound, to find it was just Aunt Bethia doing her ironing.

The summer folks mixed with the natives in those days and had some jolly good times. Every Sunday they would meet at a neighbor's house and have what they called a "sing."

At one time Fred was boarding in the W. Rogers home, and he informed all new boarders they must be in at nine as the doors would be locked at that time. They were locked, but the newcomers found a ladder and climbed in their attic room window. Not many window screens were used at that time.

Room and board was $6 per person per week. Eggs, 12-15 cents per dozen. Milk, 5 cents per quart. Corn, 1 cent per ear. Rump steak, 20 cents per pound, and 16 cents per pound for a roast of beef. A cousin from Barley Neck would drive up to South Orleans in a covered wagon to bring 2 pounds of butter at 25 cents per pound.

The clam bakes were something to look forward to. A big tent would be erected below the Blake cottage and everything was furnished to please the appetite. (All I can remember is the water melon.) Many people rowed across Pleasant Bay to attend.

Mrs. Brooks—a later arrival to build at The Narrows—often rowed a dory from her place to call on the W. Rogers family on the west side of Pleasant Bay, maybe a mile or more.

There was at one time a wooden bridge over the creek near here at Pleasant Bay, and on moonlight nights the summer folks would meet to dance.

The first carriage to arrive on the Cape from the city was too wide for our narrow, rutted, sandy roads.

The summer folks would plan hay rides to Harwich to the Exchange Theatre to see a play, leaving the children at home asleep. One child at one time was found asleep under the bed.

Uncle Tom Robbins lived to a good old age. He lived on Tar Kiln Road. Uncle Tom would mow the meadow with a sythe and then go out on the Bay to dig quahogs, to rest.

A man by the name of Uriah L. Pierce used to bring the mail. One night he got lost in the meadow, in the mud. By calling out his full name, my father heard him and showed him the way home. He lived at that time in a house by the south west of Winslows' bungalow.

From the south end of town, the children had to walk about two miles to a school house,

Webster Rogers, his wife and (middle) daughter, Emma Augusta.

where now is a boulder to mark the spot and near the Norgeot home.

The high school was four miles away, and in 1893 I began the ride, in a two-horse barge, hay on the floor to keep us warm in winter.

One hundred years ago, teachers were paid very little, and so lived with the parents of the children.

The year I graduated, school closed July 14.

The larger children helped gather cranberries, so school opened late in the fall. Ten cents was paid for picking six quarts of cranberries, and the women worked eight hours screening the cranberries for one dollar per day.

Years ago, with so little equipment, houses were often moved. The house my father lived in as a child was moved from North Chatham by scow to Namequoit Point.

Speaking of Namequoit, one time a vessel was wrecked on the beach near there, and it was loaded with barrels of flour, so many brought home flour and for some time the road was called "dough boy alley."

Years ago, there was a shortcut from now Route 28 to Namequoit, this a grove of white pines, soft needles underfoot and soft plumes waving overhead—a delightful walk.

Pleasant Bay at one time had many catboats anchored near the shore, the owners going out over the outside bar each day for a catch of fish, arriving home and dressing them and placing them in big hogsheads of brine. After due time, they were taken out and dried on flat flakes and then shipped to market.

At one time, Captain Ziba Eldredge had what was called a "fitting out station" to supply the light vessels, which at that time came through an opening in the beach just north of Strong Island. The Ziba Eldredge place now belongs to the C.F. Poor family.

On the Cross Road at one time was a very neat store and dwelling. A sign on the store read "English and West Indies Goods." The store was moved in 1898 to the south on W. Rogers land. The house was moved later across the road, now owned by R. Johnson.

At one time–at that time called the Upper Road, now called Route 39–was a building called the P.L.A. Dances were held there and plum pudding parties. The hall also had a Lending Library.

If anyone in the village needed some repairs and couldn't afford the price, everyone would get together and give a play, the proceeds going for new shingles for someone's roof. I was Rebecca at the Well one time and was paid fifty cents (for a glass of lemonade) by an artist.

The P.L.A. building was moved to E. Harwich to be used as a barn. It's gone again, somewhere.

Seventy years ago, when any one was sick, the neighbors would take turns going up to stay nights so the relations could rest for the next day's work. What a change.

It wasn't easy to get a Dr. in those days. I've been told a man started to walk one stormy night to get a Dr. four miles away. When he opened the Dr.'s door, he fainted from exhaustion. It think that man was the grandfather of a former Orleans Chief of Police.

I have been told that a seaman died of smallpox in a vessel at sea and was brought here and buried on the hill above the Poors. No one knows why.

I have been told about the salt works here. I know that the roof on the ell of my house was boards from the Saltwork. Also, boards in the Barn are all still white.

Years ago, one could row out from shore in a sharpie a short distance and catch all the flounder one wanted. Sometimes bluefish came in the Bay and on calm mornings plaice fish could be found near the islands. Where have they gone? Could it be because the harbor is so far to the south?

What Cape Codder wants to eat fish shipped in from Boston?

From Montreal, Canada to Key West, Florida, from S. Orleans to the Pacific, beauty spots in so many places, but one is always glad to return to the quietness of S. Orleans, Massachusetts and gaze on the everchanging colors of Pleasant Bay.

The sun or the moon casting its brightness over the water is a picture no artist can paint.

Emma Augusta Rogers
handwritten in 1954

(Miss Rogers spent all her life in the family house near Pleasant Bay. In 1961, not long before her 80th birthday, she said, "I hope to live here until I die, and I hope my money and my brains don't run out before I do.")

105

This house was moved from Brewster in the early 1900s. It was just plopped. I have a picture of a couple of old ladies sitting on the porch. Well, they probably weren't old at all. It just seemed it to me when I first saw it.

My father, Russell Johnson, was wildcatting in Texas. He said to his sister, who lived in Dennis, "If you see a little cottage on the water, buy it for me." They bought it in 1928 or '29—for eighteen hundred dollars, I think.

My father put in a sea-wall. After one of the storms, he found a boat in the livingroom. He decided that wasn't the right sea-wall, so he had a new one built. After that there wasn't any problem until the 1991 no-name storm. Water came right over the wall. I'd been someplace or other. I came home and had to park up on the highway. I wanted to come in and turn off the power. I asked someone to hold my sneakers. They were new, and I didn't want to get them wet. As it turned out, those sneakers were the only dry thing I owned.

There was four feet of water in the house. Pickle jars were floating. My mattress had left the box spring and was floating. There were three little fish in the kitchen.

The police kept saying over the speaker, "Trit Johnson, get out of your house!" I said, "I'm busy!" Then I couldn't get out the front—had to climb over the fence in back.

I really wasn't discouraged, though. It was better than a fire. I worried only that it would always smell mildewy. But they sprayed something on everything immediately, and it really doesn't smell.

At least I think it doesn't.

My mother and father divorced, so I came here every summer. My father was so strict. Oh, when I think about it. But I could go anyplace in my boat, which I did. Everyplace.

My father just loved it here. But in the winter there was no one around, so he'd spend a month or two at Southward Inn in Orleans.

Up over there were the Winslows. There was Grandpa Winslow, of United Shoe. He had four children, two boys and two girls. One boy married and had four children. One girl married Fred Foster and had three children. One girl married Dr. Hill and had three children. The other boy married and had four children. The two brothers married two sisters, so they all were double cousins

They had a two-lane bowling alley there with any kind of pins you wanted. They'd get the little kids to set them up. There was a seven-car garage with living quarters over it for the help.

I think it was Dr. Hill's chauffeur who would come with his family, and they'd spend the summer. They rented this house before we were here. Every year, their first duty was to shovel sand out of the house. There was an outhouse and a summer kitchen. Gardner Munsey was the son of that chauffeur.

Captain Carroll Nickerson lived where the Wequassett Inn office now is. He was Jeanette Dybing's father. They served dinner on the back porch. That's how they started. Then they bought the main building.

Josh Nickerson, Jan's father, was married to a Whitehead, I think, and her family owned the building that now is Wequassett.

Ed Dybing bought it and then built some cottages. The cocktail lounge was called "The Saloon." I ran that for a long time.

Ed was a wonderful host—very Danish-looking. Light blue eyes, Viking-looking. Is that Danish? No.

Granny Ewing lived over there across the way. She was a Winslow by marriage. Someone came to her house one day to solicit money from her. She said, "I just built the tenth tee." I think a lot of those people put money into Eastward Ho! when it was needed—to keep it going.

My father had been married again, and when he died his wife didn't want the house so—after a lot of deliberating—I bought her out. I decided to give myself three years to see if I liked it. I had a little bed and breakfast here, which I hated. I mean, you never have a minute to yourself.

I loved Judge Brooks and Susan. He'd call and say, "Well, we're here. Come and see us anytime." Then he'd call back and say, "How about five-thirty tonight?"

One year, I rented my other house over there to some sort of blowhard from Ohio. Judge Brooks said to him, "I've seen the house, but not what's been done inside." The blowhard said, "How would you and your wife like to come over for breakfast?" The Judge was a bit surprised, but he said, "That would be fine." "How about seven o'clock?" the man said. Judge Brooks said, "Could you make it seven-thirty? Sue and I go swimming every morning at seven."

Wasn't that wonderful? They were in their nineties at the time.

Ben Cahoon lived right behind here. He was older than my father. My father would go swimming once a year. So would Ben. But neither of them would go in without being sure that he was seen by the other.

I had a Baybird when I was little. They're tough. They're wet. It's hard to sail them alone. You can't sail without the jib, and that's not an easy reach. The mainsail is big. But it's a very pretty boat.

I grew up thinking that all sailing was cold, wet and hard-going by yourself.

I now have a nothing boat—an O'Day Sailer. But it's a cinch to sail.

When I was young I was forbidden to swim at night. So I built a rope ladder, and my friends and I would go down it every night, whether we wanted to or not. I was always sure my father could hear us.

Later, when I was in college, he said, "I found a rope ladder. Do you know where it came from?"

I said, "Are you kidding? You really didn't know that we went swimming every night?"

Trit Johnson
South Orleans

Trit.

107

Captain Poor and friends. From left, Gardy, Raymond and Roger Munsey.

Our family rented what now is Trit Johnson's house in the summertime. I think 1915 was the first year. Roger was three. I was just born. Our father was chauffeur for Dr. Hill. He was part of the Winslow family.

We didn't have any electricity or running water. There was an outhouse.

We never took a bath while we were there—just went swimming all the time.

We came from Beverly. That's where the Winslow family lived. When we got here we had to shovel sand out of the kitchen and living room. There wasn't a sea wall like there is now. We used to have a good sandy beach in front there.

We'd come by train from Beverly to Boston and then to Harwich—my mother and three kids.

And the dog. Don't forget the dog. Pete. We used to put him in the baggage car. That was something. All there was were sand dunes this side of the Canal.

The first thing I remember is seaplanes and seasleds all over the place all the time. And there were stories about how they fixed the bombs so they wouldn't work. We both saw the barge sink off Orleans, what was that, in 1918. My father took us down to Nauset beach, and we saw it.

There was an awful lot of activity there at the Air Station. A lot of planes went down.

Later we moved to the other end of the Bay—where Josh Nickerson built that house by Jackknife Harbor.

You mean Muddy Creek?

Yeah, Muddy Creek. Josh built that house. They had a summer kitchen and a winter kitchen, a summer outhouse and a winter outhouse. The winter one was connected to the house, so you didn't have to go outside.

In about 1929, Father built a house where Roger lives now. Roger used to have the best view on the Cape, before all the trees grew up. Now all he sees is the golf course, the country club and the ocean.

I can still see quite a bit—Strong Island, Little Sipson's. I moved there in '31, during the Depression. Well, I did carpenter work, odd jobs, like everyone else was doing. I worked at the WPA for awhile. That was Roosevelt's way of giving us money to live on. They'd hire thirty or forty men to do the work of one bulldozer. We built, by hand, Pleasant

Bay Road. That was all sand in the '30s. There were three tracks—one each way for the outside car wheels and one in the middle for the other wheels.

I've always had that argument. One track on the left was for cars, one on the right for cars and the middle rut was for the horse.

No. The middle track was for the other set of car wheels.
I had most of the waterfront jobs—wharfinger, harbormaster. Then I joined the Harwich police force.

I moved here in 1936, when I got married and my wife talked me into staying. She was from the Wilcox family in Orleans. We've been here ever since. I worked for the Ford garage in Chatham when I first came. Then in 1940, I went to work for the Winslow family. Bob Winslow built a new house.

The biggest change was having the Chatham inlet open wider. The water in here is about two feet higher than it was before the Cut. All the way from Nauset to the Cut has changed. There was a sand bar at Quanset Pond. We used to drive our cars there and leave them while we were out in boats. Now it's cov-

109

ered at high tide. Tides are higher way up into Meeting House Pond.

The parking lot at Round Cove is going to break away eventually, and there won't be any Round Cove, unless they create it artificially. That's my prediction.

I remember all the longrakers. There must have been ten or twelve boats anchored in Muddy Creek, and they'd go off quahogging every day.

There were fifteen or twenty boats going out of Quanset Harbor here.

You take a look at Round Cove, the way it looks today, and you can't imagine. Back in the '40s, there were no anchors, no moorings, nobody there. They used to drag for flounder in Round Cove, Quanset, Meeting House, Crow's Pond. We introduced a law to prevent dragging for flounder. They used to go in there to spawn, and if they caught them all, there wouldn't be any spawning. That was one of the first conservation laws, I guess. Since then, they've made so many rules.

They want to do so much for the Bay, but they just sit around and have meetings. If they'd go out with an otter-trawl right now, plow it like a field and turn that bottom over, it would make a big difference. There's so much rotten sediment there now.

My brother thinks the power boats have damaged the Bay, with the oil runoff.

I still believe they have. Not only that, but propellers churn up the water and kill all the spat.

Listen. A quahog has to be two inches to be mature

enough to throw off spat. So what do they do? They sell them at one and-a-half inches, even an inch! They're not leaving them there long enough to throw off spat. They don't want to wait.

There used to be Shellfish Constables. Now there are Harbormasters. They don't give a damn about the shellfish.

I used to have a boat, and we'd go out in the summertime and on weekends. I was out there one night, and I couldn't see another boat in sight. I thought, what the hell am I doing, trying to get these places dredged to get more boats in here?

When we first built this house in '62, I could see one light on the Bay. Now the edge is all lights.

That break down in Chatham could just as easily have happened up here, because it's so low—straight over from Trit's. The water washes right over in a storm.

Jackknife Harbor is going to come up and take Route 28 if it keeps going. Sometimes the changes happen right in front of your eyes, and you don't see them.

I can remember reading way back that there wouldn't be a Cape Cod by the year 2000. Cape Cod has managed to stay out in the ocean without smoothing off.

Gardner Munsey
Former Orleans Shellfish Constable.
South Orleans

Roger Munsey
Former Harwich Shellfish Constable.
East Harwich

110

The Gentle Heritage was built as a hunting lodge around 1915 by four men from the North Shore of Boston. It was sold to the Winslows shortly thereafter. Originally, the house had a canvas roof. It later was changed to copper.

There had been in the 1800s a Winslow—a cobbler in Brewster—who developed a process of shoemaking. The foundation of United Shoe Machinery was that you couldn't buy the machinery but had to rent it. And you had to have it fixed by the company.

The Winslows lived in Beverly, but they owned a lot of land around the Bay. Of the four children, Sidney went on to run United Shoe and kind of became the patriarch. He lived at the end of Towhee Lane.

Edward bought this house, but he died in that pandemic flu epidemic; when was that, 1917? He was about twenty-eight, and he left a young wife and four children. She went on to marry Mr. Ewing and had two daughters with him.

Ginger was a summer kid. Her mother worked for the post office in Boston. I think we met a long time before we knew we did. We'd both go up to Maurice Bessom's for comic books and candy. It was a little gas station and store at the end of Quanset Road.

This shoreline is so different than when I was a kid. It was all sand dunes. There were no pine trees, and you could see forever.

It's unbelievable the land they owned here—from Route 39 and Trit Johnson's house, all the way to Judge Brooks's house, from this end of Quanset to Route 28. It was amazing.

When I was in first grade, my mother—a young widow—had a friend who also was widowed. They had three daughters between them. We came down to a very rough cottage on Tar Kiln Road. There was no hot water, no shower. There was a refrigerator we called "Old Faithful." We thought the place was Shangri La. When we got older and started to get pimples, hot water became more important to us. There we were, five women on Tar Kiln Road for twelve summers.

We'd walk through the meadow, cross Route 28 and sit on the beach. There'd be nobody on the beach but us. I'd look over to the Winslow house. Little did I know I'd spend the next twenty years cleaning it. One day we were all out on the Bay. Later, I wrote in my diary, "Met K. Winslow today."

Kenelm and Virginia Winslow
South Orleans

The Winslow children by the Bay.

My Grandfather Bulkeley preached in Concord—sort of the birthplace of Unitarianism. He studied with Emerson and I think lived in Emerson's house while he was a student at Harvard Divinity School.

My grandfather and grandmother had two children—Alice and Mary. Alice married Sidney Winslow, and Mary—my mother—married Edward Winslow.

The Winslow fortune came from United Shoe Machinery Company. My grandfather had a sense of humor about that. He said USMC stood for "Useless Sons Made Comfortable."

Edward Winslow died very young, and my mother was married again—to my father. The four Winslow kids were absolutely wonderful to my sister and me. I was five years younger than the youngest step-brother. They referred to us as "the babies" until we were about twelve and said, "Knock it off! We're not babies."

Of all the Winslows, my step-sister Mary was the only college graduate. The others started college and then quit.

Edward, my oldest step-brother, worked at USMC and just loved it. The men loved him. They didn't regard him as a superior. He was one of them.

My brother Bobby was the brightest of the lot. He didn't go to college, but he was brilliant. He lived up on top of this hill.

My father wouldn't let us go out in boats until we could swim from the big house to Quanset Pond. That's quite a distance.

My sister and I had a little raft, and we'd float around on it. One time we decided to pick scallops. We didn't know what they were for. We just thought they were pretty. We put them in the little beach house down in front of the big house and just left them. The next time someone went in there, oh, the smell!

Right about at World War II, my sister married a P-47 pilot up at the big house. They were a perfect match—a wonderful couple. He never came home. Those P-47s were devastating. Very few of them came through the war.

I met my to-be husband when I was at Oberlin. We decided to not get married until after the war. He was a B-17 navigator and gunner. He was lucky. He came home.

I used to sail all the time—a Baybird. In the early days, that was *the* boat on the Bay.

Out there now the buoys are all the same. The Winslow buoy. The Ewing buoy. They're there.

When I was little, I just thought everyone had a place like this. I thought everyone had a Pleasant Bay.

Judy (Ewing) Kurzban
South Orleans

Stanley Smith was my late wife's father. His children were Ann and Toby, and his brother was Albert. Stanley didn't marry until he was about fifty, so he and some other bachelors used to come down here.

The Sand Heap was just a half-house with barns. About the time of World War I, he was starting a family and he brought the house from across the street and put it on the back, with an attachment that is the dining room.

He bought the place from Charlie Rogers, who had cows, and used to bring them here to graze before the gardens were put in. They helped fertilize it, of course, and now it grows too much grass. Charlie was selling land for twenty-five dollars an acre. Stanley bought twenty or so. Of course, money was more valuable back then. The Sand Heap was a farmhouse, built well back from the water, so it would be easier to heat and sheltered from the weather.

Stanley had one and a-half acres in gardens, and he'd take his vegetables to the Grange. He was very keen on growing things and giving them away.

Gerald Gilmore
South Orleans

When the original Sand Heap gunners came to South Orleans at the turn of the century, the old place still was owned by Charlie Rogers, whose son Ralph usually was on hand at the train station with the horse and buggy. Guests came and went over time, but the regulars were Stanley W. Smith, Arthur M. Jones and William R. Sears, of Boston, John Wade Willard, of Brookline and Frederick G. Hopkins of Dover.

Through 1913, the logbook of weekends and weeks spent on Portanimicut Road was kept by John Willard, who always brought to the Sand Heap his gun, camera, tripod and sense of humor.

July 3, 1910—After breakfast, we got the boats out and went over to Sipson's Island. Found a great many gulls' or terns' nests. The eggs were just hatching out. We were very much disgusted to find that some bone-head had been robbing the nests and collecting the eggs in piles to be taken away later. It also seemed as if they had been killing the young ones. Pity they could not be caught and fined.

We rowed over to the Outer Beach. Ocean very quiet and no surf running. Returned to the boats and went over to Broad Creek and went in swimming. Water was bully, so the bathers said. J.W.W. did not indulge, having to look out for his "roomatiz." In the afternoon we went for a walk and called on Lockwood and looked over his garden. The roses were superb. It is breezing up from the S.E. and looks like rain. Everybody is having the time of his life tonight picking ticks off himself.

September 4—Weather warm and muggy. To the great disappointment of certain members of our party, the Camp Quanset girls had heard of our coming and had taken an early and hurried departure for Boston. Tough luck. After breakfast, we got out the sharpie and rowed over to Hog Island after a mess of clams. In the afternoon went to ride with Charlie Rogers over to Nickerson Four Corners to see the Bunker Hill flute. J.W.W. favored the crowd with a selection on said flute, giving an imitation of his ancestor who beat a rapid retreat from that historic place. Then we drove over to Mr. Crowell's, the decoy-maker, who had some of the prettiest decoys we ever saw. S.W.S. and J.W.W. ordered largely. Clam chowder for supper. The mosquitoes invaded the house in swarms, and we had a tough night of it, being nearly eaten up.

September 5—Rain in the morning and very hot. While eating breakfast, had considerable amusement watching Charlie Rogers trying to drive his cows out of the corn field. Charlie came in all het up and said evil things.

November 19—Came down to have our annual whack at the ducks. Found Ralph Rogers waiting for us. At the house, Charlie was on deck with a good fire and everything ready.

November 20—Wind NW. The new decoys are beauts. Best we ever saw. Put the boats in the water with everything shipshape. Loafed around during the afternoon. Made a mess of cranberry jelly, which refused to jell. Turned in early.

November 21—Clear and cold. Thermometer 20 at sunrise. S.W.S. and F.S.H. doubled up and went down to the Narrows. J.W.W. went over to Broad Creek. A good many birds moving. Sheldrake around but very wild. Whistlers decoyed better. S.W.S. and F.S.H. got 2 whistlers, 5 sheldrake, 1 oldsquaw. J.W.W., 2 whistlers. Oysters, tomato soup, planked steak, baked potatoes and cranberry sauce for dinner.

November 23—Cloudy and showery. Wind brisk, S.E. J.W.W. went over to the eastern point of Hog Island, but found Fred Higgins there, so tried Broad Creek, but Eli Rogers was ahead of him there, so he hiked over to Oldfield Point. Same story again. Some galoot had swiped that place, so he tried up Namequoit River, after having rowed about all day. Did not get a shot, did not see a bird all day, but had a real good healthy 100-mile row.

November 26—Went down to the shore and hauled up the boats. A tremendous sea is running on the backside. Wind has hauled to the N.W. and blowing at a 60-mile clip. Went back to the house and made a lot of cranberry jelly. S.W.S. spent the afternoon hunting for eggs but did not have much luck. Eggs are 60 cents per dozen, and hens not laying at that. Total for the week, 22 whistlers, 12 sheldrake, 1 oldsquaw.

November 27—Woke up late and found our bad weather jinx still with us. A roaring nor'easter. All hands drove over to Asa Mayo's. Heard on the way that Mr. Taylor, Joe's father, had died last night. Arrived at Asa's and walked to the headland over-looking the beach. The place has changed greatly since we gunned there for black duck several years ago. The sea has broken over the beach and has washed the sand down, nearly filling up the creek leading up from Pochet Island. Should not be surprised if the sea cut through there sometime during a heavy gale and high tide, so as to make a permanent inlet. It would mean quick tides in the Bay.

November 29—Wind east and a pouring rain. Loafed around all day. Read, yawned, snored and ate, and then, for a change, did the same thing all over again in the late afternoon.

December 2—Decided not to go gunning today. Drove to town and made various purchases. Came back and had a novel experience in having the horse run away. J.W.W. managed to pull him in after a brisk dash. Was quite exciting. Got to work in the afternoon to get a very elaborate dinner, for S.W.S. was going to have company. Ladies! Also a Mr. Steele was expected. Great was the scurrying around. Astonished the floors by sweeping them, and everything likely to offend the critical eyes of the ladies was hustled out of the way. And the dinner. Great Scott! Oysters on the half-shell, tomato soup, roast mutton, carrots, beans, canned corn, cranberry sauce, bread, butter, wine jelly, cake, cocktails, tea and candy. J.W.W. shaved for the occasion. A general air of expectancy and agitation pervaded the house until 6 P.M. when Mr. Steele arrived and announced the ladies were not coming. Too cold, etc. Oh, woman, woman, you are ever uncertain. J.W.W. wished he hadn't shaved.

As F.G. Hopkins was coming down on the evening train, we got up a Christmas tree for him to show our esteem and admiration. A beautiful tree was selected and planted carefully in a hand-painted tin can. On the tree were hung many gifts. Tinsel glittered, nuts, apples, candy and cigars made a brave show, candles blazed and such a tree was never seen before. When F.G.H. arrived, tears streamed down his cheeks at the evidence of such loving appreciation, and with a voice choked with emotion and supper he tried to thank each thoughtful friend. The wind whistled cold outside, the fire glowed warm inside and the Christmas spirit of joy, good feeling and wassail hovered around the house three weeks in advance.

December 3, 1911—Beautiful clear day with brisk NW wind. In the morning all hands took a ride in the auto to Chatham and other places, got all snarled up in the Harwiches, but finally got straightened out and

came home by way of Brewster. In the evening, rummy, smoking and yarning.

December 10—In the afternoon, S.W.S., J.W.W. and Charlie Rogers drove over to the cranberry swamp near Dr. Davis's and picked a peck of splendid cranberries. This has been a magnificent day. A true, smoky Indian summer, as warm and balmy as any June day. The pussywillows are out, and we saw butterflies around.

May 29, 1913—An elaborate program was laid out for this day's work. The motor boat was to be launched, and after a cruise around the Bay, J.W.W. was to be left at Sipson's Island to take photos. A mess of clams to be dug and a lot of other things to be got away with. But the beans were spilled first thing in the morning, for on waking up it was raining hard.

Charlie Rogers turned up with a sack of clover seed he was going to sow and was going to get in a big day's work planting. We stopped and chatted for an hour, and then Charlie guessed he must be putting in that seed. But some interesting questions came up, and we talked for an hour. And then Charlie said he must be putting in that seed. But a very interesting subject came up, and we talked for an hour. Then Charlie said he would hurry and put in that seed. But on talking a little, he said he would harness up old Tom, drive down to the river, dig a mess of clams for us and then hurry back and put in that seed. On arriving at the river, we found the tide was too high to dig clams. As the weather had cleared, Charlie said he would drive us over to the boat house, watch us start the motor and then hurry back and put in that seed. On arriving at the boat house, we began on the engine. It ran bully. We were delighted. So Charlie said he would help us launch it and then hurry back and put in that seed. F.G.H. ran out of the creek and got aground, so Charlie and J.W.W. had to wade out and haul him off. F.G.H. tried to start the engine again, but it refused to go. So Charlie said he would help get the boat on the beach, and then must hurry back and put in that seed. F.G.H. spent the rest of the afternoon trying to make the engine go, but it was of no use. About 6 P.M., it was blow-

114

ing great guns NW and expecting rain, so we gave it up and went home, Charlie remarking it was too late to get in that seed today.

September 25—Warm and clear. Worked like blazes all day on the boat, with no result other than a faint click once. We are fit to be tied. Have telephoned Boston for an expert to come down and start it, for it is perfectly evident we cannot. Our hands are so stiff from trying to crank the engine that we can hardly close them. However, all this comes under the heading of pleasure. The harrowing details will be continued from day to day, but J.W.W. bets the expert don't make it go. For sale: one stationary engine. Owners have no further use for it.

September 26—Not much doing today. We are expecting the expert to be down this evening to fix the motor boat, and everything hinges on him. We adjourned to the beach to dig a mess of clams. They were pretty scarce, but we managed to get a mess, for we have got to feed the expert somehow.

In the afternoon we went over to Camp Quanset to help Charlie put away Mrs. Hammatt's sail cloth. While over there, Mr. Sparrow pressed us into service to move about five-hundred beds, portable houses, furniture, etc. We then went to town to get some pork for the clam chowder. So many interesting things happened, or else we were so busy rubbering at the pretty girls, that we forgot the pork and had to go back again.

At 8 P.M. the expert arrived. Brown was his name, Marblehead his home and mechanic his trade. Much to our dismay, he did not seem to have much appetite, and J.W.W. is afraid his cooking did not appeal to Brown, not being like what mother used to make.

Went to bed early, as we expect to have a tough day of it and Mr. B. is desperately anxious to get the 3 P.M. train back to civilization and Marblehead.

September 27—Cloudy. Threatening rain. Got up at 4 A.M. Mr. B. ate one of J.W.W.'s flapjacks and shied at any more. Got down to the boat and started work before 6. The first thing discovered is that we had forgotten the extra batteries, so J.W.W. rowed ashore, trotted up to the house, got the batteries, trotted back, rowed out and started work again. Mr. B., after looking over the engine and trying to start it, decided that the trouble was in the reverse gear and that everything must come apart, including the shaft. Great dismay. A large screwdriver was next wanted. So J.W.W. rowed ashore, trotted up to the boat house, got it, trotted back, rowed out and delivered the goods. Mr. B. said he could do nothing out in the Bay, and the boat must be beached. So we ran her ashore and started in,

but taking a propeller shaft out was a big job. So J.W.W. was sent for a sledge hammer.

Driving out a stuck shaft in water waist deep was too big a job, and J.W.W. and F.G.H., not being submarine divers, after getting sopping wet, gave it up and agreed that the boat must be hauled up on the beach. So J.W.W. waded ashore, trotted up to Charlie and told him to bring old Tom down and help haul her up.

After a tremendous amount of hammering and pounding, got the shaft off and found a key had jammed in the shaft and was the cause of all the trouble. Also, the shaft was an inch and a-half too long and would have to be cut off and a new key seat cut. More dismay.

By the mercy of God, Mr. B. had brought a small cold chisel with him, and Charlie had a hack saw so the shaft could be fixed.

We fell to work again, discovering, by the way, that in hauling up the boat, we had upset the big oil can in the bottom and everything was afloat in oil.

After much fussing and tinkering, Mr. B. pronounced the boat ready for a trial trip. Mr. B. gave a few scientific whirls with the crank, and away she went. It was blowing heavily from the SW. After cruising around for a while, we headed back. Just then the engine stopped. Mr. B. made a hasty examination and pronounced the pump had jammed. This time, he was the one to get rattled, for it was getting on to train time, and he did some tall hustling with hasty glances from time to time at his watch. Mr. B. started the engine up again and pronounced everything perfect.

Then, hastily jumping into the tender, he was rowed ashore with J.W.W. and F.G.H. using a pair of oars apiece. Doing a hot-foot to the house, Mr. B. made a hasty toilet and, jumping into the waiting auto, bid us a hurried farewell. Off he went with 27

minutes to spare and never telling us how he liked South Orleans, the Sand Heap or the cooking.

November 23, 1913—Very warm. Therm. 60 at sunrise. Wind very strong SW. J.W.W roasted the rib of beef that was getting pretty rank. F.G.H. put up the new weather vane, which, as soon as it was set, refused to work. Probably it needed a new battery or something of the kind. F.G.H. is putting up the windows, while J.W.W., with averted nose, is wrestling with the roast beef. Is beginning to look like rain.

The next day, John Willard became ill, and Dr. Marvel of Orleans was called to the Sand Heap. His diagnosis was "a bad case of heart trouble." Stanley Smith, it was said, was a "royal provider," and Mr. Willard "was over indulgent of a Cape Cod appetite." With him, "indigestion, nine times out of ten, ends in heart trouble." A few weeks later, Mr. Willard was much better. Accompanied by a nurse from Brookline, he took the train to South Station, and was met there by his father .

In a letter to Stanley Smith, Mr. Willard wrote, "When I appeared at the train door with a gun case in my hand and a gripsack in the other, there was a general demonstration of amazement mixed with joy. I was escorted to the auto, which fairly bristled with pillows and hot water bottles, which, by the way, were not used. The driver came out to Brookline as though he were driving on eggs. The trip was a grand one and a great success."

John Willard, writer of the Sand Heap log, died on January 19, 1914.

Lucretia Romey

Around the turn of the century, my grandfather—who was a minister at a church in Providence—got a summer place in Orleans on what now is Henson's Way. My father, in 1936, bought this property from the Taylor family, and I always knew that when I retired I'd never go anywhere else.

The Bay was our playground, and a wonderful one it was. There were few enough people then so you knew every boat on the water, knew who owned it and where it was moored.

We sailed, we crabbed, we fished, got clams, went berry-picking. There were no organized things then; we entertained ourselves and were very busy. We'd row over to Pilgrim Lake and camp for a week. The Paysons used to give us permission to camp on Hog and Sampson's islands.

There were a lot of stripers after the war. We'd catch them and sell them. The price was a quarter a pound, uncleaned. They didn't care how old they were, either. They just threw 'em in boxes and shipped them to New York.

When I was a wee one, it was a thirteen-hour trip here for the summer, with everything: people, bikes, cats. We used to put the cats in bags and tie the bags around their necks so they wouldn't scratch.

We'd get cats by grabbing wild ones here, finding a kitten in a tree or someplace. We had two that were called "This" and "That." We came one summer in two cars. A guy who worked for my family drove one car and had the cats. When we got here, my mother said, "Where are the cats?" The guy said, "Oh, it was awful! In Providence they took a fit and died." Well, he'd just pitched them out the window.

There were so few houses then on Barley Neck. One family next to us had sixty-odd acres with just three houses for various relatives. There may have been ten houses, in all, around here. The biggest change, of course, is that the Taylor fields have all been developed.

Easton and Weston were the Taylor twins. I think they were survivors of a shipwreck, taken in by the Taylors.

I went out sailing with my father when I was this high. I learned by osmosis. Nobody had sailing lessons, unless you went to the camps.

We had a Catabout, a nice little boat, about fifteen feet, a Spaulding Dunbar design. There were Comets and Penguins and Daysailers. We have a Baybird now, a replica that Merv Hammatt built. The lines are the same; he took them off a wooden one.

When Billy Gould got back from the war in around '45 or '46, he and a guy named Crane—a guy who had a potato field—started the boatyard in East Orleans. I worked there in the summer, painted boats, rigged them. There was an old geezer there who was working on a boat one day. It was turned over and propped up. Well, it came down on top of him, and he couldn't get out. Awhile later, they heard these cries for help.

We used to live on bikes, but I eventually got a 1933 Chrysler truck. I paid fifteen dollars for it, and I was robbed. It had a cracked block, which we fixed with marine glue and caulking, just like you would a boat. It didn't have a front seat—just a rolled-up mattress to sit on.

In around 1960, the area begain to change. There are no more crochety New Englanders. I remember that a lot of those old guys used to limp. They had arthritis, and were in the water all the time which made it worse.

Some of the most rabid Cape Codders just moved here. They're even changing the names. They want to call Arey's River "Namequoit River." Lonnie's Pond is going back to Kescayogansett Pond. Guess they think that sells more real estate.

They said that when Lonnie Chase died, they went in his house and all around the walls of the bedroom were his tobacco juice spits.

The Bay is a fascinating thing. It's got shoals, creeks, open deep water, islands, ocean tides coming in every day, salt ponds—just fascinating areas. Back of Sampson's and Pochet are all sorts of creeks.

The water quality used to be the cleanest on the East Coast. We're trying to keep it that way, but it's a tough, tough battle.

There is infinite variety on the Bay. It's the diversity that I love. That's why I'm pleased to be here.

Arnold Henson
East Orleans

Before the Plymouth colonists arrived, what now is East Orleans was called Pochet, which is Wampanoag for "the dividing place." This was the dividing place between the Nauset Indians of Town Cove and Eastham and the Monomoyick Indians of Chatham and Pleasant Bay.

Old records in Orleans reveal that in the town's early years, Barley Neck and Pochet were among the last areas inhabited by wolves. The Indians were paid a bounty by the town for their destruction.

In 1644, Mattaquason, sachem of Monomoyick, sold to the original Nauset purchasers the "land of Pochet with two islands lying before Potanumaquit and its beach and islands." Pochet Island was not sold, for it was reserved by the sachem as his domain. Mattaquason sold it to the white men in 1662.

According to town records of January 2, 1665, Sampson the Indian gave the town his rights to all the whale and blubber from Rock Harbor in Orleans to Lieutenant's Island in Wellfleet in exchange for "a little island lying nere poche island called Squanacut." That became Sampson's Island.

Then on April 13, 1706, the Town of Eastham—Orleans was part of Eastham until 1797—wanted land on Sampson's Island to use as common pasture. The land then was owned by Samuel Mayo, Sr., John Sparrow, Richard Sparrow, Nathaniel Mayo, Sr., Joshua Hopkins, Joseph Doane, Jonathan Higgins, Jr., Thomas Mayo, Sr. and Jonathan Sparrow, Jr.

My great-great grandfather, Samuel Russell Payson, was president of Manchester Mills, then the world's largest textile mill. His son, Gilbert Russell Payson, worked for the mills and wanted some property down here. One of his purposes was that he and his sons liked to hunt geese and ducks.

On July 8, 1885, he bought Pochet and Little Pochet from Freeman Doane and Elisha Cole for $1,200. That same year he bought Hog and Sampson's islands for $200. He bought Barley Neck Point in 1886 for $100. He didn't want anyone building a house on it. Later, he purchased the meadow between Pochet and Little Pochet for $10 and a peat swamp on the southwest corner of Pochet for $1. All told, he bought 139 acres of upland and 130 of marshland for $1,511.

In the late '40s, my grandfather, Charles Clifford Payson, told me that Asa Mayo had come to him in the 1920s and offered to sell him his house and farm for $2,500. Grandfather said, "Asa, we've got more damned land than we know what to do with."

All four islands were bare of trees and were burned off regularly until about 1915. A couple of the fires got too close to the houses for comfort. Also, Aunt Eleanor Parker wanted cover for the birds.

The Old House was moved to Pochet Island, presumably from South Orleans, earlier in the 19th century. It had been the site of a gun club during the Civil War.

When my great-grandmother saw the Old House, she was pretty horrified and did not want to live there. Grandpa Payson had the New House built in 1886 by a ship's carpenter.

In 1890, the Life Saving Service approached Grandpa Payson for land to be used for a life saving station. He sold them a piece on the south end of Little Pochet for $30, with the proviso that the land would revert to him or his heirs when the government ceased to have need of it. He used the $30 to buy a ship's clock, which he presented to the station.

The Pochet station ceased operation after World War II and was dismantled by the Coast Guard in 1961; with it vanished the clock.

Grandpa Payson lived only a few years after buying Pochet. He died of typhoid in May of 1891 at the age of 51.

The textile industry in New England was highly cyclical. Grandpa Payson experienced severe financial losses, as had his father before him and as would his son, Clifford, later on. At the time of his death, his children were able to salvage little aside from Pochet. They were able to save that because land was so cheap that it was of no great value.

My mother was Althea Payson, and my father was Eric Hakon Thomsen. He was born in Denmark. He went into the shipping business and was fantastically successful, chartering ships to the Allies in World War I. But the Germans got them all.

In my father's trips back and forth across the ocean, he ran into one of the great evangelists, who pursuaded him to go into the ministry. He went to Union Theological Seminary. Then he went to work with the volunteers at the Grenfell Mission in Labrador—St. Anthony's W.O.P.s—Workers Without Pay.

My mother was a pre-med student, and she went there to work in the Mission hospital. They were married the next year, when she graduated from Smith College. My mother died of cancer when I was four. She was twenty-eight.

In 1961, Gilbert Payson subdivided some land and offered me four and a-half acres for $12,000. Well, for a thirty-three year-old guy, that was a lot of money. In 1967, Gil offered me the same property for $30,000. Whoops! I saw the meter going up, so my aunt and I bought it jointly.

There are about a hundred living descendants of my great-grandparents, and some of us live here now. I've been a part of the Bay all my life. What's amazing is its spectacular beauty and the fact that most people who built around it have protected it. There are darned few trophy houses on the Bay. The purity of it is something. It's known as the most pollution-free body of salt water on the East Coast.

Charles H. Thomsen
East Orleans

Men of the Life Saving Service, at the Pochet station.

Photo taken by Samuel Payson in 1888, when the ocean was full of sail.

In this rambling, and for the most part, unorganized opuscule, I have attempted to describe life on Pochet Island, and in the New House, in the years between 1912 and 1920, before the Guest Book was started. These include the years when I was growing up (from ten to eighteen). It is quite impossible for me to remember things in order; however, special dates and events stand out.

The memories of 1912 are not as vivid as those of 1920; the mists of time and fogs of memory blend together, but is to be hoped that some flavor of that life has been conveyed.

There is no need to describe the familiar sensations we all know so well: the smell of the Bay at low tide, the tickling of sand fleas on bare legs, the stab of the green-head, the sound and sight of the sea with fog creeping in over the beach, the serenity of moonlight and the song of the crickets, that great hum steady as a heart beat. Doors slam, feet patter up and down stairs, a voice calls, "Anybody home?" We're back.

According to Uncle Russell's diary, his brother-in-law, Philip Stanley Parker took his family to the New House in 1912. We usually went near the end of August and stayed six weeks. At seven a.m. of a summer morning, a procession left 175 Mountfort Street (now Lennox Street), waving goodbye to Aunty and Grandpa and Grandma Parker, whose houses were first on our route. In the procession went Pa and Ma, Catherine Cook and a second maid (usually a different one every year), Grace, Eleanor and Frances, Chappie and Kiddy (in a basket). At the Cottage Farm Bridge Station we took a local to the South Station and there boarded the Cape train.

The journey took about three and one-half hours. At Brewster excitement began to rise high as we gathered together our belongings. At last the brakemen hollered, "Orleans! Orleans!" There to meet us was Asa Mayo with his horse and cart. All our luggage—trunks, hampers, the S.S. Pierce barrel, sundry large boxes and suitcases—were loaded into Asa's cart and off he jogged to collect ice, coal, and kerosene, as well as milk and eggs from his farm. He would take the long drive to Pochet and likely as not would get there sooner than we did.

The procession now formed again and straggled along the main street to the Inn. Then we had lunch, a delicious fish chowder with pilot bread. I was always embarrassed at this meal because the maids ate with us, and that never happened on any other occasion.

The carafes and shakers and cruets of condiments on the table were also mysteries. But we were very hungry, for the hour was after 2 P.M. Now, as we waited on the veranda, along the street came an old barge pulled by two thin horses whose bones nearly protruded in places. I used to worry lest they would fall down or drop dead of hunger. The barge looked like a small street car, having two long seats facing each other within. We climbed little steps at the back to get in. The driver sat behind a partition in the front end. In the early years the driver was one Walter Young. He had a coarse face of which I was secretly afraid, for it was said he drank!

Later on the driver was Old Davenport, a very dirty man, with twinkling eyes and a beard and moustache, all very dusty. On his head he wore a decrepit, broad-brimmed felt hat. I was not at all afraid of him, but wished he would not chew tobacco so hard and spit so much!

Our equipage proceeded slowly along the sandy road to East Orleans pausing briefly at Sammy Higgins' store where the Post Office was. Some small purchases were made: film or candy bars, or maybe a wedge off a huge cartwheel of American cheese that Sammy kept in his glass showcase. And so on to Barley Neck at a snail's pace until we took the last big curve before the road ran straight to the Town Landing. Up to the right was the Sparrow Farm, later bought by Uncle Russell. Shortly before reaching the water, the road took a sharp right turn under a steep bank and here the barge tipped perilously. We children all screamed as did the maids, but miraculously the barge did not capsize. On down to the shore, passing cornfields on the right, over land which was open, with a few native pines and bushes.

The barge crept down the slope to its final stop. Wavy grass and sea weed and the Bay and Pochet! Hurray! Out we piled and released Chappie, who ran round and round with delight at being free at last. The only building on Barley Neck Point was the Hearse House, which stood where it does now, and in which a rowboat was kept. Pa and the driver hauled it out and down to the shore and into the water where it began to leak. I do not remember its name (if any), or what it looked like, or its size, but we must have made at least two trips across, with constant bailing. (One year there were no oars, so Ma had to swim across and fetch some.) At last we stepped on the shore of Pochet with screams of delight. Kiddy was released from the basket to flee up the steps and disappear into a paradise of field mice.

The only building at the shore then was a block of

wooden bath houses— four or five—at the top of the steps, in use 'til 1925 when they blew down. They were used only by female bathers. On occasion I would peek through a knot hole in the partition at my naked aunts and feel very wicked!

Pa disappeared up the narrow, unmown path to return with a blue wheelbarrow from the barn. This particular barrow lasted for years and years, at least for thirty or forty, and all visitors' hand luggage went that way to the New House.

Now you may imagine Ma and the maids with hats and pocketbooks, swishing up the narrow path in their long skirts which picked up innumerable wood ticks as they passed. The children and Chappie ran on ahead to the Old House, which was shuttered and looked very deserted. Later somebody would cut the grass with a scythe. On the north edge of the so-called lawn was a bunker used for clay pigeon shooting. On the southeast corner stood the big barn where Grandpa Payson had kept a cow, its caretaker living in the Old House.

By now it must have been after three o'clock, and we marched on, the New House looming large to the north, for there were only low bushes, like bayberry, a few native pines to the east of the path and the New House, and the willows by the pond. For the rest it was low grass, wild roses, and blackberry vines covering the remains of old stone walls, relics of the days when sheep were pastured on the island. To the southeast, the Coast Guard Station, which we always called The Life Saving Station, stood out clearly, a very attractive building.

We raced up to the side door of the New House, the shutters of which had been removed previously, and waited impatiently for Pa to come with his load. We would see Asa and his horse and cart coming. Pa unlocked the side door and we all went in to scamper to our rooms, pursued by mosquitoes. One of Pa's first jobs was to put on the screen doors. Windows were now thrown open to let out the musty air, and then how delicious was the breeze blowing in, laden with the scent of the sea and grass and pine and bayberry. Delicious! The maids mounted to the third floor, Grace went to the middle room on the south side of the second floor, as did Pa and Ma to the southeast room, and Eleanor and Frances to the northeast room where Ma and Dargee had lived when they were young and had smashed some of the blue and white china with tennis balls! The west rooms were used for company and were called by us, Old Maid's Paradise and The Dump.

Asa now drove up with his load of luggage, food,

and fifty-pound blocks of ice. He had tongs and an ice pick with which to pick up and shape the pieces; in they went first for they must last till his next visit, and the boxes were still warm. Next he and Pa carried Ma's trunk and sundry hampers upstairs. One hamper which contained food remained in the shed along with the things from S.S. Pierce. They brought in the kerosene, Catherine poured the milk from Asa's tall cans into pans and put it in the small icebox on the cool, slate shelves.

No rest for Pa and Ma. (In 1912, their ages were 45 and 39.) The stove must be lit and the food unpacked. In that work we all assisted, making a chain from the shed to the kitchen closet. The wooden barrel had to be opened, excelsior pulled out and stored for kindling. Then Pa took out the packages and handed or threw them to the first in the chain.

In those days when we were pretty well cut off from means of transportation and dependent on Asa, as much as possible came with us: tea and coffee, macaroni and tapioca, tins of jam and marmalade, of tongue and chicken, evaporated milk and cocoa, a big ham, a side of bacon, a sack of dog biscuits, maple syrup and lard. Out came candies and matches, soap and sulphur napthol, mouse traps and Baker's chocolate, flour and sugar, salt pork, salt cod, and finnan haddie. All these found their way along the line to Ma, who put them away on the shelves or in the cupboards below. Not too much for a household of from eight to twelve.

Meanwhile the maid had straightened up the living room and mopped and dusted the floors, putting down the rugs which had spent the winter hanging over the railing upstairs. I do not remember that the house ever got very dirty. Perhaps someone had been in to clean the first time we went. Cobwebs were whisked away and lamps filled. Now long-suffering Pa must pump water by hand, Ma and the maid must unpack the laundry and, assisted by us, make beds. Then Ma unpacked the food hamper with stuff for supper. I remember sitting down to something that first night and being very sleepy after the long day and going early to bed. Then a faint alarm at the scurrying mice in the wall, and at last sleep.

A new day and how did we spend it? First, breakfast. Cantaloupes, maybe, and oatmeal with delicious thick cream which Catherine had skimmed off with her special cream skimmer—a flat, broad, tin implement with holes in it. Also we had hot rolls fresh from the oven, and eggs and bacon for the older ones. Every morning at 5 A.M. Catherine crept downstairs, and if one were awake, one heard the rattle of the

The Old House, 1888.

stove grate and the pouring of coal. The fire seldom went out, though sometimes an east wind would discourage it. But in general it would last for about two weeks if properly handled. Then suddenly out it would go for no special reason. I used to think it just got tired. Anyway Pa had to dump it completely before a new one was lighted with excelsior and kindling.

After breakfast Ma unpacked the trunk and the hampers, large wicker containers with metal rods holding down the lids. These held all sorts of things like children's clothes, new curtains, Chappie's pil-

low, etc. After these were emptied, one remained in the second floor hall for laundry, and the rest went up to the next landing. In those days there was nothing else up there. Catherine Cook had the seaside room, the maid the other one. Each contained a bed, a bureau, a table and chair, and a washstand. The china for them was plain white. I vaguely remember that one year we had a nurse as well, and that there were two beds in one of the rooms. We seldom penetrated up there; it was off limits!

The bedrooms, with the exception of Pa and Ma's and Old Maid's Paradise, each had two of the folding

The way to and from Pochet was via boat and Asa Mayo's wagon.

wooden cots with mattresses of horsehair and corn-husks, a bureau, washstand, two small tables and two or three upright chairs, all matching. The other two had double beds and rockers. Each room had a small wooden towel rack, the like of which I have never seen before or since. They were used to dry towels or sweaters and were easily transported to spots of sun. Now they are handy for clothes hangers. There were no pictures until later, when we used to put up cut-outs from magazines. Included also were a couple of posters advertising Pears Soap and flour. In the first, two small and practically naked children burst in on mother's posh tea party screaming, "The Pears Soap has come, Mama! May we have our bath now?" The other pictured a delectable strawberry shortcake. Some rooms had Japanese rattan hangings with birds on them, and Japanese fans on the walls. Some had Sandwich glass hats to hold burnt matches. On the floors were small rugs, dark with brightly colored flecks in them. The blankets were yellow and had blue or red stripes along the ends. The bed spreads were made of heavy white cotton with a woven pattern. Closets were doorless with hideous curtains made of a heavy brown material hung on wooden rings. Inside, the closets were lined with double hooks and that was all. The floor was used for shoes and we made shift with three bureau drawers.

Downstairs there were the same old sneakers in a heap on the floor, sticky, yellow oilskins belonging to Pa and Phil hung on the hooks, and in the corner the big megaphone, taller than the children in 1912. Pa used to take it out on the front piazza and bellow us home from the Old House. It was fun for us to try to use it. We had to tip it over to reach the mouthpiece and then it would roll away sideways.

Now come into the living room. On the first step of the stairs, below the railing, stood and stands the umbrella stand, though we had few of such things because they blew inside out too easily. The stand always contained at least one tennis ball, maybe a butterfly net, and often a dead mouse! I remember also a caramel-colored parasol. The piano was in the same place and was then as now a receptacle for people's small things like cameras and fishlines and flashlights, and usually some shells and stones. As an instrument it had belonged to Uncle Russell in his college days and so had been on the island for a number of years.

The book shelves contained a catholic selection which included classics from the Home Library Series, old novels translated from the German, the Family Flight series and many others. We had chil-dren's books like *Lady Green Satin, Down Spider-Web Lane, The Proud Roxana, The Enchanted Forest, The Enchanted Mountain, The Oz Books, The Lady of Jerry Boy's Dreams,* and *Mr. Penwiper.*

In the right-hand lower shelf were kept a collection of prayer books and hymnals, most of them with very small print, which were used on Sundays. In the archway by the dining room stood two armchairs with wicker seats, one of which I used to lick surreptitiously because it was the color of chocolate and should have tasted like it!

In the pantry off the dining room, clean papers on the shelves held the large set of Pochet dishes, said to have been the pattern used in the Pullman cars. Here too were the finger bowls, amber glass and blue glass, cut glass tumblers, sugar bowl, and two cream pitchers, etc. Up above were the platters and big tureen we used for clams, and up above them a row of lamps.

In the kitchen the stove and tables as well as the clothes rack were positioned as now, but the three-legged stool did not appear until many years after, when Ma became the cook. The kettle was always on the boil in a quiet way, for the Irish loved their tea, and so did Ma! For dish-washing, a good-sized tank was built into the stove and hot water made available to shavers of a morning; it was never used in the kettle. Pa kept a hod full of coal to the left of the stove and some kindling wood. Under the tank on the stove one could generally see a pile of drying sneakers. Even Chappie, who sometimes carried a pair home for us, was once seen putting them there!

Outside the shed, across its west end were two wooden earth closets, back-to-back, one for the maids and one for the family, reached by going out the side door. As I hopped up and down waiting my turn of a morning, I thought this was a very unfair arrangement! They were one-holers and were periodically dug out from the west side which was equipped with hinged boards below floor level. (All the bedrooms were provided with chamber pots, for who wanted to go downstairs and out on a stormy night?)

And now around the west side to the piazza, as we called it, which boasted no furniture except a couple of wooden settees. Chairs were brought out the front door for any adult who wanted one. Probably Ba had a rocker out there when the wind was north and mosquitoes negligible. At some point we put up canvas hammocks slung from hooks, but mostly the children sat on the steps. Nothing grew in front except the same old lilacs which never attained a height of more than a foot or less. We tried to grow goldenrod but nothing took. Whenever we had peaches we ate them out there and spit the stones over the railing, but no peach trees ever grew. The grass was only scythed and very tough and rough. As the steps aged, we got splinters in our bottoms! Frances and Edith sat there to play jack-stones by the hour, as they also did in the upstairs hall. On the east side of the so-called lawn was partially interred an old rowboat which I presume had flowers in it originally. Now the turf had crept up the sides and very little if any boat showed.

A short path led to the north down the slope, and Pa used to go down it to dig holes under the low bushes and bury the garbage with ashes on top. This system worked pretty well, though occasionally Chappie would go what we called "swilling," return to the house and be very sick! Ashes did not agree with him. The buckets at the back. were tightly covered so that skunks would not be attracted, though often they could be heard at night trying to unlid them. As much as possible, papers were burned in the stove or fireplace and other rubbish was taken down to a dump deep in the bushes where the wind could not penetrate. Catherine used to hang dish cloths on a line stretched between the bushes. Fascinated children watched the plumbers dig a hole in the ground to locate the drain from the kitchen sink which periodically got plugged. Once in a great while these magicians would rig a sort of derrick over the pump and pull up what appeared to be miles of pipe. Other back-of-the-house activities included wood chopping and the cleaning of flounders. Sometimes Pa cleaned fish on a flat rock near the house by Asa's path, though when possible that was done at the shore. Clams were set to soak in fresh water in the shade.

In early days the view from the back was open to the sea and to Pochet Neck. Even the flash of the Nauset Light was clearly visible to the north. To the east a clear view, save for the good old grove of native pines, showed us many schooners passing up and down the coast. Once we saw the largest in the world with its seven masts. Frances in a classic remark was heard to exclaim, "See that bully boat with a couple of sails!" These wooden ships had to go around the Cape until 1914, when the Cape Cod Canal was built, as did the New York boat whose bright lights gave us all a thrill in the early evening. Once, when we were older, we went up to the Canal to see it pass through, a great excitement.

To the south of course, we had a clear view all the way to Old Harbor, dancing in its mirage, and to the lights of North Chatham. Beyond the Old House, we could see Sampson's Island and the Bay. To the east the upland of Barley Neck was visible, and one night

in 1919, we had the pleasure of seeing Weston Taylor's barn struck by lightning and burn down. (W.T. had a twin brother whose name was Easton!)

Of course we could not have lived in the New House, isolated on the island, without a good deal of help, especially as Pa was in town so much. Our chief helpers were the maids and Asa Mayo. The so-called "back stairs," ridiculous on the face of it, symbolized the deeply engrained class distinctions of that time.

Several million Irish people, beginning around the middle of the nineteenth century, left Ireland for the U.S., driven first by the potato famines, later lured by chances of work with good wages. Many of these people landed in Boston, and a number of the women remained there to enter domestic service with the merchant and professional classes. They were pretty much illiterate, half-starved and homesick. Here they found work and homes, for they "lived in," wages such as they had never dreamed of, and plenty of tea. Their uniforms were provided so that they were able to send a good portion of their wages home to their parents. If they became ill they were cared for and treated well for the most part. It seems strange to us in this day and age that they expected and were expected to stay in their place, so to speak.

For them the back stairs, meals in the kitchen, bedrooms on the top floor (consequently the hottest in summer and coldest in winter), plain furniture, unadorned crockery, one bath a week in the bathroom, one or two afternoons and evenings off a week, and opportunity to attend the nearest Roman Catholic church. On Pochet, of course, nobody had real baths; but the maids went to church in Brewster at least every other week. This meant Pa had to row them over, hire a driver to come and convey them to and fro, and then row them back. The fortnightly arrangement came because it was not always possible to get them off at low tide and to keep their skirts and feet dry for church. Later, when Catherine got pretty heavy, it was even harder work to get them off.

I do not remember any other cook but Catherine; she lived with us for many years, until she had to cook sitting down. No one ever knew her age, which she refused to confide even to the census man! The second maids seem to have been different every year. They usually were young and found life on Pochet very dull, despite a few calls from men at the Life Saving Station. The girls occasionally walked to the shore and even waded a little, but they seemed to be wary of the water and I presume that none of them could swim. They were indeed free in the afternoons, but aside from a walk they had little to occupy their

Gunners on Pochet. Brent Dickson is second from left. At right are Samuel and Gilbert Payson.

leisure, and of course there was really no place to go.

Catherine's cooking became a legend with the family. Her bread, her doughnuts and gingerbread, her apple tapioca pudding which none of us can begin to emulate since she did not know how she cooked, and never used a cookbook to my knowledge. Somebody should have sat down and watched her, writing down each step, but alas! nobody ever did. In her last years with us her legs more or less gave out and she could not manage Pochet, but went to visit her relations while we were away. She got up early and went to bed early. She always wanted and had a cat, invariably called Kiddy; she was good-natured, though no oil painting, and developed a shuffle in her old age. To quote a description by Angela Thirkell in *Happy Return*, Catherine looked like this: "She was extremely plain and the same size all the way down, with ankles that overflowed her sensible shoes." How she managed to cook for a family that sometimes numbered a dozen, with the equipment she had, seems now like a miracle. The fact remains, however, that the coal stove, while it may have been slow at times, made a lot possible which gas or electricity make very difficult.

Our other indispensable helper was Asa Mayo, nicknamed "Asey." About twice a week his cart would appear from the southeast as he drove up, after fording the creek. Laden with our necessities, the cart left a trail of water from great blocks of tarpaulin-covered ice. He brought us mail and coal, eggs and milk, and sometimes kerosene and fish. His bony horse came round back of the house enveloped in a cloud of mosquitoes, the escort from the marsh; the only protection from them, aside from his swishing tail, were long leather thongs hanging over his face and swaying with the motion of hauling the cart. As I look back, I think he had them over his rump, too.

Anyway the pests were such that Asa usually wore a sou'wester and a coat buttoned up close around his weather-beaten neck, or if green-heads were especially bad, he draped the coat over his head. Actually Asa brought milk every day, driving in a buggy; this he left at the foot of his path which came straight up to the house from the east and which we used as our beach path. Asa was a spare, sandy-haired man of middle height with bloodshot blue eyes, red from the sun and wind. A taciturn person with abruptness of speech, he was a master of the grunt, and I was always a little afraid of him because I never knew what he was thinking. He cut salt hay on the marshes which was used for bedding down the cows. Once in a while, after they had wandered onto the marsh and eaten some, the milk tasted nasty.

Asa was ever faithful, and, I think, fond of us as a family. He fell in love with Grace; very silly of him I thought, since he was thirty or more years her senior. But he never said anything about it and simply confined himself to staring at her!

When asked why he had never married, he said, "Thems as I'd have wouldn't have me, and thems as would have me the devil himself wouldn't take." His house on Pochet Neck was full of curiosities, many of them picked up on the beach. We used to visit it once a year and be shown all sorts of queer things off ships. I was particularly taken with a glass eye! He kept his house and place in immaculate order. Later when he was, I think, in his seventies, he lost interest in it. We went to call once when he was not there and looked in the window. What a mess! He no longer invited us to come and was not the first elderly person to tire suddenly of what had previously been of great importance in his life. But to us on Pochet he was indispensable and in Pa's absence turned his hand to almost anything required except plumbing.

The family had another friend and helper in time of need, Captain Charles of the Life Saving Station, a short, tubby man with white hair and moustache, of whom we were all fond. The maids used to walk over to the station sometimes, and once in a while a member of the crew came over in the evening to call on them.

To attend a boat drill was one of our most thrilling experiences, for we were allowed to climb a tall pole and ride down in the breeches buoy. Captain Charles issued very snappy orders; the truck was run out of its shed with all its ropes and oars, a gun fired, carrying the rope over the cross-arms of the mast, the breeches buoy was rigged and the first victim saved, all in something like two minutes. It was a sort of magic to see the men moving like oil, ropes whirling off spindles, and all the other details. The equipment shone with varnish. The crew had little to do most of the year, so all was spit and polish, gleaming glass and brass, spotless kitchen and living quarters. The New House never could hold a candle to it, despite the efforts made to keep it clean.

To ride in the breeches buoy was a treat always offered to our company, although adults seldom took advantage of the opportunity, probably because of the way it was built. Literally a life buoy with a pair of short pants built into it, it was not a seat conducive to dignity, particularly if one had on a long skirt! I remember falling well down into it once when I had pretty long legs, and being very embarrassed. I do not recall seeing a lifeboat drill, but when the boat was used, it was hauled over the dunes from its shed to the water by a large and shining horse. I presume he would likewise haul the breeches buoy wagon. In his spare time, which was considerable, he could be seen grazing on the slopes behind the station.

Another local character, though not exactly a friend, was One-Arm Higgins, who lived in a shack on Barley Neck and had a large family of boys, one of whom became Orleans Chief of Police when he grew up. One-Arm supported his large family and, I suspect largely fed them by gunning. He took shooting parties down on the marshes where he had constructed a number of blinds. He had supposedly shot himself accidentally in the arm, though I doubt if we ever really knew the truth of it. Anyway he was a law unto himself as far as game was concerned and had spent time in jail, a fact that made him seem dangerous to small children! He used to skull his sharpy past the island, with an oar sticking out of a hole in the stern, and how adept he was at it! I used to try to do likewise but with very little success, probably because there was no hole.

Pa and Ma, of course, were our mainstays as children. We did not see so much of them in Brookline because we all lived with Ba (our grandmother, Mrs. Gilbert R. Payson), who did the housekeeping. We always had a nurse too. So Ma was free to give her time to Pa and the church and the Red Cross, where she worked very hard during the First World War.

On Pochet she did the planning and housekeeping, she doctored us when needed, took care of us, supervised our recreation, read aloud to us, and helped us with our summer school tasks. She could row and loved to swim, which she did clad in long stockings and a bathing suit like a dress, usually black, with a very unattractive bathing cap high on her head.

Pa spent a great deal of his time doing chores. He was not exactly a handy man, but he chopped kindling, emptied ashes, pumped water, buried the swill, all very systematically. Once in a while he would take a swim, but he did not seem to care for it much. Of course he rowed. His lot was to clean fish and not to catch them. Never having been an outdoor person or been camping, he played a good game of tennis, though of course there was no court on Pochet then.

I used to think he never had any fun, but I believe now that he enjoyed what he did down there. He had a shotgun and occasionally used to drape his head with his mosquito net and go to the marsh to sit in a blind, hoping to get a yellow-leg or some peep. I don't think he was very successful at the sport, not like the

uncles (Russell, Sam and Clifford). Of course he was in town mostly and only came down for long weekends, although sometimes he would stay longer.

On Sundays he would sit in the big rocker and read Morning Prayer, surrounded by his family and any visitors who were there. We children used to giggle a good deal, I fear, especially when we were on our knees with our heads buried in the seats, and Chappie joined us, going the rounds and sniffing at us to try to find out what on earth we thought we were doing in such a position. As we always went for the same six weeks, we became very familiar with the epistles and gospels for those Sundays after Trinity. Pa read very well and looked very handsome in his green coat which he always wore then and for meals. He was ever dignified, and while I never feared him so gentle was he, I always respected him and would not want to do anything to upset him.

He was fond of formality. Every day after lunch he would get chocolate peppermints out of his cabinet cupboard and parade around the table, passing them to adults, and popping one in each child's mouth. This became a ritual. He was the kind of Victorian or Edwardian gentleman one sees no more. At Pochet he always wore a collar and tie, even if the shirt were khaki. His bathing suit was a misshapen knit affair, typical of the time and perfectly hideous! He was six feet tall and had gray-white hair and dark eyebrows, and so handsome!

Now it is time to leave the New House, redolent with the pleasant odors of Catherine's pork and beans baking in the oven. We were clad in khaki shirts, bloomers and hats and dilapidated sneakers. When we were little, Ma went with us and supervised our pastimes. She had been thirteen years old when the New House was built in 1886, and the only girl in the family, with three brothers. I imagine that she was much more sedate than we ever were, and stayed in and sewed a fine seam! Her first cousin, Grace Train Whitney (Dargee), used to visit her as they were fairly close in age, and they raised Cain in the northeast room! But I doubt if Ma went about the shore as we did; they had a Captain who sailed the big cat boat.

Ma had been going to Pochet for a long time and knew the perils for small children, such as stepping into a soft slough or falling over-board. Though the island was open as compared to now, it was necessary to keep to the little paths to avoid the blackberry vines which could raise long bleeding scratches on small legs. Paths then were easily made and maintained with scythe or sickle. Asa made his own road through the long grass, but it was the only one at first. A little path ran off the main one to the pond. Below the Old House pump another ran along the edge of the slough to the creek where the bridge is now, and we used to wade over or walk on a board to get to the Life Saving Station. That was about all in the way of paths, except Asa's path. It was easy to go north to the mayflower patch; one simply wove in and out around bushes. The sheep hole was harder to reach, and I don't think girls went there for a long time. Some places were accessible, others not. We were there too late for blackberries, but there were plenty of beach plums.

Many years later an apple tree appeared behind the New House, and high-bush blueberries, both of which furnished fruits for Ma to make pie and muffins. Goldenrod, asters, and the Pochet sunflowers bloomed then as now, and thistles, everlasting, and Queen Anne's Lace.

On the marsh we saw marsh rosemary and on the beach sand, rosa rugosa. In the fall swallows gathered for migration, hanging and whistling on the bushes till one morning they were gone. Crows cawed to the east, and in the night one shivered in bed to hear the

Eleanor's grandmother, Althea Payson, perhaps waiting for a ride.

hoo-hoo-hooooo of the great horned owl. The bushes were full of small warblers, an occasional hawk sailed over the land looking for mice. Once in a while we would spy sinister-looking bats hanging upside down from bushes on the main path. They chattered and scared us! Another chatterer was the woodchuck at bay. Always one lived under the Old House and fed on the lawn, only to waddle away at our approach. One the southern slopes we often saw the deer. To the north of the bath house, we sometimes saw red foxes with their young playing on the small sand slides where their holes were. Before our day, they used to be a menace to the mainland chickens, so that the farmers organized hunts on the island, in which teams of men went along the shore at the bottom of the banks and bayed like hounds. Then when a fox was flushed, they shot it.

Because the Old House was mostly used for a shooting camp, it was usually shuttered when we got there. It was dark and spooky and smelled very musty—so indescribable and now gone forever in these days of deodorizers! The house was also pretty messy. Mouse-eaten blankets hung from ropes in the bedrooms; mattresses were full of mice and weasels' nests! The attic was dark and contained decoys and a lot of musty straw and things nobody wanted. The mice used it for a nursery and gymnasium!

The shore was the happy hunting ground for all sorts of adventures.

At low tide we waded aboutseeking quahaugs with our feet and finding broken shells and rocks instead, so our wounds were frequent and numerous. We found a favorite place near the mouth of the boathouse creek; in those days the mud was not so oozy as now! We chased minnows, trying to drive them on shore and sometimes succeeding. It was a thrill to see the little silver marooned fish jumping and struggling on the sand. We picked up horseshoe crabs by their tails and learned that it was safe to turn them over and push a hand among all those crawly legs which included no nippers. But we always turned them back over so they could go home to the water, not having learned that they were clam-eaters.

Indeed clams and scallops were so plentiful that there was never any problem getting all that were needed. The scallops came when the weather began to turn cold, and we loved to find them up and look at their rows of blue eyes and pretty shells which they opened and shut with most vicious snaps. Catherine would cream them for supper. Yum yum! Blue-claws we knew nothing of until the middle of the 1920s. Uncle Myron used to get them over at Marston's

Mills. Then we began to see them once in a while in the marsh creeks. In early days and for many years the shore was covered deeply with dried eel grass and the same old rocks with rock weed which was so necessary to a successful clam bake. The eel grass came sailing in on the high tide and wound itself about the anchor ropes. If a boat was anchored in the water, the weight could become great enough to move the boat off. On the shore the stuff was always a pest, but one got used to hunting for the rope under its masses.

Early we had the swimming-the-channel rule, and many a frustrating hour was spent rowing or trying to row an anchored boat! I do not remember how or when I learned to swim but have a vague memory of floating on my tummy with someone's hand under my chin and frantically pumping with my arms and legs. Anyway, once I had succeeded in swimming to Barley Neck (in those days there was no mud over there and one could walk right up on a sandy shore) and returning to Pochet, I was eligible to row alone. The other rule was that we must not do that unless an adult was on the shore. Although it seemed as if we never could learn to row, we all did and could negotiate some strong winds and tides in the bargain by using the short Cape Cod stroke, the rapidity of which prevented going backward instead of forward.

We also learned to sail the boats belonging to the uncles: *The Peep*, *The Whistler*, and *The Poke*, leaky sharpies with a sort of gaff rig wherein a pole was inserted into a loop on the peak and anchored in another near the foot of the mast. Such a wretched arrangement, for the loops were forever rotting out and leaving us with a flapping sail and no way out except to come to shore if we could! I do not remember that we had any instruction. We had to learn the hard way, which meant fighting the tide and rowing miles or getting stuck on the flats or going ashore with a bang just when we thought we were well on our way! The boats yawed before the wind and sometimes let the water in over the side; the center boards jammed or their ropes broke at crucial moments and there was incessant bailing. That they drew very little water was a redeeming feature when passing over shallow flats, and we learned how to ship the rudder and use an oar when necessary.

After a while it dawned on us that while i northwest wind made for perfectly lovely-sailing down the bay, it did not necessarily insure the same delight on return, for it was a fickle wind and apt to die away later in the day. If you were faced with no wind suddenly and an outgoing tide, then row and row and row with the furled sail and boom in the middle getting in the way. It was better to have two in the boat so that one could sit and row on each side. Later on, Pa had two boats built for Frances and me: The Owl and The Pussycat, with leg-o-mutton rigs which did away with the horrid gaff poles and were much easier to handle. Their worst feature was incessant leaking, for Pa had them built by a carpenter rather than a boat builder and he used green wood!

We never had a boat that could deal with Barley Neck Point! If you were coming in nicely with a southwest wind, suddenly there was no wind, or a peppy little breeze began to come from the northwest! So bump ashore and drag the stupid boat along the shore to the steps, stubbing toes and cutting soles in the process. The old rock by Beef's pier was higher out of water then (maybe in sixty or so years it has worn down), but it seemed to move unpredictably and appear just where it was least desired!

Pa finally got us a decent salt water canoe, and Uncle Cliff built the boat house in 1916, so that there was a place to keep it and the other boats we got. I don't remember who painted the sail on the door, but it was always there and helped encourage us on some of those long rows home.

Another realm of pleasure was that of the flats which we often roamed at low tide sometimes as far as Sampson's Island. Razor clams, scallop shells, strange eggs that grew in chains, bits of pretty seaweed which we used to make Christmas cards, all these we gathered. I remember spending many an hour putting amethyst sand into little glass bottles with tweezers made of toothpicks. Living things were captured and let loose in the water in the boats and often forgotten until we were greeted by a rotten stench the next day!

Sometimes we fished in the channel for flounders using hand lines baited with the tough parts of clams. When the water began to get cold at the end of September we sometimes caught a lot, and some of them were very good-sized. The trick in flounder fishing was to let the line down until the sinker hit the bottom. Then bang it two or three times and haul up about a foot. Then wait for a good hard tug, yank the line and pull the struggling fish to the surface. What a thrill! Sometimes the flounders weighed as much as two pounds and felt like tons! When we were young, Pa was kind and cleaned them for us.

Our pleasure in the boat or on the shore was tempered by greenheads. The only satisfactory aspect of them was the ease with which they could be slain, but always after the bite rather than before! Ticks did not bother us children, but Ba and Ma were poisoned by

them and poor Chappie had to endure long inspections, of his ears especially. We had to de-tick ourselves before coming into the house and any that eluded us and were found later, met their death by being dropped and popped delightfully on the kitchen stove. It is difficult to give an idea of how many there were in those days of long grass.

Asa brought clouds of mosquitoes up from the marsh with him, and it was almost impossible to keep them out of the house while he brought in ice and all the other things he had to deliver. That is why the doors to the living room and back hall were supposed to be kept shut—to keep out the wind and the insects.

Salt water mosquitoes came in with the wind, attracted from the shore by human beings. Others came from the pond. We children were accustomed to them and did little to repel them aside from a dab of citronella now and then. But one in a bedroom after dark was then, as now, torture, and many a gory smear appeared on the wall over our beds or on the pillow cases. The trick was to lie still, listen to the tiny song, let the mosquito bite and then smack!

As we grew up, the quality of life on the island changed very little.

When the line storms blew in from the northeast, we stayed at home and played games, or thought up practical jokes, or made fudge or sang songs with ukelele or kazoo! The games of Pounce on the dining room table were terrific! The din was so awful that I do not know how the parents stood it, especially after dark when small oil lamps were bouncing up and down among eight or more yelling demons!.

By October the nights were turning cold and great blasts blew up into the kitchen from the pump hole. Northern lights shivered across the sky and stars hung almost low enough to touch. Extra blankets came out, and reluctantly we went to bed; the fireside was so cosy. Now the "goldenrod was yellow and the corn was turning brown." Purple asters bloomed and red rose hips shone in the sun.

It was time to go back to school, and so much did I hate the idea that to this day I remember nothing of the return journeys.

Eleanor Gilbert Parker

Born in 1902, Eleanor Gilbert Parker was to grow up and old with abiding ties to Pochet Island. The family presence that continues today began in 1885, when her grandfather decided to buy some land.

Much has changed in my lifetime at the New House. No more maids to beat the rugs, so the rugs are over the bannisters instead of on the floors. The china wash sets are for decoration or stored in a corner; again, no maids to bring hot water to our rooms or to empty the slop jars. The thunder jugs still are around, however.

A solar-heated shower takes the place of a small pitcher of hot water left outside each room in the morning. The red curtain over the big window on the stairs is gone. The orange parchment, accordion-pleated shade has disappeared from the tall glass kerosene lamp, but the lamp still lights the dining room table, supplemented for reading by two propane lamps.

The wicker table is under the window now—still covered with the old cloth with tiny mirrors sewn into its design—but no longer in danger of being tipped over by the wind. Now we can use the front door! The coal stove dominates the kitchen with the mural of the pond behind it, but a white propane stove sits next to it and a propane refrigerator is in the shed near the ice box.

On the third floor, the two bedrooms have gone from one bed in each to a playroom and storage area and now to three-and four-bed dormitories. On the second floor, double beds with colorful bedspreads have replaced the camp beds with their one layer of springs and horsehair mattresses.

Outside, the brush has grown ten to twelve feet high. Where we have cleared and cut back, a huge lawn has been reestablished, cut now by a forty-inch riding mower. The apple tree, now freed from the thick growth of viburnum and honeysuckle, is producing lovely blossoms in the spring and apples galore. The blueberry bushes have access paths, and the harvest is easy to acquire.

Down the path toward the Old House, the matching pairs of pine trees planted by Dad fifty-odd years ago have reached thirty to forty feet. Some have died and all were being choked by honeysuckle, viburnum and poison ivy—now slowly being cleared.

The newer boats are made of fiberglass instead of wood, and the design of the sailboats is sleeker, but they still tip over with regularity.

Things have changed at Pochet. But the peacefulness, the unhurried pace, the love for the place and the love we have for each other, down to fourth cousins—not many families even know their fourth cousins—has not changed. That's the beauty of Pochet.

Helene (Parker) Barrington
East Orleans

The New House on Pochet Island was built by Gilbert R. Payson in 1886. The Old House already was "old" when it was moved to the island from the mainland much earlier in the 19th century.

Pochet Island, about the turn of the century, with the "Old House" at left and the "New House" at right.

133

Listed and pictured here are more residents of Pleasant Bay. Some are year-round, some move in for the summer and some stop by on their way to other places. But for all of them, the Bay is important to the cycle of life.

Red-throated Loon, Common Loon, Pied-billed Grebe, Horned Grebe, Great Cormorant, Double-crested Cormorant, American Bittern, Great Blue Heron, Great Egret, Snowy Egret, Little Blue Heron, Cattle Egret, Tricolored Heron, Green-backed Heron, Black-crowned Night Heron, Yellow-crowned Night Heron, Glossy Ibis, Mute Swan, Snow Goose, Brant, Canada Goose, Green-winged Teal, American Black Duck, Mallard, Northern Pintail, Blue-winged Teal, Gadwall, Eurasian Wigeon, American Wigeon, Canvasback, Greater Scaup, Lesser Scaup, Common Eider, Oldsquaw, Black Scoter, White-winged Scoter, Common Goldeneye, Barrow's Goldeneye, Bufflehead, Hooded Merganser, Common Merganser, Red-crested

Merganser, Osprey, Bald Eagle, Sharp-shinned Hawk, Cooper's Hawk, Northern Goshawk, Broad-winged Hawk, Red-tailed Hawk, Rough-legged Hawk, American Kestrel, Merlin, Peregrine Falcon, Ring-necked Pheasant, Northern Bobwhite, Clapper Rail, Virginia Rail, Black-bellied Plover, Lesser Golden Plover, Semipalmated Plover, Piping Plover, Killdeer, American Oystercatcher, Greater Yellowlegs, Lesser Yellowlegs, Willet, Spotted Sandpiper, Whimbrel, Hudsonian Godwit, Marbled Godwit, Ruddy Turnstone, Red Knot, Sanderling, Semipalmated Sandpiper, Western Sandpiper, Least Sandpiper, White-rumped Sandpiper, Baird's Sandpiper, Pectoral Sandpiper, Dunlin, Stilt Sandpiper, Buff-breasted Sandpiper, Short-billed Dowitcher, Long-billed Dowitcher, Common Snipe, American Woodcock, Red-necked Phalarope, Laughing Gull, Little

Lucretia Romey

Gull, Common Black-headed Gull, Bonaparte's Gull, Ring-billed Gull, Herring Gull, Iceland Gull, Glaucus Gull, Great Black-backed Gull, Black-legged Kittiwake, Royal Tern, Roseate Tern, Common Tern, Arctic Tern, Least Tern, Black Tern, Black Skimmer, Rock Dove, Mourning Dove, Black-billed Cuckoo, Common Barn Owl, Eastern Screech-Owl, Great Horned Owl, Snowy Owl, Long-eared Owl, Short-eared Owl, Chimney Swift, Ruby-throated Hummingbird, Belted Kingfisher, Red-headed Woodpecker, Yellow-bellied Sapsucker, Downy Woodpecker, Hairy Woodpecker, Northern Flicker, Olive-sided Flycatcher, Eastern Wood-Pewee, Willow Flycatcher, Eastern Phoebe, Great Crested Flycatcher, Western Kingbird, Eastern Kingbird, Horned Lark, Purple Martin, Tree Swallow, Northern Rough-winged Swallow, Bank Swallow, Barn Swallow, Blue Jay, Black-capped Chickadee, Tufted Titmouse, Red-breasted Nuthatch, White-breasted Nuthatch, Brown Creeper, Carolina Wren, House Wren, Golden-crowned Kinglet, Ruby-crowned Kinglet, Blue-gray Gnatcatcher, Veery, Swainson's Thrush, Hermit Thrush, American Robin, Gray Catbird, Northern Mockingbird, Brown Thrasher, Water Pipwit, Cedar Waxwing, European Starling, Solitary Vireo, Red-eyed Vireo, Blue-winged Warbler, Tennessee Warbler, Northern Parula, Yellow Warbler, Magnolia Warbler,

Cape May Warbler, Yellow-rumped Warbler, Black-throated Green Warbler, Pine Warbler, Prairie Warbler, Black-and-white Warbler, American Redstart, Ovenbird, Northern Waterthrush, Common Yellowthroat, Canada Warbler, Northern Cardinal, Rose-breated Grosbeak, Indigo Bunting, Rufous-sided Towhee, Chipping Sparrow, Field Sparrow, Savannah Sparrow, Sharp-tailed Sparrow, Seaside Sparrow, Song Sparrow, Swamp Sparrow, White-throated Sparrow, Dark-eyed Junco, Bobolink, Red-winged Blackbird, Eastern Meadowlark, Common Grackle, Brown-headed Cowbird, Northern Oriole, Purple Finch, House Finch, Pine Siskin, American Goldfinch, Evening Grosbeak, House Sparrow.

The above list was compiled for Friends of Pleasant Bay by Blair Nikula, a Harwich resident and former Regional Editor of American Birds, a publication of the National Audubon Society.

Heaven

The skunk was diggin' in the lawn for beetles,
The woodchuck was complainin' of the heat.
The clams were squirting gaily near the marshes,
And the greenheads flying 'round to bite bare feet.

The tick, he was roostin' in the beach grass,
The quahog, he was settin' in the mud.
The midges, they was nippin' and a-ticklin',
And the miskeeter had gone out after blood.

The yellowlegs was running 'round the slough-hole,
The flicker, he was pecking at a blind.
On Rocky Point the herrin' gulls was squarkin'
And eatin' everything that they could find.

On the Outer Beach the rollers was a-tumblin'.
In the Bay the little ripples washed the sand
Where the hoss-shoe crab was crawlin' on the bottom
And the little peeps was running hand in hand.

As I looked around the Bay where I was rowin',
At the tall dark cedars scattered here and there,
With the beach plum patches purplin' in the sunshine,
The prospect that I seen was mighty fair.

I've cruised to lots of places in my lifetime,
Landed in ports on many a distant sea,
But this skeeter, skunk and tick-infested heaven
I tell you, folks, is good enough for me.

Gilbert Russell Payson
1868-1939

136

I've been here only fifty-two years. There has not been one year in that time that some part of my income hasn't come from Pleasant Bay.

When I first came here, I was in Harwich Port and I got a job on a boat at the Snow Inn. The Thompson brothers—Frank, Biddle and Edric—were top dogs then. Their father was on the way out.

Frank was a man of about five hundred pounds. When he died, he had to be buried in a piano box. Biddle was kind of a hard guy to understand. He was married to a beautiful blonde—Mary.

Edric, I got along with. He ran down to the dock one day and said to me, "Tig, you know what my stupid brother did last night? He died." I thought that was a strange way of putting it.

My job on the boat was to see that Frank got a whole bucket—a twelve-quart bucket—of cod tongues and cheeks. Don't make a face. Frank would eat the whole thing. Maybe twenty-two to twenty-four pounds of tongues and cheeks.

He said, "Tig, what do you think? Would a clam bar go here?" They started the Clam Bar and did a hell of a job with it. The significant thing was the setting.

When I first landed there, thirty-six trawl boats were at the dock. Most of the men were Newfoundlanders or Nova Scotians. Only two or three guys were affiliated with the town.

Later, Jackie Our said, "Hey, Tiggie, you want to come with me?" We went fishing for many years and had many, many close calls.

We went right out of the Chatham Fish Pier, and we were the only boat with an anemometer. It measures wind. One time in a nor'easter, Jackie said, "Uh-oh." When he gave you one of those "Uh-oh"s, it was a bad sign. I said, "Jackie, are we going to make it?" He said he thought so. Then he said "Uh-oh" again. The anemometer had been ripped right off the roof. Jackie said, "Well, if we don't make it, I don't have a goddamned mortgage payment on my boat or house to worry about anymore."

About the middle or late '50s, we were getting one-half cent for cusk, two and a-half cents a pound for market cod and five to seven cents for haddock. One time, during Hurricane Carol, the boats didn't get out for four days, the seas were so high. The next day the price for haddock was seventeen cents—the highest ever paid.

If you worked on land, say, clearing lots, you made a dollar an hour. No more than forty dollars a week. If you went fishing, you maybe made sixty a week. So it was better than working on the land. In between fishing trips you did all the crazy jobs you could to get by.

Jackie Our was a tradition, really. One time, he was having a little conflict with my brother-in-law, Sten Carlson. Pure b.s., you know. Well, Sten had gone to college, and Jackie hadn't. They were in a little debate, sort of. Jackie said to Carlson, "The trouble with you is" this and that. And Carlson said back, "Jackie, the trouble with you is you're excessively paranoid."

Well, everyone was waiting for Jackie to land a punch. But he didn't say one word—just walked away. About fifteen minutes later he came back. He put his finger in Sten's face and said, "Look. I didn't know whether you were complimenting me or insulting me, so I went home and looked it up and I am *not* paranoid!"

Meanwhile, I started quahogging in Pleasant Bay. I had married, and I was scalloping, but there's good scalloping only once in ten years. I was making about ten dollars a day quahogging. Then I went striped bass fishing.

We were out in a storm one time, and lightning started. Seven or eight of us went ashore to sit on the beach. One guy laughed at us, sitting there. He stayed on his boat, got hit by lightning and was killed. Nobody laughed at us after that.

One time my partner fell overboard, right in front of Little Round Cove. We couldn't find the body. His family offered a thousand dollars to anyone who could find it. We borrowed a net from Charlie Chase and dragged and dragged but couldn't find it. A few days later, somebody saw a foot sticking out of some seaweed on the inside of the beach.

Quahogging is funny. One year, it'll be bad. Next year, it'll be better. But you won't do any better, because there'll be too many guys going out. It all ends up just as bad as when you started.

I used to go flounder fishing in the fall. They'd bring fifteen to twenty cents a pound, and I could get from two-to four-hundred pounds a day with my little handline. I haven't seen one in three years now. The seals eat all the larger ones, and the cormorants eat the little ones.

When you were long-raking for quahogs, you'd have a basket in the front of the boat and you'd get some flounders, some blue crab, sometimes a tommy cod. So you'd have three or four meals. You don't get anything now.

Things are altogether different now. There's all this instrumentation on the boats. I had a sounding lead and a Big Ben alarm clock. I'd allocate money for two of those clocks a year. They'd get rusty.

If it weren't for this instrument stuff, some of these guys wouldn't be able to go out. That's how stupid they are.

But then you've got guys like Jay and Jim Harrington. They're great quahoggers.

One of the big things that comes out of the Bay is horseshoe crabs. They take, say, five hundred at a time to Woods Hole. Then they bring them back and put them in a different part of the Bay.

People have blamed horseshoe crabs for the demise of shellfish. That's a bunch of crap. Jay can fill you in on that.

One day I'd been out fishing for bass. I'd lost eight in a row. If I'd caught them all, I'd have had a five-hundred dollar day. I was coming back from Strong Island in such a funk and a rage, I couldn't see straight. Then I said, "Tiggie, what are you doing? You're in the most beautiful place—the prettiest estuary system—probably in the world, and you're just sitting and sulking, looking down at your knees and feet like a jackass."

Well, that's when I got ahold of myself.

Charles "Tiggie" Peluso
Eastham

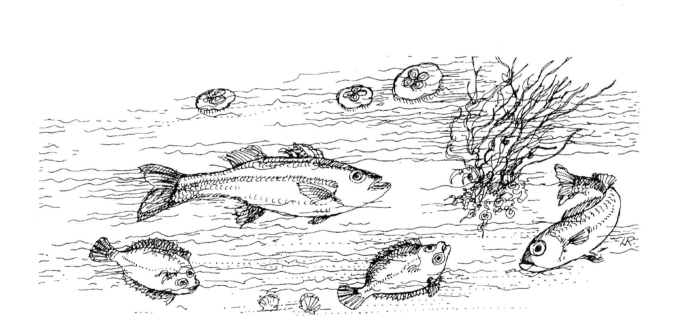

Tiggie, awhile back.

My parents moved here when I was three. My grandfather owned camp Quanset at that time, which was started by his mother. My Dad was working in a Dupont plant and got lead poisoning. We came here for a year—for his health— and we stayed.

He worked as a commercial fisherman for about twenty-five years, out of Rock Harbor. At the time, we owned a house about a half-mile up from the end of Portanimicut Road. We could see the water.

I learned to sail when I was six. That was an experience. My grandfather–he was Francis Parkman Hammatt–put me in a little sharpie. He told me how to put the sail up, how to do this and that. Then, right when I thought he was going to get in the boat, he just pushed me off. He stood on the dock and taught me how to sail, what to do, how to get out of any trouble I might get into. I've been sailing ever since.

I went to Pleasant Bay Camp when I was really little. That's where I learned that I didn't like to swim. I worked mornings at Quanset when I was about seven—in the garden and bailing out boats. He had about thirty wooden boats that all leaked, so in the morning I'd go bail them out. In the afternoon, I'd sail or row. We rowed an awful lot then, going from Portanimicut over to Hog Island. We'd hike around, bring lunch.

I never was into real beaching. When we were at the water, we were sailing. You hung around with the kids in the neighborhood, because you didn't have any transportation. I grew up in a family of three brothers and myself. I think there was only one girl on the whole road—Betty Smith. Friends then were David and Marty Rich, Dick and Betty Smith. Peter and Skip and Mark Norgeot lived up the road. In the summer it was different. There were Gilmores and Cunninghams.

I had a beautiful model sailboat in Paw Wah Pond. It was about four feet long and stood about five feet high. One day I was out rowing in a big dory. I put the model in the water and saw it going away from me. I tried to turn that dory and get to it in time. But I saw the mast going down. I spent a week out there with a grapple hook, trying to get that model. It's still out there—stuck in the mud.

When I was fourteen, I designed and built a boat out of fiberglass. I called it a Bandit. I was going to make my fortune off them; I built just one. I had been drawing pictures of boats. This one was a combination of a bunch of different boats. Sort of like a Baybird, sort of like a Whistler. You draw on your experience.

I took a mechanical drawing course in school. Bernard Collins was the teacher, and he was interested in boats. He knew how to draw them in three dimensions. I carved a model out of wood and took the lines off—just like the old guys did.

I went to Rhode Island School of Design and studied industrial design. When I left college, I knew I wasn't going to Detroit and design hubcaps. I went into the Coast Guard and spent three years as an officer in Virginia. When I came home, I was manager of Arey's Pond Boatyard, then worked at Nauset Marine. I started my boat-building business five years ago. I should have done it right when I left Arey's Pond. I knew enough to do it then, but sometimes things take awhile.

The *Tioga* was the big boat the camp owned. She was a thirty-two foot Crosby Knockabout that had belonged to H.K. Cummings, the photographer, as a yacht. She was built in the late 1800s, and she's still sitting in our back yard.

In the mid-'50s, the *Tioga* was leaking so badly, they had it rolled over by a crane on the beach and covered it with a layer of fiberglass.

We'd put thirty kids on it and sail to the Outer Beach. She didn't have any power—strictly sail, gaff-rigged, with a mast that had to be thirty feet long and as big around as a telephone pole.

At one time, it turned over in Pleasant Bay. I've no idea how they got it upright.

I spent an awful lot of time duck-hunting on the Bay when I was a kid. I got my license when I could; I think we had to be fifteen back then. The MacKenzies—John and Don and Ralph—probably were my best friends. Even though we weren't in the same grade, we were in Scouts together. They lived on Meeting House Pond then. We'd go hunting all day, then go to their dad's shop and build decoys for three or four hours in the evening.

We hunted all over, around Hog Island, Sipson's, Strong Island. We had a big, octagon-shaped boat, with a box in the middle of it that was big enough to hold two people, guns and a dog. It had a little outboard, so you could maneuver it. We'd set it up on the flats. You'd pull the sides of the box up, and it would be like a blind.

We hunted black ducks, geese, sometimes brant. There were a lot more whistlers around then, and sea ducks, diving ducks.

When you look out on the Bay, nothing has

changed. It's when you look back in at the shore that you see what's different.

There used to be a lot of boats out there—all the camp boats. The only catboats you saw were Beetlecats. Now, most of the ones you see are catboats. There's been a real resurgence of interest in catboats themselves.

A catboat is a generic term for a single-sail vessel. A Cape Cod cat is gaff-rigged and half as wide as it is long with a very shallow draft. They're anywhere from twelve feet up to thirty feet; a thirty-foot cat normally would have a cabin. They're very stable and easy to handle, having a single sail, and the shallow draft allows them to go into bays and rivers.

The Beetlecat was designed in the 1920s and generally was used as a yacht club trainer. The Arey's Pond fourteen-foot cat is a boat I designed when I was working there. It's a little bigger and little more comfortable than a Beetlecat.

The Bay changes every day, with the weather, the seasons. Over the years, I've been over or on every part of it. For sailing, there are so many places to go. It's very safe for boating. Nothing can happen to you.

We used to tell the kids at Quanset, "Just stay with the boat. Absolutely nothing can happen to you." Most places, if you overturn you can stand up.

My wife, Pat, and I go out there all the time—usually in a little Whaler. We run at quarter-throttle and just poke along, around Strong Island, into Ryder's Cove, make the loop along the shore in Big Pleasant Bay. We take the dog. It's a great afternoon.

We came down along the back channel one day last summer, just chugging along. Pat said, "I wish I could see some bass." All of a sudden, we were in a school of them—hundreds and hundreds, with silver streaks going out off the bow. We went about a quarter of a mile through that. It was beautiful.

We always have a bet about when the Buffleheads are going to arrive. Then we have another one on when they'll leave.

One day they're here. Then they're gone.

Mervyn S. Hammatt
South Orleans

In 1897, my grandfather, John Wilson, and George Kent and George Pratt wanted to have a healthy, economical place to raise their children and to practice their profession—the Unitarian ministry. They decided to form a cooperative. Pratt must have dropped out early on; I never heard my mother speak of him. But that's why this is called Minister's Point. There were two Cape Cod houses here then.

They came here in the summer and preached at different churches. I've never known how they got from church to church, but they took the barge—that is, wagon—here from the train station.

In 1914, the sills on the house gave out, so my grandfather built a new one and he built it on stilts, because he was afraid it would wash away.

Eventually—between 1900 and 1910—it came to a point where the Unitarian ministers couldn't get along. That was that.

There was one little road that went down to the fish shanties. At the end of Old Wharf Road, the packet boat came in from Boston. The road went up over the bluff and to our yard.

They got everything at Atwood's: paint, groceries, lines for the boat. Plus, my grandmother would never arrive before Atwood's laid in her supply of chicken feed. She wrote her son, saying, "If Atwood has the feed, I'll come down."

They'd also sail in the family catboat down to Clafin's Landing—just beyond Chatham Bars Inn—for things Atwood didn't have. Or they'd sail the other way to Orleans and go for ice cream cones.

There was the rumor that the Germans did come ashore and get ice cream cones.

There were various delivery people who helped those who didn't drive, including my mother and her mother before her. The ice man came several times a week, as did the Cushing's bread man. The Fosters brought fruits and vegetables. After the '20s, when we collected milk from Mr. Atkins up the road, we had a milkman, either Noble's, Whiting's or Hood. The laundry was picked up by Acme.

When the airplane hangar was built in World War I, my mother and sisters got up on the roof and waved to the pilots. They used to entertain them—invite them for supper.

If you lived here in the summertime, you knew everyone; you knew who was sailing or powering by.

My mother or her mother used to sail down to Cochrans—or Davis Point at that time—and have a cup of tea. They all knew each other.

Up until the hurricane of 1944, there were four fish shanties down here. They belonged to Bert Baker, Allie Griffin, Joe and Rufie Nickerson—who had the biggest one—and Eugene Eldredge. I think it's an "e" Eldredge. His father was William. When they weren't off fishing, they were lobstering. Those men were very much a part of our lives. When they'd been seining for bass, we'd be sent down with a quarter to get a fish for dinner. They were wonderful men, and we all grew up with them.

We'd go sailing around the lobster cars. They were boxes about twice the size of this cot on the porch, made with slats. You stored your lobsters in them until you took them to market. There were three of them. Inside the line of fishing boats were the lobster cars. When you were just learning to sail, they were a real hazard!

In 1928, my uncle, Donald Wilson, decided there was too much family in this house. He built himself a boathouse. It had fifteen feet of beachgrass in front of it.

The fishermen told him, "If that house isn't taken by water, it'll be taken by wind." Sure enough, the wind did just what the men said it would—sometimes wind, sometimes water. It scoured under it. You never could get boats in there, because it was too high. In 1944, the hurricane took it. Uncle Donald put the house in the wrong place. He had to learn. Nobody talked about a revetment.

We've lost a lot of land, going from four acres to less than two-and-a-half.

Mrs. Loveland owned all the way up to where Grandfather Donham bought in 1880. Sometime after 1911, a piece of property was sold to a maiden lady. She had inherited $10,000 and bought land to build a house. Her family told her she was crazy, that it was a bad investment. Last year the property was sold for about $900,000. Some bad investment.

When I was little, nobody was going to buy Strong Island because it had so many bugs. It had horseflies, greenheads, no-seeums. It was awful. We'd row over and explore the marshes and rivers there. It was a long row from here, but you didn't think anything of it. You just rowed.

When the Depression hit, and all through the 1930s, there were a lot of vacant houses. I will admit that as teenagers we investigated them. We could get in and explore. There were wonderful places. On one property was a playhouse.

Minister's Point.

Betty Summers, 1924.

I'd better tell you right now, *nobody* had an outboard motor. You'd sail or have an inboard. My Uncle Willard was a double uncle. He married my mother's sister, and he was my father's brother. He brought down an outboard that had been in fresh water. It would work only in the rain barrel or for just a very short way in the Bay. They'd take a beach umbrella in the boat. When the outboard quit, they'd put up the beach umbrella to catch the wind on the way back.

When Mother was first here, the Outer Beach didn't extend as far as the Old Harbor Lifesaving Station. One of the first things you did when you got here in the summer was go to the lighthouse and see how far the beach had grown.

The Outer Beach—called North Beach by some—used to be very different. It was quite a way across. First, you went over a dune, which ended in a low area with clay-ey sand and a line of telephone poles strung with wires going to the Coast Guard Station—the Old Harbor Station now at Race Point. Then you climbed another sand dune, and finally the beach appeared.

Occasionally, in the winter, there would be shipwrecks, and the boats and their cargo were spread on the beach for us to climb on and explore. The last one was the blueberry boat from Maine in 1937.

In the late '30s, we all sailed to the Outer Beach. The war came along, and we had to have an I.D. to go anywhere on the beach. You got your picture taken at the telephone office. I had a plastic card about the size of a credit card with my mug shot on it. As far as I can remember, we never were challenged.

Did Midge Guise tell you about her mother and me learning to drive an ambulance? We went to Exchange Hall in Harwich and learned how to repair automobiles. We were given instructions in first aid. If a ship was sunk here, we were to go and pick up an ambulance. We were told to eat prunes to give us energy. It was wartime, of course, and there wasn't much sugar.

I can remember my mother waking me up in the middle of the night. "Betty, there's bombing out there! Here are your prunes."

The house here boasted a piano and a pump organ. If we were good children, we were invited to the hymn sing at the organ. The real show here was the sunset. Weren't they smart to build this porch? The sunset was entertainment. The other show was any phenomenon of nature: thunder, lightning, a hurricane.

When we were teenagers–between fourteen and sixteen–we invented the North Chatham Sailing

Association. We'd race, and some family or other had to make fudge for the winner. People knew how to mend their own boats. That sounds so foreign to people today, but we did. And if there wasn't any wind and the tide was against you, you'd get out and pull the boat. Sometimes we got only as far back as the Rogers house and would go in and have hilarious lunches.

We lived on our boats. We had to do our own chores, do the dishes, fix the boat. We weren't on the cocktail party circuit.

Sometimes, children were here after summer ended. If there was an infantile paralysis scare, you stayed here. Why you weren't supposed to get polio here, I don't know, but you weren't.

This house has come down through the distaff side. My mother bought out her relatives. Then it came to my sister, Dolly Howell, and me. Now our children own it.

We all grew up together. Then we had children together. Some new people have come, some families have moved. But mostly we're still here.

There's a list on the wall. There are rotating jobs. You have to do your job before you go off sailing.

We're summer residents. As Dolly says, we're not vacationing; all we've done is change dishpans.

Betty (Summers) Cary
North Chatham

Grandmother steadies herself, Betty steadies the boat and her father, Colin Summers, pushes off, 1936.

From Scatteree Road, looking northeast to Cotchpinicut Neck, 1922.

M any, many years ago—back in the seventeenth century—my family started off as immigrants and ended up in the South Precinct of Eastham, which turned into Orleans. Then they went to Barnstable and eventually off-Cape, because after the Civil War the economy here went down the tubes.

My great-great grandfather was killed in the Civil War. My great-grandfather was born in Barnstable, but his children were born in the Boston area. My grandfather ended up living on the Cape again. I have a picture of my father, Andrew Young, at age two, being held up in front of a sign that said, "Twin Lights Tea Barn." Sounds like a tourist trap, doesn't it? I haven't been able to figure out where that was.

After World War II, my grandfather, Robert, and his two sons, Andrew and Robert, looked for a place on the Cape that could be a summer hangout for the family. In 1950, they bought the Loveland place, so that was where we spent summers, no matter where we lived in the winter. My father was in business, and I grew up all over the place. But Chatham was the singular place—the anchor.

The house had been Rufus Nickerson's. We know that. He had a big family. We know that. The Lovelands at one time ran a pony camp.

Although my grandfather was not terribly clear on the details, it was clear we had Cape roots. Every once in a while, he'd drag some of us children off to go through cemeteries. It sounds interesting now, but it was pretty awful when you were ten.

He'd talk of going hand-drailing for plaice in the surf and of his ability to walk out there. The North Beach was attached. Maybe he did that on one of his trips with his wife to the Twin Lights Tea Barn.

At one point in the erosion cycle, there was a vast expanse of meadow bank at low tide. It had been buried in the sand for years. There were wheel ruts with hoofprints. That was somewhere between Holway Street and Andrew Harding's Lane.

It was interesting to be driven around by my grandfather as he'd talk to his grandchildren. Unfortunately, his grandchildren were too young to absorb it all.

Like most young people, I went off to school and then to work. In 1981, I had an opportunity to come back here, and I took it. You bet. We bought the old place from my mother.

But back when I was little, I hung out with people like Bill Chapman—also a summer resident, by the way—with Jamie Alcock and my brother, Brian, who has since died. We were absolutely a team, and had more fun than a barrel of monkeys. My uncle's family was here, too, and they had three girls.

You arrived as soon as you got out of school. You were here—in residence—and you didn't leave until after Labor Day. The in-between times were ping-pong in the barn on rainy days, neighborhood-wide games of Capture the Flag and being on the water.

Summertime here, for a kid who was interested in the outdoors, well, what more could you ask for? There's no question that getting to spend the summers here meant you were privileged.

My father had some experience with boats, so we had a boat; sometimes that grew to a fleet, then back to one boat.

The little place across from the end of Joe Nick's driveway used to be the North Chatham Post Office. The Wescotts lived in that cottage and ran the post office. Bill Wescott ran an engine repair shop.

Well, my father cut a deal with Buddy Henderson, and we got an old, used Sturdee Sea Skiff, fourteen feet. We got a many-times rebuilt fifteen-horsepower engine, and that was the ticket to freedom, right there.

Before then, we'd been rowing in a dinghy. We'd learned how to swim, learned how to go gunk-holing. We'd get around on bicycles, and we'd walk everywhere. But it wasn't until we got that skiff that we got out and explored on our own.

Gunk-holing involves salt water, a shallow estuary, exploring and—by necessity—a boat. Gunk-holing in a place like Pleasant Bay means poking around in shallow places. It almost always means getting hung up someplace, maybe spending the night somewhere or coming back far later than you'd expected. But to me it means actually seeing the physical makeup of the Bay.

Our boat was outfitted with a couple of lifejackets—maybe—a set of oars, oarlocks, three or four bottom rigs, a quahog-scratcher, a clam hoe, a couple of face masks and snorkles, anchors, wet t-shirts and some dried up squid guts.

We'd go crabbing and snorkeling and terrorize the little fish. I called them sticklebacks, mummichaugs, I didn't care. They were little fish. Minnows!

You could scare them into a little place you'd dug and torture them. No, we were not into little-boy torture games.

You could spend many, many hours out there every day. You could try spearfishing, and it was cool. You should have seen us when we finally figured out how to get flounder. We'd go out near some of the wreckage, let out the anchor, roll over the side with a mask and homemade spear. We'd see these little beady eyes. Those flounder would look so damned big through our masks!

Camping out on the beach was an absolute gas. It was always done in a somewhat disorganized kid-like way. We'd forget that we wouldn't always find wood for a fire or that a whole chicken took an extraordinarily long time to cook. Invariably, you'd want a Coca-Cola at three o'clock in the morning, so you'd jump into the boat and come over to the fish pier, hoping that the soda machine was working.

One thing I really miss is the way the Bay was connected through the creek to Stage Harbor. It was sure a lot easier to get to downtown Chatham for me, not having a car.

Despite the fact that you could get around with a boat, the horizons were awfully close. Chatham was North Chatham and Downtown. You didn't go too darned far. Bicycle or boat. That was it. It meant that I didn't know a lot of year-round kids.

Those were terrific summers. We really took advantage of a lot you could do here. Also, the population was lower, there were a lot fewer houses, fewer trees and a lot of the roads were narrower. I distinctly remember what seemed like an interminable car ride coming here. As soon as we got on Bay Road, you couldn't hear tires on pavement anymore. It was sand, and you'd wake up.

It doesn't bear a lot of close analysis, but I'm convinced I just love distant horizons. The Bay is a great venue for that. It has a lot more interest than just the surface of the water body, because it's shallow. It has lots of edges to explore. You feel that you're at least observing if not connecting with a lot of the natural life around the Bay.

It's something to look at, play on, play in, play under. It allows us to think we're on the water without presenting the threats of the open ocean. I don't mind the ocean, but in January you'd rather not be out there.

It's a wonderful spot. The edges, I think, are what's so very attractive. It's a shame that a great many of those edges have had their mysteries stripped away by development.

One of the best parts of Chatham is the number of town landings we have. People say we don't have enough, but the fact of the matter is we have quite a few ways for people to get to the water. Some are regular town landings. Some were just informal arrangements or easements to allow someone who had business on the water to get there.

Do my kids do what I used to do? No. Life is different. For one thing, they're not on vacation here as much as they're on summer vacation in the place they live. They like to do all those things, but it's not the preoccupation that it was with me. They have lots of other things to do.

It's also more congested, faster, more dangerous than when I was a kid. When we went out on the Bay in the summertime, the number of recreational powerboats and sailboats was one-tenth of what it is now.

Besides, we were boys. I have two girls. That's different. You worry more.

Andrew Young
North Chatham

148

Ifirst came here as a kid—I was seven years old—as a guest of the Place family. Ann Place's father was Clyde R. Place, the man who built Rockefeller Center. I believe Mr. Place traded some land to give Eastward Ho! enough land to build an eighteen-hole course.

He had a house up on Fox Hill Road. It was the most wonderful house, with a huge barn that had about a mile of model train track in it. Their chauffeur was the trainmaster.

We'd come for Thanksgiving and Easter holidays. I lived in Greenwich Village, and I had one pair of shoes–polished for parties–and one pair of scuffed-up ones for play. I remember their maid came in and asked where my good shoes were. I said I didn't have any. She took my shoes and did the best she could to make them shine.

That's as close as I got to Pleasant Bay in those days.

Later, I had joined General Motors overseas operations, and we were living in Europe. We'd come back on home-leave every couple of years. We had three kids, all born while we were living in South Africa.

About 1960, an aunt of mine had bought a house on Shore Road; it still has the prettiest view in town, I think. We were invited for a weekend, and it was like this morning—impenetrable fog. But we woke up and looked out at the harbor, and I realized I had forgotten all about Chatham and how gorgeous it was.

That Sunday morning, my aunt said, "I'm going to call Huddy Eldridge." She called him at Eastward Ho! He was at the bar, probably having his gin and tonic after eighteen holes, and he was so mad he walked into her house wearing his spikes.

He took us down to the Cow Yard. There was a house for sale and a lot for sale. We decided to buy the lot, then and there. I noticed a brick foundation and asked what it was. Huddy said it had been the coffin-maker's house.

The whole area used to be a pasture with a big corral for cows. I don't know what kind of cattle—but eating cattle. They were hoisted onto ships with block and tackle. Ships came in there, and, of course, someone might have died on-board, so business came right to the coffin-maker.

Back then, there used to be seven feet of water at low tide. Now there's not seven inches. Now it's a hornet's nest of jet skis. Last summer it was just starting, but now you can't drive down there for the jet ski trailers.

I've talked with some of the jet skiers, and I said, "There's nothing wrong with you guys except attitude." It's sort of a motorcycle syndrome.

So we bought the land and went back to Europe. We didn't build until 1966. We did this, in part, as an anchor for our kids. We'd been told that kids who are born abroad need to know who they are and where they come from.

The good thing is, they worked here every summer. Bill, my oldest, worked for Tom Ennis at the boatyard. Then Barry Eldredge hired him to run the harbor patrol. Patrick worked for Bob Ford, doing landscaping. He said, "I've cut the grass at every church in Chatham." And Tony worked seven summers for Willard Nickerson at the Fish Pier. Of course, my kids spoke different languages, so every time a Canadian came into the market, Willard would yell, "Tony! French!" so he could go talk to them.

The kids knew more people and knew more about the town than the parents. When I retired and moved here, people would say, "Oh, are you Tony's father?" or "Are you Bill's father?"

My kids grew up with Sam Rogers' kids. That's a wonderful family. Big Sam is a fantastic sailor. Patrick, who now is six-feet-something, was Sam's crew for years, and they always won. Tony and Sam, Jr. were great pals, and they sailed together. If they weren't in at least third position in a race, you'd see them with their feet up on the gunnel and a six-pack.

The Bay is such a safe place for kids to sail. If they get blown over, they'll come ashore. I think parents

149

feel—at least they did before jet skis—that their kids are safe.

Our kids learned to sail at Chatham Yacht Club. When it comes to recent history of the Bay, that little place is the key. Sam Rogers' mother was Commodore of the club—probably the first women commodore of any club. It was created, I think, by a group of dissidents who left Stage Harbor Yacht Club. It's a place for older people and teenagers to be together—sailing together and against each other. I know it sounds elitist, but there is cultural appreciation and politeness, and almost never a serious protest after a race.

What that place has done for kids is just tremendous. I think my kids made more friends there than anyplace they've been—forever friends.

I thought I had a million friends when I was in business. But when you leave the corporate world, you see just how fast people disappear. If you end up your life with five good friends, that's a lot. I think of my kids as come-latelys down here, but each one of them has five lifetime friends.

Parker "Pete" Wiseman
North Chatham

Photo by Richard C. Hiscock

My grandfather, Roy Everett Tomlinson, came here in the late '20s and bought the property. He had two children—my mother, Betty, and my Uncle Everett. As time went on, their families came along and my grandfather expanded the buildings here to accommodate us, thankfully. We were able to spend the summers of my childhood on the Bay, and those summers were very much water and sailing-related.

"Paca," as we called my grandfather, joined Nabisco as a lawyer, worked his way up to president and eventually chaired the Board of Directors. He must have been very effective, but you wouldn't have known it from his demeanor. He was a very gentle person—very quiet. We used to go up to their house after supper and have readings. Pretty much the whole evening, he'd sit at his desk playing solitaire—listening to the family activities.

Obviously, Paca had large business responsibilities, but he'd manage to drive or be driven from Montclair, New Jersey to the Cape every weekend on those old roads. It must have been a very long trip. His wife, Eleanor, and my mother and uncle stayed here all summer.

My grandfather was a founder of Eastward Ho! He came in at a point where some financing was critical; otherwise the land would have gone to another use, probably development.

Irving Doane, who I loved as a person, worked for Paca. He did boat maintenance. He taught me sailing, and he did things that were intriguing to watch—like cleaning fish on the beach. He was a big part of my growing up. I'd go down to the boathouse and watch him put on his boots; he'd take off his socks and change from his shiny land-shoes.

His motorboat, the boat that was so beloved to him, was lost. Might have happened in the '38 hurricane. It washed ashore out here—a very sad day for him.

I think he may have been the first captain to shift from sail to motor. Carroll Nickerson was the opposite extreme. He kept on fishing in his catboat *Gladys* without a motor.

Merrill Doane used to help with large projects around the property here. We knew him through Chatham Yacht Club, where he patrolled races. Merrill's boat, the *Big Scat*, was an almost entirely

Roy Tomlinson and grandson, Howard Van Vleck.

open inboard with a little windshield on it. It was a roomy utility boat. He also had the *Little Scat*, something like a Cape Cod Knockabout.

I loved knowing Alan McClennen to the extent that I did. I sailed with his kids at the Club, and he's done such good work with the Friends of Pleasant Bay.

I used to go fishing and buddy around with the Baker kids, Gordon and Skippy. Their father, Milton, worked for my grandfather and lived on the property

Howie, captain of his world.

year-round. We used to fluke-fish out here—wonderful summer fluke. We'd take them down to Willard Nickerson at the Fish Pier and sell them. My mother would go in later and buy them back.

Willard was someone we knew and regarded highly.

Tern Island used to be a big part of our summers. It had a very healthy nesting population when we were growing up. Dr. Austin, at what now is Audubon in Wellfleet, would come band the birds. At the end of summer, we'd go over to the island and find all the birds that had died. We'd take the bands to Dr. Austin. He seemed to appreciate that.

That Halloween no-name storm [1991] was a memorable one. Bill Hammatt's beach camp ended up here. It was intact, but was carried to the end of Cow Yard. And we had three feet of water in the boathouse. There are two rows of racing pennants on the walls in there, beginning in 1925 from what then was Chatham Country Club. Those pennants were pretty badly damaged by that storm.

I always like to see the activity at the Fish Pier. It's a living resource, with the fishing, lobstering, scalloping. It comes and goes, of course. When I was growing up, there were huge eelgrass beds in front here. We'd watch the growth of scallops over the summer. Now that's gone—not that it's gone for good.

Those are the changes, and we must accept them. Things come and go.

Howard Van Vleck
North Chatham

Roy, Howie and the Baybird.

I never take the Bay for granted. It's sort of my morning prayer when I look out there every day. And I don't feel I've earned this; it's been my good fortune.

I think it was 1928 when my parents first rented the Slocum house here. They did that for two or three summers. Then "Far End" came on the market—the house on the hill. My childhood was spent up there at the big house. My brother Sam lives there now.

Being here was great. We lived in our navy-blue woolen trunks, period. Bare feet. Bare tops. We were in the water or on the beach all the time and were sailing independently by the time we were seven or eight. We couldn't sail alone until we passed a swimming test. And we were taught to stay with the boat if it capsized. If it's drifting, it'll fetch up eventually, so always stay with the boat.

Our first ones were Rookies. They were rowboats about seven feet long with a sail. We went from Rookies to Beetlecats to Mercurys to Whistlers and then to Daysailers.

I have very vivid memories of camping overnight on the Outer Beach. That was the big thing every year. We'd set a date. Maybe what was big was that Dad was here on his vacation, so we'd all go. Ordinarily, he didn't come down on weekends. There was no Mid-Cape Highway, so the drive from Newton could take about five hours in the summer. But I remember pitching tents, eating corn, collecting wood for the fire. One year we camped in the wrong place. The tide came in, and we were in about six inches of water. A loaf of bread was floating away. Oranges were floating.

Skunks would come around when we were camping. One time we were squirted in the tent. We burned the tent and came home.

The first thing in the summer—before we moored our boats—we'd get a carton from Atwood's Store and pour a cement block then put a ring in it. That was our mooring.

My father and his friends made all their own boats—little ones—duck boats, kayaks. Dad built his boathouse from wood he salvaged when they tore down the Naval Air Station. He floated the wood to Bassing Harbor. We kids used what was left over to build our own little boathouse.

From a fishing standpoint, we used to be able to go out anytime and pull up flounder or scup. We'd dig clams, put meat on the hook and catch something. Anytime. My father had made us a raft to swim from, and we could just sit there and catch fish. Now the seals and cormorants have wiped out those bottom fish. I'm not really sure who was responsible, but I suspect it's the seals.

We'd catch bass and bluefish regularly behind Strong Island. Back when I was little, the fathers would get together and go fishing. They never went outside the Bay, because they all had homemade boats—little ones. But they did quite well with bass right in the Bay.

I can remember when the Naval Air Station was still there. We'd play on the beach at Bassing Harbor and would hear the sound of a little tiny motor. We'd all run over to look, because it was a motorboat! And the seaplanes used to land right in front of us, this side of Strong Island.

I remember Ernie Kendrick fishing here. Of course, the professional fishermen didn't want to live on the water. They wanted to live in town where it was warm and sociable.

Ernie was colorful. He earned his living out of the Bay. He quahogged, clammed, lobstered and spearfished for plaice. He trolled with a handline out of a sailboat, and on Sundays he'd take his wife whose name was Florence.

He took each of us four kids out at least once in the summer. His fishing boat was really a dory with a motor. We'd have to get up at five in the morning to go out with Ernie and haul pots. We thought we were big stuff.

This was a good place for duck hunting. The men built their own duck boat and would row over, usually to Strong Island marsh. We kids were all taught how to shoot—at least a twenty-two and maybe a shotgun.

My brother Ray and I used to go out the door and walk around to these marshes and see if we could shoot a Canada goose or something. That's not something I'd do now.

We learned about boating, about guns and tools and about cleaning paintbrushes. If you had a tool of some kind and left it out to rust, well, that was too bad. You didn't get another.

We had one pair of sneakers that had to last until we grew out of them—if we wore them at all. They had slippery bottoms and many holes, with our toes sticking out.

During the war, everything for us was by sail. We either walked to town or sailed to Chatham Bars Inn and walked from there to get groceries. We were allowed three gallons of gas a month. My mother would save up gas coupons for the drive down from Newton. Once here, she'd start saving up for the trip

Sam, Lucia, Horatio and Midge Rogers.

Race day at Chatham Yacht Club in the summer of '48.

back at the end of the summer.

When the Nazis marched into Poland, then kept right on going to overwhelm France, Denmark and the Low Countries, there was nothing left between them and me in Chatham but the Atlantic. What could prevent U-boats from surfacing off the Outer Beach and discharging flotillas of rubber rafts full of armed soldiers? The possibility was acutely real to me at age eleven, and I knew what I was going to do about it.

Our house was perched on a high, sandy bluff. Close by at the front edge of this great lookout point was a well-camouflaged little depression, actually a secret rendezvous that we kids called "Sleepy Hollow."

I had already figured out that I could lie there, hidden, propped on my elbows, with my brother's rifle at the ready and watch to see if any rubber boats were dragged across the beach and re-launched in Pleasant Bay. If any raft paddled within range, I would shoot holes in it to sink it. I worried about having enough ammunition if there were more than five or six boats. If they reached shore and started to climb up my steep bank, I'd scramble down the back side, run across the salt marsh, jump the creek and disappear into the woods beyond. Eventually, I would alert the Navy and Coast Guard in town. I might be a heroine.

In Chatham there were lots and lots of Navy and Coast Guardsmen. Up to five thousand men filled the Old Harbor Inn, the Mataquasson, the Hawthorne, Wayside and Chatham Bars Inn. Uniforms were everywhere, as were Jeeps and small trucks with Navy insignia on the doors. I got to know some of the men when my brother Sam joined the Auxiliary Patrol to monitor the harbor entrance from a commandeered yacht. Many seventeen-year-old boys volunteered to do that the summer before being drafted.

I also knew some of them from picnicking on the Outer Beach and visiting with the walking patrols from the Old Harbor Lifesaving Station and the Orleans Coast Guard Station. These men carried pistols, radios, binoculars and usually had a dog as well. On four-hour cycles, they walked toward each other from their respective stations. Where they met was our chosen spot. They'd stop and visit with us, we'd give them cookies and then they'd jog to reach their stations in the allotted time.

Along with these servicemen came some war-like regulations. Each person in town got fingerprinted, photographed and issued identification tags. Mine was a steel-link bracelet which I was ordered to wear. We also were ordered to be off the beaches and the water by 6 p.m..

The Navy took all our photo albums during the war. They didn't want pictures of the area getting to the Germans, and they suspected that was happening somehow. We were investigated one time, because our blackout curtain was flapping and a light showed from inside. Our house was on such a high place, it looked like someone was signaling.

Until about 1946 or '47, Chatham Yacht Club had no clubhouse and no pier. We just sailed off the beach. I've got a picture showing the pier in 1948, but still no clubhouse. When it was cold and wet and stormy, we had no place to go inside. That was OK. We got toughened up. We all loved to race.

I can remember Alan and Weezy McClennen sailing their Mercury, called *Vivace*, with their baby asleep forward of the mast on a pile of lifejackets and their other children running around the boat. Sometimes you could hear the baby crying through the whole race course.

I'm looking northeast from here, across at Strong Island. To the left is Bassing Harbor and Fox Hill. There were no houses anywhere there when I was growing up. None.

It's difficult to convey to anyone but another sailor the exquisitely gentle relaxation that overtakes you as the shore, the house, the business of family and town recedes out of reach, out of earshot, out of mind. For awhile, the v-shaped wake suggests there still is some connection with those landmarks, but once in the open Bay I could be anywhere. I *am* anywhere. I am just here alone with me, my boat and these glorious, timeless open spaces.

My parents used to let us sleep in the boats overnight, at the mooring. I was astonished to find out later that some people don't like the dark. They're afraid and want a light on. Light ruins your night vision. We'd lie there looking at all the stars, listening to the sounds.

Chatham is the continuity in our lives. Children grow up. They move away. Homes are sold. But this is the reunion place. It's what we all have in common.

Amelia "Midge" (Rogers) Guise
North Chatham

There weren't many fishing boats out there when I was a boy. The only ones you saw—most of them twenty-six to twenty-eight feet—belonged to Ernie Kendrick, Ben Baker, my father and his brother Rufus, Allie Griffin, Willie and Eugene Eldredge and Bill Speight.

Ernie had a little dory with a one-cylinder engine.

You could always tell when he was coming—"putt-putt-putt-putt." Ben Baker had his boat moored three-hundred yards up the channel. It'd be flat calm, and you could hear him up there—"goddam, goddam." Willie and Eugene were father and son. They'd argue like a son of a gun over anything. Bill Speight was a comedian when he had not more than two drinks in him. Anything over that, he'd get foolish.

In the morning—after a late night—Bill would get out there in the boat, stand up and take deep breaths.

Fish shacks on Scatteree shore around 1900. The shanty at left belonged to Rufus, Joe and Willard Nickerson, Sr., and the one on the right was Willie Eldredge's.

One morning when he stood up to do that, he said, "I can't breathe! I can't take a deep breath!" Well, he opened his shirt, and he had a bra on under there.

Willard Nickerson and I used to work at Old Harbor Inn. I washed dining room dishes, and he helped his father washing kitchen dishes and such. I was fourteen. Willard's grandfather Rufus owned the place first. He sold out to his son, and then Willard kept it until 1962. We'd go out in gunning skiffs—just big enough for two guys to get in. All through the summer, we'd go every day to the east end of Strong Island and troll for bass. We'd get as many as twenty-two and bring 'em back to the inn.

To look back on it, the most amazing thing was there was nobody else out there. Oh, you might see Ernie Kendrick—hear him coming.

Ernie and his brother had a fish weir on the west side of the Strong Island meadow. It was made of poles driven in the ground and chicken wire. They used to catch quite a lot of flounder there. My grandfather and father had a trap down off Sam Rogers' point. They weren't monster big things like they have out there in the Bay.

Ernie used to love to talk, if he could keep his teeth in his mouth. He'd tell of going codfishing in the harbor. The most he ever caught was at Fox Hill. That channel was full of cod that winter—probably around 1890. The mouth of the harbor was way up here then—in North Chatham—not where it is now. Ernie was a nice old guy. He never swore. He'd say, "Well, I swan" or "My gracious." He's been dead probably twenty-five or thirty years.

He used to go fishing with his father when he was about nine to twelve years old—in a catboat called *Raleigh*. They were out one time when the wind came up as they came along the bar. All Ernie could see was white water all around, and he was scared. His father told him, "Come sit next to me and hold on." So he did, and the sea came up behind them and lifted them right over the bar and into the harbor. Ernie's father said, "Now that wasn't too bad, was it." Ernie'd never forgotten that.

You never saw any stone walls around the shore back then. They're all over the place now. That old water does a lot of damage, even if it's in the Bay. You don't get a running sea, just wind and waves. From about 1930-1940, we'd go flat fishing every Spring. There'd be thirty-five to forty boats out there. You'd sit half an hour and get all the fish you'd want. The water depth was probably eighteen feet deep then. I was there a few years ago, and at low tide I could touch bottom with an oar. The tide goes out like a son of a gun.

The whole shore has changed. It's dropped in height, and that's especially noticeable at Minister's Point. It doesn't look any different. It's all stones there, but the sand has gone and the stones have dropped.

They started calling that place Minister's Point because there were three ministers living there at one time during the summers. Before that, it was Amos' Point, because Amos Nickerson lived there.

Up 'til 1932, they'd go seining for bass up here in the harbor. My father, Rufus, Eugene, Allie Griffin and Bill Speight were the seining crew, and I used to go with them a lot—until I was fourteen. My uncle was treasurer for the outfit. He'd keep all the money 'til fall, then they'd go to his house to settle up for what they'd done all summer. The last year I went, they gave me a twenty dollar bill for helping out. I thought I was a millionaire.

They'd go up by Strong, Sipson's islands, maybe half or three-quarters of a mile past the town line. As I remember, they weren't supposed to go up there, it being out of town. They'd go in a thick fog.

The only place they stopped bass-seining was Barnstable—in 1932. You could go anywhere else along the east coast, but not here. That used to gripe the oldtimers quite a lot.

In about mid-May, the men would start putting pots in, and they'd go lobstering in the harbor and outside until about the end of October. In the 1920s, they'd go plaice-fishing a lot. On calm days, there'd be three or four feet of water over the flats in the harbor. They'd see the outline of the plaice in the water. The plaice just disappeared sometime after that, then came back in the '50s.

As far back as I remember, the Naval Air Station still had planes flying in and out. Once in awhile a car would go by here, but not often; my mother would let me walk down to the shore and wait for my father to come in to Scatteree. He had a shanty there. So did some others. Those planes would fly a hundred-and-fifty feet over my head, and I'd hide in the bushes so they wouldn't see me. They'd go by, and I'd run like hell to the shore. I'd be so afraid they'd drop bombs on me.

One day along about that same time, I'd been to the shore to meet my father. I had a little tricycle, and I'd left it behind the shanty. My father said, "You ride up the road, and I'll meet you." I got that tricycle, and there was a dead seagull tied to the handlebars. I let out a yell and ran screaming for my father. Eugene Eldredge's father was watching me through the shan-

North Chatham, with the Bay beyond, about 1891.

ty wall. He said to my father the next day, "I guess I shouldn't have done that."

Back a long time—roughly between the 1880s and 1910—there were a bunch of catboats out there, probably eighty-five to a hundred of them.

Carroll Nickerson was the last one to go out of here with a catboat—*Gladys*. He was the only one who could sail over the bar and into the harbor. He could keep her going with little or no wind and the tide against him. To me, he looked like an old sea captain. He had a pointed beard and a moustache and always wore a yellow oilcoat. He always went fishing alone.

I remember going lobstering with my father one time in a dense fog. We couldn't see a thing. All he had was a compass and his watch. He said to me, "Look now, you're going to see a buoy just ahead of you on the right in a minute." Sure enough, there it was. I don't know as anyone could do that nowadays with just a compass and a watch.

Joseph A. Nickerson
North Chatham

In 1961, Dr. Horatio Rogers, George Benson and Dr. Marshall Bartlett, longtime summer residents of Chatham, began taping conversations with a man whose voice and language and stories they didn't want to forget–one of the last of the true watermen.

Ernie Kendrick was in his nineties.then. Together with his brother, Ed, he had spent all of his life sailing, rowing, motoring and fishing on the Bay and outside the Chatham Bar. Among a thousand other things, he talked about ships going down offshore, about wrecking crews attempting to right them, about going after spilled cargo and about how folks made do in a time when money was in short supply.

Here is a bit of what Ernie had to say, just the way he said it.

Why, Ed and myself was setting eel pots over here to the beach late one afternoon. We towed our big dory. I stayed in the dory and Ed in the powerboat, and I hove the pots as we went along. I noticed a man rowing for dear life across the channel in a skiff. Well, I knew pretty near who he was, and I knew he wouldn't be doing that for fun.

I hove those pots over fast as I could, and we made for the beach. Wasn't a great ways off then, no more'n a quarter of a mile. Joe had disappeared over the bluff, just hove the anchor off his skiff and went on the run across the beach. I knew something was up. Hadn't heard of any vessel anywhere. We got to the beach and when we riz over the bluff, we seen what it was. The whole surf–the surf and the whole beach–was lined with bundles of laths. Bundle after bundle coming ashore. There was a little sea on, and if they hit on end, there they go, break right open. There was loose laths so that we couldn't walk, but we wasn't interested in loose laths, not then. We picked up bundles as fast as we could.

All the loose laths, the underwriter's agent said, you could have free. He called me up. Well, I guess I was a little short with him; he was an Orleans man. I told him how many we had. He said, "How about eight cents a bundle?" I said, "All right, that's all right. I would have had a lot more if it wasn't for your Orleaners coming down the beach with a horse and team and carting them off."

Perhaps he didn't like that. He was kinda mad over it.

We had to lug them laths across the beach on a hot summer afternoon. Went over on the high tide, loaded them up on the dory and brought them back over to the shanty. Laths was scarce. They was selling for one dollar and one dollar and a quarter a bundle, and we sold off all our laths. But it was a job. Took those laths–they was water-soaked, full of sand–put them on a pair of oars and lugged them between us. Three bundles was about all you could stagger under, and then you wanted to set down and fight the mosquitoes. They was biting terribly. Used both hands. Well, we done pretty well off that.

I was on the beach gunning, and as usual I was shore-birding. After awhile I got kind of tired of laying still, and I went over the back of the beach. The wind was off here to the east'ard. Hadn't been no vessel in sight and no vessel ashore that I knew of, but the first thing when I got over the back side, there was a dory coming through the surf. It was rugged. She come through bottom up, side to. She struck. She split. Just like that.

They was trawl dories, big ones, and they kept a-coming. The shore was covered with oars. Oars and thwarts and bailers, gaffs and all their gear. I wasn't interested in the dories, because I couldn't do a thing with them. There was five or six or seven of them, close together, and I knew they had been nested. They must have all come out of one nest aboard the vessel. Then I see the name of her–*Mary P. Mosquito.* She had been run down offshore and gone to the bottom. Saved most of the crew somehow. I don't think they lost more'n one or two men.

The next thing I see was the station crew coming on the dead run. One fellow got a dory that was fairly good.

I piled up the oars and thwarts and the bailers and all that stuff on the back of the beach, over the rise. Uncle Hezekiah from the station crew come up, and I told him what I got there. Uncle Hezekiah said, "Those go to you."

So we had all the oars that we wanted for a long time. I don't know but I got one or two left in the shanty now.

One night they said there's a vessel ashore, but she wasn't ashore. It was the *Calvin B. Orcutt*, laid right off here close in, northeast snowstorm. Went to the shore, the boys did. Couldn't get across and couldn'a done anything if they had.

When morning came, what there was left of her was in the harbor here. All over was pieces coming by the channel that was bigger than this house. Great chunks of her tore right to pieces. Don't seem as though the sea could be so powerful. Those big iron bolts–bigger than your arm–was twisted right up as though you'd tied them into a knot. Everybody lost on her. Nobody saved. Not a soul.

We had a square rigger strike the Bar. Stove herself right in, but somehow or other she got around and headed for the beach and she fetched up on the Bar. That morning at daybreak, one of my neighbors came and hollered below my window and said, "There is a vessel ashore."

I said, "Where is she laying to?"

He said, "On the Bar."

And I said, "All right, it's no use to go. You can't do anything with her at all.

And they didn't. Pretty hard work if the vessel is on the back of the beach where you can get out and in. But when the vessel is out on the Bar, there at the mouth of the harbor, there isn't much to be done. She was a barkentine.

Sometimes they would get the stuff out of a wrecked vessel and hold an auction of it. I did get some china from the *Horatio Hall*. [*The Horatio Hall* went down in March of 1909.] When a vessel sunk like that, the fishermen would go out and grapple around. One time they got whole bales of dress goods. They brought it home and carried it up to Chathamport and put it in those freshwater ponds and got the salt out, first thing. More new dresses around town. You couldn't tell one woman from another; woman had a dress for every day in the week, pretty nigh.

Now the ocean is barren of vessels. You might stay at the Light there for days and never see a vessel only once in a while. Only once in a while in the spring there is a three-master comes from Nova Scotia, but nothing like they did. Never will again.

Take it in the spring of the year, when the southern mackerel fleet was going down. It was a sight to behold. A fleet of beautiful vessels, carrying everything they could put on, coming before a nor'wester, with a seine boat on deck and towing another one.

A beautiful sight. Everything is power now. The beauty has gone. The beauty of sail has gone off the sea.

We always had one cow, always a cow, and we had quantities of milk. We had one or two pigs. We kept hens, ten ducks, and at one time we kept turkeys. When I was a little fellow we had an old Tom who hated me. Why he did, I don't know. I wasn't very old. I should think probably around four years old. Let me go to the yard with that fellow and he would get red in the face and start for me, and I was scared of him. He chased me all over the place. Great big old Tom Turkey.

Mother would make a pudding, what we called a hasty pudding, made out of country corn, white meal. And you know why I think things tasted so good? The utensils they were cooked in; they were cooked in iron kettles. Big iron kettles, and that beats all this fancy shiny stuff we have, you know. A big kettle of hasty pudding. We'd eat that with milk and cream and sugar for supper and then mother would scrape the kettle all out and put it in a big dish, a platter, and when that got cold we would slice it off in slices and fry it brown with molasses turned over it. Lovely eating. Lovely eating.

Another thing Mother made was what we called molasses tops. Some of the people call them Joe Sloggers. Funny name, but we called them molasses tops. She would have a kettle of boiling fat and we would cut them out on her kneading board. Well, they weren't got out round, they was cut kinda diagonally. They were made of flour , and I can't tell you what else, but they tasted delicious. They was dropped into this boiling fat and they puffed right out. When you put them in they was flat, about as wide as two fingers. And they popped right out, all hollow inside and they browned right up. Took them out just as soon as they got brown. Something the way you would fry doughnuts. And then dipped them into a whole kettle of boiling molasses and take them out onto a big dish to let them cool. Well, they was the most wonderful eating stuff I ever ate. Wonderful

We never lacked for quantity of food. We always had a great variety. Meat, we had quantities of meat. Father raised a steer, and when he got two years old had him killed and we kept practically all of him to eat ourselves. Hung it upstairs in the attic where it froze solid. A big hind quarter. Pretty heavy beef he was. And it was a good thing we got clear of him, because he chased Father out of the field one day and if it hadn't been for Father broke a cedar rail over his head I guess he would have killed Father. He got quite wild.

We had a lot of chicken pie. Now I have bought some chicken pies and they, you know, had peas in them. Peas and potatoes in the chicken pie. Never heard of such a thing. You never had vegetables in that chicken pie. You had chicken from the crust right down to the bottom. Solid chicken. Put two chickens in one big yellow dish. All the dishes was large and

Ernie Kendrick, 1935.

deep. It was good, and Mother would make a gravy to go over that and that was something nice. And then they had Indian pudding. We went over to Harwich on Thanksgiving. They had Indian pudding, and that was from an old recipe but it was different than they had when I was a boy. That one was made in a different dish. They turned it right out, bottom up, turned the dish right over into a platter and sliced the pudding right off. Come off in slices. And then we put cream over it because we had an untold amount of cream to home and made butter.

I used to churn the cream for mother to make butter. She used to have a stamp, a sheaf of wheat, pretty. When the butter comes out of the molds, and then stamp that with that sheaf of wheat, handsome. We also had a big sea clam shell alongside the dish, and the nicest thing about cream— the pantry was cold in summer and it was a lot colder in winter and the milk would freeze, and every time we went in there we would take that sea clam shell and skim off a great chunk of that frozen cream and eat it. Better than ice cream any day.

No house had any central heat. Our house was het by stoves, wood stoves mainly. A man's wealth was estimated, apparently, by the size of his wood pile, because I know one man, he told his son, he said: "Look, you see that wood pile over there? That man is getting along. Look at the size of that wood pile. That

is something to go by," he says. And the coal that we had was many times coal that we got out of the sea. A coal vessel would be lost off here and of course it would be close in to the back of the beach—-and take a smooth time, go out and tow a dory and take a rake and rake a dory load of coal and bring it in.

They had a meat cart around, and of course in the summer time there was more or less flies chased the cart, but just the same, this meat man came from Harwich. We had steak for fifteen or twenty cents a pound. It wasn't cut the same as it is today. There was a chunk cut off here and a chunk cut off there, but it was good meat, and if you wanted stew meat or anything like that it would be about eight cents a pound.

And we had apples untold. Always had a great quantity of apples. Always on the table set a dish of apples.

Another thing I raised, I had a garden down here, over in that hollow there. Planted it with popcorn. Just popcorn. Sold quite a lot of popcorn. Everybody bought popcorn by the ear. I forget what I got a pound. Not very high. I might have got three or four cents a pound, perhaps five. I always popped a lot of corn every night. I had a dish of popcorn and a big bowl of apples on the table, all the time, and mind you, money—real money—was not plentiful. It was scarce. Very scarce.

We had plenty of everything but money.

Going nowhere.

Photo by Richard C. Hiscock

164

My brother Jim was at the University of Massachusetts the same time Bob Wilcox was. Bob said, "Hey, Jim, you ought to come down to Orleans." That probably was in 1969. We had lived in Charlestown and Boston, then Stoughton.

Jim came down and lived for a summer up off Freeman's Way, in a shack kind of thing. I guess today people would call him a homeless person. This was back when Freeman's Way was still dirt. We used to come visit him, and we started enjoying the area. The place had a roof, there was a pond, birds, it was quiet. We thought it was great.

That was Jim, who's older than I am. Then there's Bill, who's older than both of us. He had just gotten out of the Air Force in 1970. That winter, we said we should live together.

We rented Sam Peck's house on Arey's Pond and did different carpentry jobs. Then I got a job working for Arthur Finlay, a buider in Orleans. He also owned Little Sipson's Island.

Arthur said there was a house in the middle of Sipson's Island—that it was sort of abandoned. We wrote the guy who owned it and said we'd caretake the place and fix it up in exchange for rent.

In the spring of 1971, we moved to the island. I was about nineteen. I lived there with my brothers for a number of years. We probably left around '79 or '80.

We had no electricity. There were gas lights, a gas refrigerator and a pump with a Briggs and Stratton engine. In the winter, we'd have to drain the whole system every night. We had a wood stove and burned coke—sort of baked coal. Near where we lived in Stoughton was Murphy Coal and Oil. There were old piles of coke with grass growing up through it. We'd put it in burlap bags, drive ninety miles, row to the island and put it in the stove.

There were gigantic mounds of eelgrass all over the island. We'd bank the house with it—halfway up the walls—for insulation.

The year we lived on Arey's Pond, we didn't know anything about fishing. We saw some people spearing eel on the pond and thought that looked pretty interesting. When we moved to Sipson's Island, it was kind of the heyday of longraking for quahogs in Big Pleasant Bay. There were scallops, striped bass, flounder.... Seeing as how we lived in the middle of it all, it was easy to start pursuing it.

Tiggie Peluso helped us with quahogging and scalloping, in particular. You had to learn certain tech-niques, tide direction, all that. It was all brand new stuff.

I think there probably were a lot of people like us then—sort of back-to-nature types. People who said, "I don't want to wear a tie." And the place was so beautiful—phenomenal—with an abundance of fish and shellfish. And there was peripheral stuff going on around you—bird life—eagles—all kinds of things you didn't know existed when you were a kid and wouldn't have been interested in. Now you see it all and find it fascinating. You're young, you're doing all this physical stuff, you feel good and you're surrounded by this amazing place.

I owe a lot to Arthur Finlay, who first reached out with help and with a suggestion about where to live. His family pretty much lived off the Bay. They raised their kids on the island. They saw it all.

The Finlays' boat was called *Crab-Crab*. When one of their kids was little, he saw two horseshoe crabs mating up. He said, "Look! Crab-crab!"

The Finlays' house disappeared in the Hallowe'en storm in 1991. Jeff Norgeot was walking along the beach after the storm and found photos of the Finlay kids.

When you start out, you just observe what's going on. You see what other people do. I think all the good fishermen go looking for fish and not other fishermen. A lot look for other fishermen, but the good ones don't.

It's hard to miss when all of this is right under you. Pleasant Bay is so shallow, it's easy to see everything.

One of the big fisheries for me used to be flounder fishing—winter blackbacks. I had a permit from the State to harvest winter flounder from the Bay using a net. A lot of winters you're out there breaking ice; you smack out your little piece of the Bay.

Even though all these little boats took less than one per cent of all flounder taken in Barnstable Country, the State took all permits. Seemed that way it could look like it was doing something about the fishery—protecting the resource.

The Bay's still got probably more bass and bluefish than I've ever seen. There aren't as many migratory winter flounder as there used to be. The seals are there to eat fish, and the fish have to run the gauntlet of those seals. Now we have a year-round population of these predators.

In the mid-'60s, there was a massive set of quahogs in the Bay. People fished on that set for about fifteen years. It's hard to say what the problem is now. There are so many predators. But we still get good sets in the ponds and rivers where there aren't as many conches

Jay Harrington.   *Photo by Patrick Wiseman.*

or horseshoe crabs or green crabs.

The Nauset Fishermen's Association is planting about 30,000 quahogs in Meeting House Pond. It was closed to shellfishing for years because of all the drainage pipes coming in. Now it's the best shellfishing pond on the Bay.

Tiggie Peluso likes all the peripheral stuff, too. You're fishing, so you can see all the rest that goes on—migrating shorebirds, maybe an odd seagull once in a while. You try to remember to look it up when you get home, so you can figure out what it is.

And you look over the side of the boat in Meeting House Pond and see millions of moon jellyfish. And there are comb jellyfish that glow in the dark. And you look around and see turkey buzzards and egrets and heron and ospreys—all kinds of shorebirds on the flats.

A lot of people would say, "How can you go out there in the winter when it's freezing?" Maybe it doesn't make sense to people, but if you like what you're doing you're out there. You're warm because you're pumped, and they do make good clothes now—the miracle of fleecewear. You get salt on cotton or wool and it rots, unless you come home and soak it in water.

All the species here are interrelated. I think some people look at a resource and say, "If it's not a clam, oyster or quahog, it's not productive." Working with horseshoe crabs, I've learned the potential value of something.

There's been a lot of research at the Marine Biological Laboratory in Woods Hole. It was discovered in the late '60s that the horseshoe crab has a protective element in its blood to prevent infection.

If a horseshoe crab was damaged and started to bleed, as soon as its blood came in contact with seawater—which is full of bacteria—it would clot. So now they can use a little horseshoe crab blood to test for bacteria in any flu vaccine, insulin or injectible

pharmaceutical. You have to make sure there's no bacteria in any of those. The blood also is used to test for bacteria in heart valves, catheters and syringes. Now it's the standard, worldwide, for injectible pharamaceuticals.

So we drive them to the crab lab in Falmouth. There, a needle is put into them, and they bleed into a jar. The next day, they come back to the Bay.

That's an animal that was considered a nuisance, a predator. There was a bounty on it, because it ate shellfish.

The horseshoe crab also has value in a system like Pleasant Bay. It's plowing through the bottom, so it turns over sand constantly. Clean, jagged sand is the perfect host for a lot of juveniles swimming around.

Through MBL, I've learned a lot about things that might have been considered lowly life. Spider crabs in the Bay, for instance, can grow back a leg and reproduce nerve and muscle tissue. What does that creature use to do that? They're studying the spider crab. The horseshoe crab also is important in vision research. The comb jellyfish is used in cancer research, the squid for research in Alzheimer's, epilepsy, heart disease and kidney disease. Those are just a few things that are going on.

I consider Pleasant Bay incredibly, astoundingly productive. The estuary is the beginning of the food chain. There's been a lot of talk, particularly among people who want to privatize part of the Bay for aquaculture; if an area doesn't have a clam, an oyster or whatever, it should be considered unproductive. There should be a place for aquaculture, but everything in moderation.

We should say, "We really don't know what this is good for." Maybe it's good for only one month of the year. Being cautious is a good thing.

There's a worm called the "lugworm." You see their egg cases in the Bay. I was reading a Rachel Carson book and learned that an acre of lugworms turns over four million pounds of sand in a year.

There's got to be some kind of balance in this big web of life. Nobody really understands it, and nobody's really studying it. Somebody like Tiggie, who's observant, or somebody like me, who watches—we know just a fraction of what's going on. I do a lot of videotaping to document what's going on. I like that; you can show what's what.

I think it would be good if an in-depth assessment was made a part of this Bay management plan. Poeple should come out and look for different species, even though whatever they see would be only a snapshot of that particular day.

I hope they find out what the resources are before they try to manage them. If you don't know what's there, you don't know what's needed.

What I've suggested is that there be no more private shellfish grants anywhere from Hog Island—which is all National Seashore public access—to the Outer Beach, over to Strong Island—which again is all public access—to Little Sipson's Island. That's all public; anybody in the world can go to the land that surrounds this little piece of the Bay. The sand flats here are very popular. People can put ashore or anchor up and get out to explore, observe birds, shellfish, fish off the flats into the channels and swim off the edge of the flats. It's a great place for children; they can spend hours on the flats. This area has a history of public use for recreation, navigation, fishing and fowling.

Some of the aquaculturists don't agree, but I don't care. For one thing, this is where I spend most of my time. Because I make my living off horseshoe crabs, there is some resentment, I know. But certain things are good for certain areas. I believe they should have their historical areas to feed, and those shouldn't be paved over with nets. There's still all kinds of room for aquaculture areas—to expand what we have—if people choose to privatize the Bay.

It's up to the selectmen in the towns. They can give away parts of the bottom for shellfish grants. But then you get new selectmen all the time, many of whom don't have the faintest idea what goes on out here. So it depends on who lobbies the loudest and longest.

Just to be on the safe side, why don't we just say, "This will be open to everyone—forever" If they don't want to make it forever, try the next twenty years.

It's these guys who say, "I want it. Gimme it. Why can't I have it?" Usually, the people who claim there's nothing going on here are the ones you never *see* out here.

Conservation and environmental groups would seriously look at spending a lot of money to protect maybe twelve acres on Sipson's Island. People don't seem to look at what we already own out here on the water. They just think of land as open space—not water. The true common wealth of Massachusetts is the tidelands.

I know it's easy for me to say. I have a shellfish grant. I have my private place. I had two acres and gave one back to the town. I'm not anti-aquaculture; I'm very pro public access, public enhancement. Now they want to change Chapter 130, Section 57, so you can sell these grants you've been given. If that happens, nothing will ever be returned to the towns.

I'm out here all summer, so I don't see the hordes of people on the Cape. We went snorkeling on the Fourth of July—went through this school of bass. Coming face to face with these big fish was really something.

The next day we played volleyball on the flats. The tide goes out, the flats are there. The tide comes in, game's over.

This place kinds of puts people in a mood. People in boats wave to each other. You go up to the Stop & Shop parking lot, and they'll cut you off. But out here it's "Hello!"

It's because nobody owns it. It's all ours.

It's a very nice place.

Jay Harrington
South Orleans

168

The Friends of Pleasant Bay was formed in the summer of 1985, and in the minutes of those early meetings is a passion and concern that continues to this day.

The Cape is changing before our eyes. As the population grows, so do pressures on the fragile resources of The Bay. How do we protect this precious place?

Recently, the Friends developed a condensed version of our original mission statement. It reads, "Our mission is to preserve and enhance the natural, visual and historic resources of Pleasant Bay." If the words have changed somewhat, the goals have not. We are committed to balance between past and future, preservation and improvement, with stewardship the abiding responsibility of us all.

If we are to protect and care for this wonderful resource, some rules must be made. Doing that requires patience; no one ever suggested that democracy is efficient. But there have been more gains than losses, and the first of those occurred in the late 1980s, when The Friends of Pleasant Bay was instrumental in having the Bay designated by the Commonwealth as an Area of Critical Environmental Concern. This was the first step in a very positive and hopeful direction.

Next came an all-important resource management planning process by Orleans, Harwich, Brewster and Chatham—the four towns that touch the Bay and must care for it. With that effort grew an understanding that Pleasant Bay is a regional treasure that requires unified rules based on area-wide concern.

Earlier this year, The Commonwealth of Massachusetts approved the plan that resulted from years of hard work. Now it's being put to work.

As with all environmental concerns, we have to be ever-vigilant. If complacency settles in, exploiters won't be far behind.

The Friends of Pleasant Bay is dedicated to the Bay Management Plan. We commit both our energy and our resources to making it succeed. We hope this book will help the public get to know the Bay, to understand what it has meant to people over the years and to learn why it is so remarkable. With knowing and understanding will come affection for the place and realization of its importance.

I joined the Friends because I wanted to help—because the Bay was—and is—important to me. It's been my pleasure to serve as president these past two years, a job made easy by the many dedicated people involved. We share a common bond—a complex, visceral and deep relationship with Pleasant Bay.

We have become Friends of the Bay, because the Bay has become our friend. As with all friendships, it does not benefit from over-examination. It is simply there. It demands our respect and support.

We give both without hesitation.

John Kelsey
East Orleans
President, Friends of Pleasant Bay

The Friends of Pleasant Bay was organized in 1985
as a private non-profit corporation:
to promote education, research and public awareness of the Bay as a
place of critical environmental concern;
to preserve open space and retain the visual quality of the area;
to preserve the environmental integrity of the shore;
to ensure native species habitat protection and the continuance of the
Bay's rich biological diversity and productivity;
to retain and enhance public access to the shoreline;
to preserve natural and historic sites
and to promote awareness of historic Indian culture.

Midnight Dreams

Some night when the moon rises o'er the bay,
I will snatch a moonbeam and sail away,
To the misty clouds where the stars shine through.
In the glorious heavens of midnight blue
To the winsome land of my dreams.

I will find where the boom of the sea begins,
And the home of the sparkle that edges the rim
Of each murmuring wavelet that drifts along
On the tide of the sea like a mermaid's song
In that wonderful land of my dreams.

I will look for the sea-fog's mantling wrap,
In the misty depths of old ocean's lap,
And I'll find where the sea urchins hide their pelf
In the recessed rock of some cavern shelf
Midst uncharted land of dreams.

Then I'll pin my shimmering moonbeam bright
A pink coral star, ringed with seaweed light
Picked up from the harbor of midnight blue
Then back where the stars are shining through
I will sail away on the bright moonbeams
To the beautiful land of my midnight dreams.

**Geneva (Nickerson)
Eldredge**

Mon Cochran, a Pleasant Bay man all his life. When it froze, he drove his mother across it for her 90th birthday. When it froze again, he skied to the Outer Beach. Mon went for his last sail in July of 1997.

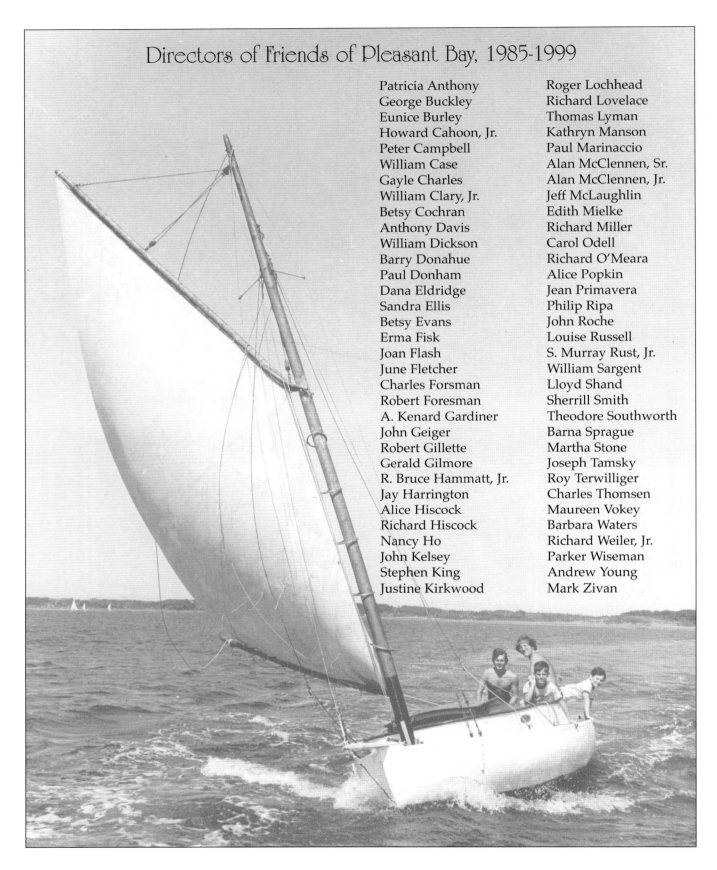

Directors of Friends of Pleasant Bay, 1985-1999

Patricia Anthony
George Buckley
Eunice Burley
Howard Cahoon, Jr.
Peter Campbell
William Case
Gayle Charles
William Clary, Jr.
Betsy Cochran
Anthony Davis
William Dickson
Barry Donahue
Paul Donham
Dana Eldridge
Sandra Ellis
Betsy Evans
Erma Fisk
Joan Flash
June Fletcher
Charles Forsman
Robert Foresman
A. Kenard Gardiner
John Geiger
Robert Gillette
Gerald Gilmore
R. Bruce Hammatt, Jr.
Jay Harrington
Alice Hiscock
Richard Hiscock
Nancy Ho
John Kelsey
Stephen King
Justine Kirkwood

Roger Lochhead
Richard Lovelace
Thomas Lyman
Kathryn Manson
Paul Marinaccio
Alan McClennen, Sr.
Alan McClennen, Jr.
Jeff McLaughlin
Edith Mielke
Richard Miller
Carol Odell
Richard O'Meara
Alice Popkin
Jean Primavera
Philip Ripa
John Roche
Louise Russell
S. Murray Rust, Jr.
William Sargent
Lloyd Shand
Sherrill Smith
Theodore Southworth
Barna Sprague
Martha Stone
Joseph Tamsky
Roy Terwilliger
Charles Thomsen
Maureen Vokey
Barbara Waters
Richard Weiler, Jr.
Parker Wiseman
Andrew Young
Mark Zivan

More Stories from Pleasant Bay

More Stories from Pleasant Bay

More Stories from Pleasant Bay